DATE DUE

DE 3 '96			
MY 1 '97			
~~128'9~~			
OC 4 99			

DEMCO 38-296

MEXICAN SOCIAL POLICY

Affordability, Conflict and Progress

Bruce Nord

UNIVERSITY
PRESS OF
AMERICA

NOV '94

Lanham • New York • London

Copyright © 1994 by
University Press of America®, Inc.
4720 Boston Way
Lanham, Maryland 20706

3 Henrietta Street
London WC2E 8LU England

Library of Congress Cataloging-in-Publication Data
Nord, Bruce.
Mexican social policy : affordability, conflict and progress /
Bruce Nord.
p.   cm.
Includes bibliographical references and index.
1. Mexico—Social policy.   2. Social service—Mexico—Finance.
HN113.5.N67   1994   361.6'1'0972—dc20   93–42083 CIP

ISBN 0–8191–9418–2 (cloth : alk. paper)

ACKNOWLEDGMENTS

These are my best wishes for the Mexican people, who I have learned benefit and suffer from the same sets of circumstances as anyone else. I'm sure my helpers - Judy, Char, Harold and Curt - feel much the same way.

CONTENTS

Acknowledgments

CHAPTER I

INTRODUCTION: THE RELATIVITY OF "AFFORDABILITY"

Quote from Jimmy Durante; Comedian, Social Commentary:

"For years we slept 4 in a bed, dressed in hand-me-downs, had fruit only at Christmas, --- and then came the depression."

The main purpose of this volume is to understand how financial support of social policy comes about in modern Mexico. After a decade of "austerity" we must ask whether the support of social policy and development has become more or less affordable? "Affordability" of support for one governmental service versus another leads to variation and relativity. Changes in the size of the total budgetary pie over time does likewise. This current volume deals with the nature of social policy in the last half century and the general expenditures to optimize this policy given the competitive nature of such funds.

In this volume there is an attempt to explain the general emphasis on "footing the bill" for particular social expenditures as well. There can be a great deal of variation in the types and costs of social policy expenditures (social security versus nutrition versus education, for instance). Different groups can be the target for social development expenditures, and one suspects that the middle class are more likely to be recipients now than 50 years ago. The scenarios can change of course.

As this volume proceeds in it's historic account of social policy developments there will be a political accountant's assessment of the costs, their relative affordability and their latent political functions within the larger context. We will look at social policy areas separately and also by periods for all areas at a given time.

The real basis for the relativity in affordability have to do with the real motives for supplying any kind of social policy support. The finite amount of money available never kept countries from having one emphasis or another. There are real economic parameters of course, but "who gets what" is still the bottom line. Affordability may translate into a social-political control function if we are not too cynical. Researchers like James Wilkie and more recently Pedro Aspe and Paul Sigmund have gathered the statistics and began the analysis of the political economy of social policy. We hope to add to this literature by suggesting more of the specific connections at work.

The Social Policy Areas Apart From Their Costs

> As in other countries of Latin America, in Mexico the state has historically been zealous in matters concerning economic development and the welfare of its citizens. (Merilee Serrill Grindle, 1977, p. 3)

The purposes of this present study are mostly universalistic, although many of the forces which strongly affect the emergence and routinization of social development are, of course, uniquely Mexican. To develop the human capital necessary as a solid basis for economic development should be a universalistic motive and prerequisite, which such matters as the effects of the structure of presidential politics and succession may be particular to Mexico as in the six year (sexenio) presidential term. The heightened need for a national identity in order to fuse Mexico's Indian and Spanish strains may not be a universalistic condition either. Likewise, we can see the struggles over the secularization of education as a somewhat unique Mexican experience as well as the additional struggle to secure affordability hopefully is not universal either.

Excellent studies exist of the totality and of the separate aspects of social policy and social development in Mexico. The Wilkie studies of social expenditure in Mexico (1970) note the overall slowness of such social spending, and observe that the motives involved need not be progressive ones either. Hence our problem with "Affordability." Our current volume will initially examine several forces that may help explain the existing pattern of social enhancement and policy in Mexico - including the pace of its expansion. A simplistic "theory" that blames under-developed peoples for their own lack of social enhancement will not be stressed in the following chapters. That is, the factors to be examined are mostly systemic and social structural in nature. As to the key processes leading to social development, we will summarize the overall pattern in relationship to background economic and political affairs. We shall also examine each of the dozen areas of social development separately in order to try to understand specific forces at work. Thus, the emphasis in this volume will be upon the total pattern of social development, with individual chapters on such social desirables as health, income, nutrition, education, employment, and beyond. We will deal with historical pattern of emergence of what Mexico has achieved to date, and attempt to understand the main forces at work.

We must also then try to explain why its process of economic and "social development" seems to have led to the "marginalization" of nearly half of Mexico's population. The reader of this volume will have the chance to try out a variety of hypotheses concerning this pattern, but we will stress one that focuses upon the control of a viable work force, and alternatively upon the goal of maintaining "stability." After a brief summary of social development in Mexico, we will examine several other factors that might separately or additionally help "explain" the current extent of social development in Mexico with special emphasis on "Affordability." At the end of each discussion of separate areas, we can try to assess the motive forces in them as well. Additionally we can examine Mexico's fiscal crisis after 1981, with an eye toward our thesis, and how the austerity measures were handled and whether or not social development became less affordable.

We will not spend much effort defining social policy or social development. These concepts are both linked with economic enhancement, and their relationships will be traced in a later chapter. Policy refers largely to governmental efforts, either planned or incrementally achieved. Policy is sometimes referred to as a standing plan. Clearly it is the adoption of one amongst several courses of action; it implies choices. Policy is supposed to be a guide for decisions, and may stem from values or philosophies. Social policies in our usage will stress the economic as part of what some have called social modernization. Services, amenities, cash transfers or social alterations may be some of the outcomes in what we have generally referred to as social development or social enhancement. We must of necessity deal with the "political context" of such social policy and development as well as the economic.

Lastly as part of this introduction, let us briefly deal with an issue which this writer is sensitive to. While it is quite possible for an outsider to accurately describe and evaluate a foreign society's cultural and institutional pattern, there is, bluntly, the issue of by what rights are such critical judgments made by outsiders. Here we have another Gringo attacking prostate Mexico; who also ignores the role of the writer's own country in determining these shortcomings on the part of Mexico. On the other hand, the present author is well aware of the military, economic, political, cultural and social impacts from north of the border upon Mexico's attempts at national enhancement. These impacts are somewhat beyond the scope of this volume, but may constitute a source of invalidity. It is fully realized that the larger context is one in which such phenomenon as dependency, aggression, threats, and symbiosis and other inter-systems effects occur. Mexicans would be the first to cherish their independence, however the "Colosus of the North" has impacted them. Such obvious independence means that there is an arena that can be legitimately analyzed on its own. The present author is also aware of the social development shortcomings of his own native land; and suspects that some of the same types of forces are at work in both countries. The austerity crunch, affecting affordability, was supposedly based on a need for capital concentration, and hence a move to better economic performance. Most students of the 1980's now realize that something else happened, and human development issues were sacrificed as well as economic development on some other alter. The issue of affordability in this author's mind must be a tool for re-prioritizing the agenda in many areas of the world, not just North America.

CHAPTER II

SOCIAL POLICY & DEVELOPMENT IN MEXICO: IN BRIEF

Conflicting opinions of the value of the form and of the extent of participation have emerged concerning social development in Mexico. The precedents for high expectations are to be found in Mexico's progressive constitution of 1917; its dedication to popular education in the 1930s; its elaborate social security programs of the 1940s and 1960s; its support for indigenous culture and civic art; and its CONASUPO program helping producer and consumer. Greater pessimism is to be found in evaluations of the national adequacy of its diets, the limited participation in the social security system; the incredibly unequal shares of income and wealth; and the harsh repression of students, workers and peasants. The conflicting opinions and perspectives also depend upon whom you ask and what period of Mexico's history you are referring to. After we briefly relate the progress in social development and its attendant social policies in this metamorphosing country, we will then examine possible motive forces at work.

Early Achievements: 1920-1940

Although the pre-Hispanic Aztec welfare policies for their own peoples were supposedly outstanding (see Gordon Schendel) the modern elaboration began with the missionary (in a secular sense) efforts to educate the nation in the 1920s. Great idealism was generated which impacted many areas outside of education. The regime of Lazaro Cardenas paralleled in many ways the New Deal north of the border, but had its own indigenous roots. Political observers of Mexico, however, have seen the pendulum swings between social enhancement on the one hand to economic "growthmanship" on the other side. Seemingly there were applications of money that differentiated these regimes, but the period after 1940 was more austere until a "balancing" was arrived at in the next decade.

During the Cardenas regime, the social budget accelerated (James Wilkie says it was not breathtaking, however) and social development moved off its meager base. Public health victories enabled the population to find the strength for the economic tasks of the 1950s. Labor laws as in 1931 regulated the conditions of work, but such mandated improvements in income as profit sharing did not arrive until several decades later. Probably more gains were made in this first 20 years of social stability in bringing Mexico to a unified political entity than in attaining social development. The view from the north of the Rio Grande (Rio Bravo to Mexicans)was that great revolutions were taking place as "Socialist Education" was confronted by anti-revolutionary groups such as the "Sinarquistas." The expropriation of the foreign owned oil companies contributed to the thesis of great radical transformation. Imagery north of the border may have been distorted in many ways even though a clear attempt to implement the constitution was being attempted. The indigenistas, who sought to protect the Indian and help preserve their heritage, also helped form the social policy of this period. A plateauing of effort would, however, occur after 1940 as the country consciously moved to industrialization.

The Supremacy of Growthmanship: 1940-1960

After the consolidating, war time Camacho regime came the single-minded surge toward industrialization of Miguel Aleman and of the Alemanistas. Many economists from Myrdal, to Hirchman, to Celso Furtado have noted the unbalanced sector, wedge quality of this dualistic surge to social development. Social policies worked to implement economic development, and Aleman stopped the growth of social amenities or reduced them slightly in several spheres. The dualism of economic aid and social benefits was exacerbated, and only token funding of programs was offered. Social Security was legislated and inaugurated after 1942, but was not extended very far - even though it had many "cradle to grave" features. Carmelo Mesa-Lago has noted the much earlier coverage of working groups, the military and so forth, but only a small segment of the population was covered.

Table I shows (in cryptic form) the scope of social policy and development achievements in Mexico. Very little was initiated in this two decade period, and if you were not in on the bite, or "mordida," then your social benefits were meager indeed. Wilkie notes the following expenditures as opposed to projected expenditures, the social outlay from Cardenas to Camacho to Aleman to Cortines (1935 to 1958)

TABLE 1
A SUMMARY OF SOCIAL POLICY AREAS IN MEXICO
(See Peter Ward, D. Acuna, T. Sanders, M. Grindle, C. Mesa-Lago)

POLICY AREA	PRIORITY	EMPHASIS	DESCRIPTION	COMMENTS
Education	"A central aim of planning"	Much technical-vocational emphasis, not graduate school	Decentralization to states, alternative sites	75% literacy as of 1985, only 10% over 8th grade
Health	Public health high since 1930, clinical up	Medical care via IMSS, ISSSTE, SSA	Benefits, services big, outsiders self-prescribe	Life expectancy up to 76 in 1990, struggling for universality in our time
Economic Well-Being	Need labor intensive activity, make a NAFTA do this?	Labor laws of 1931, 1970, regulate contracts, wages, women	Some profit sharing, subsidies cut in 1980s	Extreme inequality, GINI coefficient over 50, redistribution resisted
Pensions	Universality for workers	Private workers since 1944 via IMSS, public workers via ISSSTE	In 1989 44% of workers have some benefits	By underfunding a "surplus" is created (C. Mesa-Lago)
Age Groups	Via IMSS & ISSSTE children have done well	Aimed at points of passage	INPI - Child care institute since 1961	As with rehabilitation adults get much less
Nutrition	Has varied programs come and go	Too much for export, not enough corn and beans	SAM dismantled, high production not distributed, subsidies for growers or consumers?	Much type II & III malnutrition, data via children's hospital, etc.
Justice	As elsewhere deals with current concerns	Recently on corruption, tries to avoid desocialization, hostility	A great range in services, Santa Marta was showcase, still can buy 'good time'	Much arbitrary authority, drug laws misused?, human fights problematic
Urban Development	Reduce over-concentration	Planning as a hopeful guide, some community planning	Planning still ignored, Federal district taking hold, and elsewhere	Increased compliance, 1985 earthquake stimulated?
Housing	Loans/self help	Ownership stressed	5% payroll tax of minimal help	Reproduces ineqaulities (Peter Ward)

moved from 15.0 pesos per capita, to 17.0 under Camacho, to 19.5 under Aleman to 26.0 under Cortines. (See page 36 in James Wilkie's The Mexican Revolution.) That social expenditures were being retarded was obvious to many, but with the Lopez Mateos regime (1959-1964) the peso level jumped to 47.0. We would have to see little change in the 1940 and 1958 period in actual expenditure for social services. Political pressures were building and it was only a matter of months before a more "balanced Revolution" would be proclaimed. The emphasis, as Wilkie observes (page 38), was an economic expenditure, but when the Mateos' change took place after 1960 it was to increase the administrative aspects rather than social development, per se.

Yet the initiation of social security after 1943 with its broad scope, the emergency measures to get literacy, and the expansion of technical training were considerable accomplishments. The fact that Mateos was also trying to break strikes, with very severe repression, should also be kept in mind as the end of this economically oriented period saw a supposed rise in "social expenditures"

The Period of "Balanced Revolution": 1960-1979

We have chosen the need for available labor force and the additional needs to maintain political stability as the two interacting key factors that help explain the level of commitment to social development in this activist state. The post 1960 period has indeed offered a range of new and augmented programs. The latter included the coverage of civil service workers with social security after 1960. ISSSTE (Institute de Seguridad y Servicios Sociales de los Trabajadores al Servicio del Estado) kept government workers in the fold during this critical period of reaction to previous growthmanship. Carmelo Mesa-Lago is one who believes that groups with political-administrative control or muscle could forcibly include themselves in the charmed circle of benefits. In any case, the early 1960s saw other program enhancements. In 1961 the INPI (National Child Care Institute) meant greater protection for children. School lunches and breakfast programs were much expanded after 1961, as well. Much of the emphasis upon children may have ignored the problems of maimed adults, however. Let us spend a moment on each area of social development in order to systematically review the progress or lack of it.

Income Distribution in the Last Two Decades

Table I shows a summary of the achievements and shortcomings of the most recent years in Mexico. As to minimum wages, these were reaffirmed for government workers after 1959. Many critical observers note that real wages for the middle group of workers went up in the decade from 1960 on, even though laws protecting the bottom standards of income for the poorest workers were much ignored. Kreps and Kuykendall believe that the position of the poorest, as to income, has deteriorated both relatively and absolutely between 1958 and 1968. (See "Growth Without Equity: The Case of Mexican Income Distribution, 1958-68.") Mexico's Gini coefficient, a powerful tool for measuring shares of income, shows Mexico to be very unequal. It may be true that Mexico's poor are more alike in their lack of affluence, but there are great gaps in shares of income - much greater than in the U.S. (Gini coefficient for U.S. - 39 versus 53 for Mexico.) Exacerbating the income situation is the unfairness of taxation, where U.S. citizens pay about 20% of the GNP in taxes, the Mexicans pay 6-10% in a more regressive fashion. Some observers argue that redistribution by services is taking place, but if you are outside of the social security umbrella, then you are outside of the service sector for the most part.

Health Factors in Modern Mexico

Although as noted above, public health victories are claimed and are apparent, the basic approach was reorganized in 1959 and again in the 1970s. The horrendous maladies of the tierra caliente have been reduced except for water borne diseases, which are no joking matter! The causes of mortality still reflect the underdeveloped nature of parts of the country; that is, the uneven distribution of food, the lack of portable water, the pollution of unbridled industrialization, and the lack of investments in better sanitation. Pneumonia, dysentery, and gastroenteritis still compete as hydro-headed reasons for death in Mexico, and the "modern" maladies of cardiovascular and carcinomic diseases are also gaining. Yet the life expectancy has moved steadily into the sixth decade. This is surprising given the fact that only 35% of the population has access to modern health services. Daniel Lopez Acuna (In Mexico, Hoy, 1979, page 200) sees a "pathology" of health planning as leading to the nearly worst statistics of a 27 county sample of similar nations in the mid-1970s.

Apart from the demographic measures of the physical well being, there are clinical measures, and measures of needs for rehabilitation that might be inspected. Much of the health problem remains in rural areas which have not been reached by the "Casa de Saluds." What we know about the problems from other sources says that they are preventable maladies, and stem from malnutrition and from bad water. However, personal prevention (as opposed to public health measures) is found mostly in the larger cities and it is built into the policy in this fashion. (See Adalberto Meneses, 1979, page 244.) Some interesting consequences stem from this pattern of access to health prerequisites and access to medical services. First there seems to be overall improvement in life expectation (nearly 65 years) and there are more services to those who qualify. Many critics of the distribution of health amenities note such health contradictions as the 3rd world pattern of causes of mortality despite their affluence in other realms; and some claim an actual worsening of such health indicators as infant mortality.

Yet the gleaming I.M.S.S. hospitals in Mexico City and the effectiveness of the Casa de Saluds, where they are established set a model - which more Mexicans will demand for themselves. One of the problems with the spread of the "houses of health" is that the shortage of funds allocated means that the offered incentives to local communities go begging because they do not have the matching funds. Upcoming budgets are not likely to reduce the share which rural communities have to come up with.

Nutrition: Corn and Beans as Slow Death

In the land of abundant food supplies, one would expect people to obtain the needed averages of 2600 calories and 72 grams of protein per day (as of 1969). Yet the United Nations says that over 1/2 are suffering from some degree of malnutrition despite (because of?) Mexico's exportation of considerable food stuffs. Some see the problem as a shortage of protein, while others see it as a lack of calories and a-vitaminos. It is not only a rural, but an urban phenomenon as well. Migration, as well, brings on "Acculturational malnutrition"; but it is government policy which many critics point to. The export food production means that less domestic basic foods are produced; the incentives are elsewhere. Production of cotton, sasal, and coffee do little to feed people and even much of the rice crop from Michoacan is sent out of the country.

What has the government done to increase food supplies? Much of a substantial nature has been recent, but there is a 40 year history of attempts to encourage food production, improvement and distribution. The redistribution of land to the ejidos in the 1930s has the best intentions in mind. There was much cooperation with International agencies in the early decades in order to avoid mass starvation. Food improvement programs as MICONSA which was to improve corn and tortilla production go back three decades. Fish supplies were augmented with programs starting in the 1960s, and LICONSA was the agency which tried to modernize milk production after 1961. Mateos in the

1960s pushed very hard to end goiter by forcing the use of iodized salt. Wheat production had been a constant area of concern and TRICONSA was the agency which tried to get low income users and government institutions to use this food. By the late 1970s food importation has grown monstrously and we must discuss such actions as the Mexican Food System (S.A.M.) and the Agricultural Development Act of 1981 later.

Probably most active in the battle against malnutrition were such agencies an I.N.P.I., the National Child Care Institute, which stressed school breakfasts and lunches. In 1965, CONASUPO, the national Staples Products company, was initiated with its many subsidiaries. One of the strategies in this attempt to get food distributed more effectively was to eliminate the intermediaries or "coyotes!" The whole CONASUPO program with its 5000 plus retail outlets and 1250 rural warehouses was to help the peasant farmer market their products and to keep food obtainable to the consumer. Physical distribution problems have been partially ameliorated but one wonders if inflation may not have led to more persistent problems of lack of access. Persistent problems as we will see, lead to policy manipulations in the mid-1980s.

Social Security: A Broad Concept for a Limited Few

With industrialization in the early 1940s the broadest application of social security began, even though it was not until 1961 that a segment of civil servants was covered. Carmelo Mesa-Lago has detailed the earlier groups who acquired social security, first under state provisions, then under Federal provisions as each occupational group acquired the importance to the system or the clout to protect themselves. Meas-Lago notes that "marginal groups were (and are) in great need." (1976, page 255) Presently the main groups benefiting from social security are connected with I.M.S.S., ISSSTE, PEMEX, various occupational groups, or the military.

Association with I.M.S.S. or some of the other agencies can bring "cradle to grave" benefits; including clinical health benefits, pharmaceutical services, preventative medicine, old age pensions, layettes for infants, burial and survivor's benefits. There are also athletic and theater programs for participants. Truly I.M.S.S. is a model for the world and Mexico to follow! The problem is that Mexico does not have a large proportion of the economically active, not to mention the total population. Yet 3/4 of the health professionals work for the government in these social security programs and it implies that there are too few resources focused on too few people. Actually one interesting feature of I.M.S.S. was the policy of the investment of over funding into materials (clinics, labs, etc.) needed for sickness-maternity functions.

Mexican Education: A Promise Realized?

Mexico is a country where educational services have gone somewhat beyond what is needed merely for the industrialization process. Still the overall pattern of education is a flattened one, with few students until recently going on into higher education; and as late as 1965 there were less than 10,000 graduate students in the country. Allocations for education have followed the levels of economic growth, but there have been concessions to the revolutionary goal of a liberating education for all. Let us briefly detail the history of this struggle for an education that goes beyond the mere objective of vocationalism.

Education was a battle ground of early policy struggles, but it produced the early "casa del puebloes" and the idealistic "socialist education." There were and are strong forces toward a free, secular and liberating education, and for many of the "missioners" into the mountain villages it meant martyrdom. The Federal schools were to be the agent and instrument of the Revolution, and the community based schools were not merely for the children. This surge of idealism came in conflict with the more narrow goals of industrialization in the 1940s however, and it was not until the 1970s that rural education moved ahead, and one suspects that the lags in agriculture had something to do with this changed focus.

The Federal Government is still the main engine for educational attainment, and 70% of the money for schooling at the elementary level is federal. At middle levels of education the 1970s show a strong Technical-Vocational push. The latter quadrupled in the first half of the 70s decade. In 1975 there was a national plan for adult education, and this followed earlier administrative reform and the establishment of a broad agency for the coordination of higher education. In order to take the pressure off of the incredible level of enrollment at UNAM in south Mexico City more support for three other metropolitan autonomous Universities was given, for instance.

Generally it is clear that the overall national goals have been reflected in educational policy. Clark Gill of the University of Texas has noted how the creation of national unity in the 1930s, and the subsequent support for Technical-Vocationalism have mirrored "national goals." (1974, page 2) Higher education has been the scene of policy battles, and under Vasconcelos there were attempts to link the National Autonomous University of Mexico with the Revolution. This effort became too successful for the aging Revolution in the 1960s and 1970s, and violence, intervention and bad feelings persist between University City and government officials. Still a governing elite will eventually be drawn from UNAM's graduates or from the excellent poly-technic colleges elsewhere in Mexico. (See Mabry, Camp and Smith.)

Critics of Mexico's educational system stress shortfalls in universality, drop-outs, underfunding and attempts at repression. But Mexico's system have gone beyond mere vocationalism, and its higher education is world class in many ways.

Employment: To Be Employed or Not To Be Employed

There is much unemployment and underemployment in Mexico, and this topic has become an important policy issue for their friendly neighbor to the north. With 5 to 30 million Mexican nationals being seen by various analysts as working in the U.S., it has become a policy issue in both countries. The recent concern for oil production has obviously become linked in several ways with policies about employment as well. Mexico's developmental priorities do not seem to be centered on creating labor intensive and socially valuable jobs, but rather on basic industrial growthmanship with the "surplus" population being left mostly to its own devices.

Mexico's policy answer does not involve a jobs oriented policy as they more clearly wish to enter the next century as an industrial giant - not a labor intensive form of peonage to the major powers. In the short run most of the huge petrochemical, steel or chemical complexes are set up to employ very few people, and the notion of spin-off or "trickle down" jobs has already become a bad joke to those who know what is going to happen. There is, according to David Gordon, an Economist reporter, an agreement with labor not to "expand the workplace in line with production." (1978, page 24.)

Perhaps underemployment would be an adequate form of employment in such a country as long as services and benefits proceeded apace. Work in the industrial sector is not an end-all for any society and the creativity involved in eeking out an existence, although smacking of social Darwinism, can be ameliorated. In any case, other social policies clearly will have to compensate for lack of jobs. A positive impact on jobs will come if a president can embarrass the dominant party enough to consider another compromise with extreme growthmanship. Another policy move would be to pressure the U.S. to accept a stance more like Europe's "guest worker" policy. The educational door is open, and this will allow for a flood of graduates who want good jobs as well, not to mention women who are overcoming their special handicaps. The so-called "employment fund" as such has not been a central factor in creating new or better jobs.

The Subjectives of Mexican Social Life

Any reasonable assessment of Social development in Mexico and the role of social policy would have to note the state's activist role again. To unite the diverse groups it has always been necessary to provide a public or civic art. Much was borrowed from El Indio as well as from Europe's salons, but it often competed poorly with the landscapes of the Alto Plano. Modern industrialism has clouded the horizons and polluted the scarce water, but there have be efforts to renew the human environment. As much in reference to the tourist, there has been a continuous building process in the central zones of Mexico's major cities. New housing, whether modest or immaculate, has striven to achieve vistas that are human in scope and personally inspiring. Meanwhile public art and architecture will be the major basis for national exhilaration. And, for stimulus deprived gringos, it is a riot of sensations! It almost allows the visitor to forget the squalor, interpersonal violence, and threat of repression. The pell-mell rush to economic development has created raucous activity, which is not unpleasant to those who believe that it means personal progress. And the middle class has buffered its position, thanks to government policy.

Summary of Social Development and Policy in Mexico

As an activist state, if no longer a "Revolutionary" one, there is much effort to better social existence. One would have to mention the limited scope of those who benefit, however. The breadth of benefits is perhaps greatest in education, and least in economic sharing. Health services seem headed for near Universality in this century, but potable water, adequate housing or adequate nutrition seem many decades off. Each regime tries to reorganize a key sector, but the various interest groups that make their mark along with the powerful business groups leaves the outcome one of great marginalism for half of the population. One does sense an urgency in executive politics which may yet turn the country from its uneven and heavily troubled course. Let us next look at a variety of strategies by period effecting social development.

TABLE II
MEXICO'S SOCIAL DEVELOPMENT: THE BOTTOM LINE

SOCIAL DEVELOPMENT AREA	SUB AREAS OR CONCERNS	IMPORTANT GOALS OBTAINED: EXAMPLES	ROLE OF POLICY IN IMPROVEMENTS	SIGNIFICANT IMPROVEMENTS NEEDED
Income Distribution	Minimum Wage	Government workers covered in 1959	Good gains 1942-60 (Purcell, p. 65)	Laws Widely Ignored In May Areas
	Agricul. Salaries	Min. wages up 6%, 1950-60 (J.M. Rios, p. 11)	In the 1970s Echeverria emphasized them	Income Still Lags By 60%
	Profit Sharing	In 83 firms shares to $137 (Purcell, p. 129)	1963 commission implemented 1917 Constitution	"Not Radically Redistributive"
	Fair Taxation	Reforms, 1971-72 (Mexico 1973, p. 211)	Minimal: 1973 = 4% of GNP vs. 16% in U.S.	"One Of Worst Areas"
	Redist. Services	Cover 1/4-1/3; better in 3 of 8 regimes	IMSS & ISSTE cover 1/4 of workers	3rd Lowest Budget In L.A.
Health	Public Health	Reduced infectious diseases; reorganized in 1959	Malaria and Yellow Fever = early victories	Leprosy & Cholera Persist
	Clinics	For 35% of public in 1976 (Acuna, 1979)	1351 clinics and dispensaries in 1971	Universalize Via COPLAMAR, Etc.
	Drugs	Price controls on drugs	Self-medication common; diseases resistant	"Peoples Drug Stores"
	Rehabilitation	Free services (See Mexico 1973, p. 239)	Mexico Institute for Rehabilitation = free services	Focus On All, Not Just Children
	Prevention	Cities over 200T have it (Menases, p. 245)	Portillo stresses prevention in Type A units	Work On Chronic Causes
Nutrition	Infant Programs	Avitaminosea deaths down = 21 per 100T, 1972	Via National Institute for Child Protection	
	School Lunches	Started early; have own capital after 1961	INPI after 1960' cost = 2¢ per meal	
	Consumers	2600 calories, 72 grams protein in 1969	CONASUPO expanded after 1975	Focus On Needy, Not Middle Class
Education	Elementary	3% of Federal Budget; 70% is Federal money	Primary up from 6m in 1963 to 16m in 1976	Goal: "Each A Primary Education"
	Vocational/Tech	Gill notes push here in 1970s (p. 9)	Up 4 fold, 1970 to 1975	Still Short Of Skilled Workers
	Adult Education	Use of local schools for adults and community	See Plan Nac. de Educ. para Adultus 1075	
	High Education	Administrative reform after 1970, 1990	ANUIIES coordinates higher education	Claims Of Low Resources & Deter.
Social Security	Occupational	States started 1904-28 (Mesa-Lago)	IMSS in 1943; ISSSTE in 1959	Governmt. Workers 6X Blue Collar
	Pensions	1/4 covered; military = 1926, petroleum = 1935	44% covered in 1990 (Mesa-Lago, 1989)	"Surplus" Related To Underfunding
	Invalid-Depend.	Industry sector covered and some rural workers	IMSS and ISSSTE cover some workers	
Employment	Jobs - Private	8.5m of 17m "unemployed" (Fortune, 1975)	Development policy dictates goals here	Remove Asymmetries = NAFTA
	Jobs - Public	Mateos helped public employees much	Federal Labor Act of 1970 governs all	Privatize. Need Not Remove Jobs
Housing	Credit	Payroll tax of 5% since 1970 law	INFONAVIT builds for some workers	Avoid "Reproduction Of Inequality"
	New Units	12.8 million units over 40 years	National Housing Finance Plan and Trusts	Housing Deficit May Be 6mil
Child Welfare	School Centered	Rehabilitation and school lunch programs	INPI after 1960	
	Other	Neglected and abandoned have program	IMAN after 1963, for those outside	
Aesthetic Quality	Cultural	Indigen. crafts, archit. and published art helped	Even IMSS supports cultural goals	Stress National Culture
	Water	40.4% benefited by potable water	States and Municipalities do little, Feds some	Remove Toxic Hot spots
	Air	Industrial pollution abated; some auto	Federal District, M.C. in action	Extend Monitoring

Social Policy Strategies Into The 1990s and Their Costs

> However, while the potential for conflict exists, so does the propensity for state intervention to defuse, coopt, or ultimately repress working-class movements. (Ward, 1990, P. 5)

The last decade has seen its ups and downs, by anyone's definition. Periods of different strategies do exist that seem to be attempts at managing these fluctuating conditions. A long view back to the attempts at stabilizing the nation of Mexico reveals a variety of efforts, some styles which may repeat themselves. Different types of social enhancement will be found in these various periods as well. Public health issues do not go away, and even as yellow fever recedes an illness like AIDS may pose equal problems. A stress on primary education may give way to needs for technical education and professional training at higher levels. With increased longevity, clinical medicine can focus upon chronic illness patterns and possible prevention. Our Table II lists several periods from 1925 up to the mid-1990s, their general natures, and cost and conflict potential characteristics. The battles with austerity, the oil glut (so-called), and the foreign debt from the early 1980s to the present may justify the naming of a "period" with distinctive qualities. Costs, projected and actual, can be generalized about in the aggregate, and the major locus of conflict can be noted. We must admit over-generalization in the analysis contained in this table, but it seems that not a lot of resources were spent in any period - some with more potential to have utilized them, and some with different kinds of potentials for open conflict.

Harold Lasswell's concern for who gets what in the political system encompasses the notions of affordability and of conflict and its management via social policy manipulation. Many have claimed to have seen cycles or pendulum movements of the political system in response to these fluctuations. No one who knows Mexican history would deny at least the attempts to manage the nation's destiny with a minimum of economic costs or open conflicts. In our discussion of each area of social policy we will deal with these elements. Let us next look at some other factors that are supposed to determine social policy.

TABLE III
SOCIAL POLICY STRATEGIES/COSTS AND CONFLICTS

ALTERNATIVE STRATEGIES (By Periods)	QUALITIES, NATURE	COST CONDITIONS	CONFLICT POTENTIAL
National Integration Supportive (1925-1950)	- High subsidization of Public health, etc. - Labor intensive work - Primary education	Relatively high	Business sector somewhat subdued
Economic Development Supportive (1950-1970)	- Medium Levels for pensions, clinical health, technical education, etc.	Skimping on all services, hidden surpluses	Pushed sectors, peasants, students, workers may revolt
Balancing Strategies (1970-1982)	- Recognition of new class constellations - More high level services	- Done on-the-cheap - Potentially high costs	With business sectors and multi national corporations
"Modernization" Supportive Strategies (1983-1994)	- Austerity - Cutting of the "safety net" - Infrastructure develops to the outside	- Low cost Public sector - Pay-as-you-go more common	- National interests vs. non-national
?Neo-Balancing? Strategy	- Reduction of foreign debt - Equalization of wages, benefits after "free trade" - Social solidarity?	- Medium costs - More taxation of non-productive processes	Middle class expectations versus other groups

CHAPTER III

FACTORS WHICH COULD AFFECT MEXICO'S SOCIAL DEVELOPMENT

> Revolutionary institutions are being used to regulate the poor.
> (Susan Eckstein, The Poverty of Revolution, 1977, p. 220.)

The following list of elements have oft times been cited as being generally important in the Mexican setting and in other national contexts with respect to the specific aspects of social development. These elements seem to have a common sense quality. After all, do not constitutions; mass political responses; needs for political stability; the structure of the presidential or congressional term; the progressivism of neighbors or their potential coercion; the machinations of an internal elite; the needs for a productive labor force; all have their possible effects upon social development practices and policy? We want to be able to attest, however, to their relative weights in the Mexican policy process as a whole or with respect to particular issues. In the general literature on Mexico we find political, social, cultural and economic writers of various persuasions taking one or more of the above as their key mode of explanation. This current author favors a combination of human capital functions and political "stability" functions as a source of understanding, but let us discuss the various factors and their merits.

The Mexican Constitution as a Source of Social Policy

Since Latin American constitutions are classically honored only in the breach, why emphasize the social goals expressed in the Mexican document? Because, as is most often the case, the Mexican experience is sui generis. In the first place, the Mexican commitment to improve standards of living and the life chances for

the peasant and the laborer was made in a country in which the
social, economic, and political "dominance" had been broken.
(Roger Hansen, The Politics of Mexican Development, 1971, p. 91)

Being a less vague document than the U.S. Constitution, the
Mexican Constitution of 1917 and its accretions could be looked upon
as a direct source of social policy. In fact, implementation of the
agrarian and labor aspects of the Constitution in the 1921 to 1940 years
gave this period the title of "reformist," according to the Colegio de
Mexico's A Compact History of Mexico (1974, P. 151). Agrarian
improvement, support for mass education and indigenous culture were
high points of the social policy of this period. There are writers, as
Susan Eckstein, however, who see the Constitution as having little
impact - at least in some specific areas. To quote Eckstein (p. 172), "In
view of the potential payoffs of education and in view of the fact that
primary school according to the Mexican Constitution, is free and
compulsory, why have over half of the men not completed 6 years...".
Based on her interviews, Eckstein says that the lack of education was
not a matter of personal choice either.

Still the Mexican Constitution is not without great consequence.
For instance, the sentiments for agrarian reform and the support for
labor unions found in the Constitution has been implemented in a
variety of ways. Irving L. Horowitz notes that Mexico has one of the
highest union membership rates in Latin America, except for Cuba and
Argentina (Mexico = 44% versus 80% for Cuba and 48% for
Argentina). Obviously the struggle for agrarian reform goes on despite
its support under Cardenas, Lopez Mateos, the Luis Echeverria.
CONASUPO programs which aided the selling and buying problems of
many, both rural and urban; the extension of social security to some
rural areas in the 1960s; and the ruralization of centers of education,
health and social services; all show at least partial implementation of
the Constitutional goals. Problems of implementation do not
completely negate the influence of this powerful document. What if
unions are "coopted" as Bo Anderson and John Cockcroft claim, and
what if 2/3 fail to benefit from the social security system? In all the
social-political systems there are slips between lip and cup. Can we
also not allow for a changing interpretation of the common welfare?
For instance, if the collective land ownership of the Ejido is not able to
produce efficiently, should it be encouraged to expand? It seems true
that constitutions seem to be utilized after the fact as it's articles are
mentioned when legitimation for existing policies is sought. But we
can't be completely cynical here.

Organized Mass Political Pressure as a Source of Progressive Social Policy

As one of the few genuine revolutions in the western hemisphere in the 20th century, we could see the social gains (or other outcomes) as a result of the popular surges against "pofirioism" with its more backward social system. Societies have a way of "evolving" or at least changing without decisive political thrusts or movements; but let us assume that the populist's faith in mass political clout can move systems to greater social enhancement. However, the social fruition of the Mexican revolution has been very slow in materializing, many note. Clearly, contemporaneously organized political power has more to do with a payoff than past rebellion, "machetismo," or the burning of the hacienda! The logic against and for arguments about the efficacy of rebellion or of current organization again is circular. Whom-gets-what from the total resource in the Lasswellian rhetoric depends upon whom is in the politically advantageous position, and whom has the efficacious political clout. In the U.S. of the 1960s, the ignoring of the immediate demands (not the potential strength) of the Black marchers on Washington indicates that a modicum of legitimacy and plenty of firepower behind you determines which policies will prevail. Let us give a Mexican example.

Rosa Elena Montes de Oca has written of "The State and the Peasants" which documents that transformation of the Zapatista-Villa type movement into organized political power. In an appended list, MS. Montes de Oca lists the most important peasant organizations. These include the Partido Nacional Agrarista in 1920, the first "Congreso Nacional Agrarista" in 1923; and the Liga Nacional Campesina in 1926. Almost every four years new groups such as the Union Nacional Sinarquista in 1937; the important Confederation Nacional Campesina (CNC) in 1938; the united UGOCM in 1949; the break off faction "Jacinto Lopez" in 1972; and the reuniting Facto de Ocampo" in 1974, emerge. There has veritably been a blizzard of peasant organizations at the national level in Mexico; and to what avail? Montes de Oca (see pp. 59 & 61 in Reyna and Weinert) observes that:

The agricultural crisis has been very serious. The highly satisfactory rate of growth of Mexican agriculture started to abate in the last half of the 1960s, and in 1972 became negative.

The "crisis" was seen as marked by and partly caused by the peasant land seizures. The possibilities of change are seen in the following context: (p. 61) "That progress depends on how willing or how able the agricultural bourgeoisie is to support such an apparatus and to give small concessions that will allow it to work." Rural unrest and dispora nevertheless continue into the mid-1990s.

The argument about the efficacy of political organization is analogous to the arguments about achievement of class consciousness. That is, if you have enough of it, then the outcome is assured irrespective of the less-than-sufficient opposing factors. Also, the outcomes include divisive strategies that are counter-effective; annihilation; failure to follow through; and cooptation of lenders, to mention a few.

With respect to the latter outcome, Bo Anderson and James Cockcroft have discussed cooptation as a more-or-less private solution to social deficiencies - when either political muscle or rewards make themselves felt. This outcome is especially possible when the Mexican system offers two carrots in a row and, then, a murderous stick! Payoff can still be less than universal even as a result of successful political organization. The political system in Mexico is defined by Anderson and Cockcroft as "a complicated system of exchanges between interest groups' with an oligarchy which prevaded "stability" by "decisive and even ruthless" actions. Such actions include cooptation - even as it could be construed as selective social policy (that is, less than universal application). If this theory were correct, social development could be more determined by the party mechanisms of political coalitions than by the limited state as such. Also organized politics would not have universalistic outcomes in mind, but rather partial inclusion into the realm of party dispensables and largesse. The uneven nature of social distribution as to education, employment, health services, etc., leads us to question the efficacy of any factors!

The "Piven-Cloward Effect": Social Development as the Dampening of Unrest and the Manipulation of Labor

A version of political determinism which we will now examine involves the attempt to counter spontaneous unrest rather than the more deliberate institutionalized buildup of power. This type of response to the distribution of available rewards can include deliberate fermenting of unrest, but more typically arises out of collective discontent without the benefits of a clear ideology or the structure of party or movement. Arguments could be made about whether "guerrilla" activities meet these criteria of mass, spontaneous unrest; and land takeovers by peasants may also be viewed variously. It is likely that the increasing, yet unfulfilled, expectations of the landless is an igniting factor, not merely a vacuous ideology about the agrarian reform. The Echeverria land distribution, such as it was, seemed to have its target in the unrest amongst the landless. Indeed many of his 160 initiatives may have shared this intent. True to the Francis Fox Piven and Richard Cloward thesis (see Regulating the Poor, 1970) the regime's response (in terns of initial land transfer) is just-sufficient to dampen unrest and probably continues to reinforce existing low wage relationships as well. How can we correlate unrest in Mexico to see if it is matched with such minimal dampening and reinforcing tendencies? What would be the result if we went from government to government since the 1930s and asked if policies had been made or implemented on this basis? There must always be the existence of such push factors but must the response be the way Fox and Cloward characterize it? T.H. Fehrenbach's history, Fire and Blood, is reasonably sensitive to such conflict factors in recent Mexican history. For instance, what was the situation with respect to the potential for mass unrest during the Cardenas regime? Fehrenbach observes:

> Cardenas was not a confirmed Marxist, but he was subject to enormous political pressure by his supporters, who were determined to take over the profitable plantations. The millions of unemployed, underemployed, and landless rural people, whose hopes and aspirations had been delayed so long, created danger for the party. (See p. 591.)

In this case the "danger for the party" was also a danger for the state as it was constituted, and for the social classes which had emerged at this point. The governmental response in terms of transferring 1/5th of all the arable land to the landless could hardly be described as meager, but many large plantations survived - despite public opinion. Necessary credit and technology were also subsequently denied the peasants, and the huge, rural labor supply was eventually animated in the previous pattern. The direct application implied in the Fox-Cloward thesis does not seem to be so clear in the Mexican setting, at least concerning the subsequent train of events. Perhaps, the train of events associated with the transition to industrialization was the more important determining factor in the fate of rural labor than other goals and machinations of the regime. An urge for industrial productivity and social stability were said to characterize the next decade of the '40s, according to Fehrenbach. The profits and wages of the war years also kept unrest to a minimum. With the rural crisis headed off, the new president Camacho redistributed only seven million acres (see p. 607).

And, without severe threats during the war years the government did little. Fehrenbach notes:

> New ejidos were authorized only if they were proven to be
> productive... to win rural support, schools were erected elsewhere,
> and in 1943 a social security system was promulgated to pacify the
> proletarians. Because of a lack of funds, however, the program was
> delayed until the 1950s. (See p. 608.)

These comments reveal that <u>not much, even symbolically, is done with social development unless the pressure is there</u>. The state-capitalist thrust of the late 1940s created new pressures by the early 1950s, just as it did in the U.S. A combination of political repression of leaders and mild improvements in social services did seem aimed at holding the lid on in the intervening years. Also, a tremendous surge of legal (50,000!) and illegal migrants went north each year, and some of the pressures for mass unrest were muted. For a variety of reasons, ideological politics declined or were suppressed; but even the conservative unions became aggravated by the late 1950s. Fehrenbach observes:

> By 1957 most of the PRI leadership recognized these dangerous
> pressures and agreed that government must again turn to rapid
> development policies, huge and expensive public works, and the
> diversion of more capital into social service. (See p. 626)

The presidency under Adolfo Lopez Mateos would now respond to the possibilities of mass unrest, especially since the left was gaining credibility again. Hence, according to Fehrenbach:

> He (Mateos) took office in December with promises to expand
> social security, to regulate prices to offset the effects of inflation on
> the poorest classes, to redistribute more land...

Strikes now were followed both by repression and by moves toward social development in the form of social security advances, profit sharing schemes. public works employment and other "pacifiers." We now seem to be tracking a bit closer to expectations of the Fox-Cloward theory, but the "mass unrest" factors have changed from the kind of examples the latter authors utilize. Administrative "fine tuning" also kept pressures from getting out of hand.

Only two other "threats" to the stability of the system remained. Students in 1968 brought their protest demonstrations off campus; their causes centered on the failure of the revolution to bring social justice to over half of the Mexican population. Over 300 were slaughtered by Army and security forces while engaged in a demonstration at Tlatelolco square. This incident has relevance for the Fox-Cloward hypothesis, but only as the mailed fist backs up all other capitalist systems. Another threat of mass unrest in recent decades has been the peasant revolts and related guerrilla activities. Most of the latter involves peasant-landlord conflicts over land and high handed behaviors in general. Some of these were addressed by the early Echeverria administration in a way that would support the Fox-Cloward thesis. One theory (Anderson and Cockcroft, p. 369 in Horowitz) has it that the only significant group that could threaten the regime are the urban workers, and they already share in (somewhat unequally) low cost housing, subsidized foods and federally regulated wage structure. Hence, they will not take to the streets in protest as they have other channels. If the anticipation of unrest is involved, then we would have to modify the Fox-Cloward dynamic.

The "Asian-like poverty" of south Mexico's peasants could supply the motivation for a better test of the Fox-Cloward thesis. An article in the left-wing magazine, Mother Jones (May, 1978, p. 23) talks about "a war in the Mexican jungles." The jungles in the states of Michoacan, Guerrero, Oaxaca, and Veracruz offer possibilities for insurgency of the kind found in Asia in the 1950s. Our question remains, what extensions of social policy have these threats or activities involved? What governmental moves are being discussed to meet this popular unrest? Speculation, as we noted above, was that the slight "left-ward slide" of President Luis Echeverria in the early 1970s was an attempt to head off more serious mass popular unrest and the possible linkage of various groups and issues.

The Sexenio: The Effects of the Six Tear Term on Social Policy

In analyzing public careers of presidents and bureaucrats, Merilee Grindle noted the role of the six-year incumbency of successive Mexican leaders (1977, p. 41). Briefly, as her thesis goes, the behavior of both presidents and the public administrators is discontinuous with the previous administrations. First, the new administration goes into a period of innovation, then one of consolidation, and finally in the fifth and sixth years there is a search for security which stifles policy improvements. One would suspect that it may conservativize the last two or three years as well. A game of musical chairs comes into being in the late years of the six year term as bureaucrats become "flexible" to anticipate the new administration.

While Grindle has some evidence to document the effects of the sexenio - which are not all regressive as with the "political responsiveness" it allows - we must examine its overall effects upon policy. Basically, changes in direction or at least in packaging do come in new administrations and these alterations are often perceived as improvements. Political pressures can be acknowledged, and "balanced growth" between economic and social development can be achieved. The "pendulum" swings of policy noted by some observers of Mexican government can seemingly be accounted for by the periodicity of the sexenios. Changes over six years are, thus, possible because the bureaucrats, government agencies, and politicians anticipate the end of each six year period. But, to repeat, what is the effect overall upon social policy content, and is this the major dynamic?

Perhaps the "left" to right swings from Cardenas (1934-40) to Aleman (1946-52) to Mateos, to Diaz Ordaz, and then slightly to the left with Echeverria are to consolidate what social gains and economic gains the "balanced growth" theory allows. Few outsiders are privy to the "real reasons" for such fluctuations around the center, but many of the reasons no doubt rest on the basic economic and political processes. The sexenio thesis of Grindle and others seems to stress the bureaucratic system. Others stress, instead, the personal motives of the actors. Doubtless there is a periodicity about the flow of policy making, just as in the U.S. where legislation has special timing (as with lame ducks). The specific nature of the policy changes are less well explained by the sexenio thesis however.

The Demonstration Effect Hypothesis

"He (the Mexican) has never had a choice since 1521 but to emerge as part of a greater Western, Latin, Hispanic civilization. The Mexican has no choice but to speak an Indo-European language, live under Roman law, operate within a European derived money economy, and accept or reject a totally non-indigenous Judaeo-Christian religion." (Fehrenbach, p. 578.)

"...Since Independence the societies have industrialized, to different degrees within an adapted corporatist-capitalist framework, with heavy reliance on foreign capital and technology. In these countries, particularly in the semidependent ones, capitalist forces have produced more or less paralleled effects on the structure of economic

opportunities and access to those opportunities as in Mexico."
(Susan Eckstein, 1977, p. 214.)

"The new road, which passed along the edge of Queretaro, brought
with it new relationships and new opportunities, and when the
highway to the north was later opened to connect the city with San
Luis Potosi and the northern border, still another stimulus was
added. (Two Cities of Latin America, Andrew H. Whiteford, 1964,
p. 250.)

Gringos to the north may feel flattered, somewhat threatened, or
ignored by Mexico's moves. Cardenas was no imitation of F.D.R. in
the 1930s, but times called for strong measures in both cases. There
are common historical forces that, of course, affect both nations. The
war years played down many social policy urges as well, but some
policy areas moved ahead in any case. The most striking parallel
between Mexico and the U.S. was during the Aleman regime when
capital expansion (as well as labor repression and red baiting) were
found in both countries. Our interpretive problem regarding such crude
parallelisms is that it can be equally construed that there was some
"imitation" by Mexican regimes or at least that the two countries were
reacting to common stimuli (that is the rush for capital dominance and
the repression of opposing interests).

Of several strong arguments against a "copy cat" view of Mexico's
policy elaboration, one is that proud nationalism would forbid slavish
attention to the Yankee style or forms in any area. Many Mexican
social policy developments also have preceded those in the U.S., as in
areas of profit sharing, the labor laws, medical care, day care, funeral
benefits, government sponsored cooperatives and many other
progressive developments! Additionally, the forms of social policy
implementation often do not particularly resemble those of the U.S.

Perhaps a better argument for the existence of "demonstration effect"
can be made in the sphere of economic development. The technological
model set by the U.S. in some areas for Mexico is well established, but
as with Mexico City's "metro," (which was from France) the whole
industrialized world is its source. But, to ignore Mexico's independent
moves in the area of social development, human capital, human rights,
or even technology, is to fall victim to Yankee ethnocentrism.
Perhaps, the common evolutionary problems of institutional and
industrial convergence bring all societies to common social
developmental stages. Clearly artistic and intellectual breaks from the
"Europeanization" of art and thought in the 19th century began after the
revolution. These nationalistic breaks came in social policies as well,

even though external progressive social thought was sought and incorporated into constitutional documents. The modern synthesis is Mexican in any case. One must remember the experiments (as in collectivization and nationalization - whatever their origins) which were modified or discarded. The need to convince foreigners of the country's progressive (or stable, or solvent) nature may have been an important motive for many of the country's leaders, however. Related to this notion of external influence is the idea that external arm twisting may be involved, as via the International Monetary Fund or threats of indirect or direct military intervention.

External Constraint as a Delimiter of Mexican Social Policy

There was repeated insistence on the need for land reform, for social progress, for raising rapidly the income and the standard of living of the needier sections of the population, for a more equitable distribution of national income, and for industrialization ...But the United States delegates insisted on the inclusion of other phrases as well, for example, a clause in the Punta del Este Charter that commits the signatories to the promotion "of conditions that will encourage the flow of foreign investments." (J. P. Morray, "The United States and Latin America," 1968, p. 108.)

Close to the previous attempt at "explanation" stressing voluntary modeling after foreign sources is the idea that the "modeling" may involve varying degrees of external coercion and direct intervention. As the 1980s wore on, international observers were aware of the range of coercive alternatives the major powers have - including direct violence. Efforts by the U.S. to get Mexico to comply on matters of emigration, oil spills, gas prices, drug control or on general border policies do not initiate horrendous discussions of intervention as they would have barely 50 years ago, but other typical forms of retaliation are implied. The use of muscle by the U.S. concerning "operation intercept" which repeats itself, directly implies escalation of coercion as well.

Obviously it is not true that Mexico knuckles-under readily! The "Estrada Doctrine" which Mexico followed (named after the foreign minister who espoused it) allowed the country independence and flexibility in pursuing its interests. There is much evidence to indicate that Mexico will not typically comply with either economic or political pressures from abroad, much less the effects social policy considerations which they yearn for. The reaction to the embargo after Cardenas' oil nationalization showed much early stiffness of spine, at least up front.

It was clear that Mexico had no intention of closing Cuba out of the world either, as the U.S. wanted in the 1960s. Also the willingness to entertain Hortencia Allende after the U.S.' dismal involvement in Chile, showed no lack of political spunk either or at least we can view it in that fashion. Then, how would a thesis of external compliance be laid out to accommodate the facts that we have at hand? What kind of scenarios would find foreign intervention based on antagonism to Mexican social development? A Castro-type Mexican revolution would see blood-shed and National-International goals sought, one might expect. But what about a significant redistribution of national income, if that, unbelievably became feasible? What about a significant modicum of improvement in general social development that upset feeding at the existing hog trough? There is some evidence that the latter is actually favored by segments of Mexico's powerful neighbor! Much of the moneys for social improvement in the 1960s and 1970s actually come in the form of foreign loans, and such improvement for peasant and proletariat takes the pressure off in many places and must be repaid in real funds!

Let us pursue one of these scenarios a bit farther. What would transpire externally if there were a significant change in the international distribution of Mexican income? A scenario of external reactions might be laid out as follows. A grossly unequal distribution of wealth in both countries infers the presence of a group or groups which would fear further left-ward moves by Mexico, and would apply restraint in many jugular oriented forms. This view of external constraint would have to see the high costs of many forms of social development as also threatening the economic or political preconditions for foreign investment in Mexico as well as the economic stability in the U.S. This situation could exist with a Mexican elite of the same mind or with one that is cowed into submission by the barrage of diplomatic interventionalistic attacks. But, in fact, neither Echeverria or Portillo have looked cowed, and Echeverria added many controls on external capital that stressed autonomy. The U.S. is probably asking Mexico to partially alleviate its social and employment problems before they complicate political stability in the U.S. as well. Perhaps no other long-term orientation toward Mexican social policy can be read into U.S. foreign policy at the present time, although President Clinton's policies (shared we hope!) keep the interaction worthy of press attention (as with NAFTA). And, there are other matters of external concern.

The proposed building of concrete walls on the borders to replace the vulnerable wire fences will not change the basic fact that we have common human concerns, that must be approached with substantially progressive social policy outlooks in both countries. The Mexican mobile labor force with its attendant brace of human concerns clearly has a forcibly shared quality, and, indeed, the economic development of the two nations is more mutualized than either country admits publicly. Even political demands for U.S. social security returns for Mexican nationals are probably not far from achievement. Also, U.S. cities are, de facto, becoming bilingual. Mutualism will probably overtake scenarios of compliance as well. There is little doubt that 70 years ago when the University of Wisconsin social psychologist, Ross, came back to a tenure-threatening situation after eulogizing the Mexican social revolution, the Gringo temper was again totally reactionary.

An issue by issue approach to social policies in particular may find that specific labor wage policies are such that significant demands or accessions to change may invite foreign economical and political muscle. A common "drug policy" could be evolved as well, especially since coercion here has offered the U.S. some return on the operation intercept type operations. Former President Carter's rebuffs from Lopez Portillo are not only for the Mexican home folks; these gestures represent a genuine spirit of independence by Mexico's leaders. But, what about the role of Mexico's internal elites in determining the shape of its social development. Lest we fail to cover all of the obvious vectors, let us proceed.

Mexican Elite Machinations as an Explanation

Elite theorists were very popular with social scientists in the 1950s and 1960s. They have faded partially because they are not easy to define. Each set of writers had their own favorite, malevolent elite as well. Was the elite an ethnic enclave, a close knitted class, office holders, bureaucrats, the bolstered military as such, and so forth? Did the elite have decisive "power," decision making opportunities, sufficient weapons, go-betweens, or super-control of public opinion processes as their source of dominance? Were they legitimate or illegitimate?

And, which particularly elaborated elite theory should we apply as a guide to Mexico? Clearly the criolles of Spanish Ancestry are visibly conspicuous in upper middle class and in leadership circles. One observer, Robert Scott, stresses more diffuse "interest groups" - or rather a more pluralistic elite. Anderson and Cockcroft assume (p. 375 in Horowitz, 1969) that these interest groups are secondary in importance. Instead:

The ruling class group considers and arbitrates the conflicting
demands of many, often rather militant interest groups, but also has
rather explicit long-term plans for how Mexico is to develop
economically, politically and socially. (p. 381)

Still the elite must "coopt" some of the dissenters, if not with a
carrot, then with a well aimed stick and issues can smolder for long
periods making counter strategies problematic. Even though the C.C.I.
from the Baja was clubbed almost literally into submission over land
and salted water (from the U.S. Colorado River) issues in the 1950s,
the popular resentment of this issue came up again in October of 1979
as an answer to reparations over the oil spills on Texas coasts. In this
latter case it is not known which groups used the issues, however. It
seems that dissent may be squashed by the powers that be, but the basic
issues can fester on in one form or another.

Other views of elite machinations include those held by Martin
Needler, who is closer to Robert Scott with respect to the role of
multiple interest groups rather than the notion of a united ruling class.
Needler's model of policy making is as follows:

The political limits on the President's power are of special
importance. The major interest groups and important figures in the
country have an influence on policy, roughly in proportion to their
capacity for causing trouble for the president. As is true of all
modern governments, government policy in Mexico is made by a
process of interaction between political leaders and pressure group
leaders...refusal to cooperate (may cause a) resort to violence.
(See P. 43)

Needler claims that the legislature is a minor and technical entity,
but the judiciary is seen as having some autonomy (p. 42). Needler
offers several versions of power in his book, Politics and Society in
Mexico; in a real sense he equivocates about how policy becomes
established. Needler's view may be another example of the liberal,
pluralistic muddle which denies power anywhere in particular in the
system.

Pablo Gonzalez Casanova in Democracy in Mexico, 1970, (p. 67)
offers another version of elite control:

Finally, a relatively new power in Mexico has become apparent -
that of native financiers and entrepreneurs. They along with the large
foreign enterprises and the great power that supports them, hold the

real power which the Mexican state must take into account in important decisions...

The state is still seen as an active entity in this version, and there seem to be possibilities for conflict between native and foreign entrepreneurs as well. Democracy, however, is not seen as being high on the agenda of either elites or "conformists," according to Casanova The most representative assessment by this writer of the power of the state to develop independent policy may be encompassed in the quote below:

But there is no doubt that the state and institutions are limited and their limitations are apparent in implementing the policy of independent development, especially in dealing with underdevelopment as an internal phenomenon and with the internal forces of inequality. (p. 69)

There is little optimism here that the genuinely universalistic social policy or income redistribution is going to get by the ruling groups. Still, advances in social development occur and they may be chalked up to considerations of political stability. Apparently, under Echeverria, the typical pendulum swings from left to right and return (claimed by Needler, 1971, p. 47) was thrown off its "normal" path. Whether an elite correction was made, or whether the independent power of the executive was involved is not clear at this point. We just are not privy to the maneuverings of an elite, as critics of this approach for the U.S. have noted (Robert Dahl, etc.,). Correlation's with obvious class interests still see odd forms of progressive advance that were to be attributed to "pluralism", "cooption", "stabilizing", or "humanitarianism." But there are reasons why even Scrooge had to put more warming coals on the fire - the worker, Bob Cratchett, would have died of hypothermia otherwise! The next hypothesis will stress the needs for human capital as an explanation of social development.

Social Policy as the Development of "Human Capital"

The school is the agency through which the fertile masses are being cultivated so that the social and economic reforms which the people demanded may be established. (George Sanchez, 1936, p. 187)

In this section we will briefly examine the idea that social development changes in Mexico were inspired mostly by the needs for a healthy, somewhat educated and viable work force. Table II in the second section shows nine areas of social enhancement and what progress has been obtained in each of them, and may help us to choose amongst our competing explanations. Basically the argument being examined here is that, after 1942 especially, the main basis for social enhancement were the needs attendant to industrialization and the development of a labor force for this purpose. Actually some of the data we will look at on social security shows the support for some groups going back 20 years earlier. Of course, pulling the country together in the 1930s and heading off challenges to this "growthmanship" strategy in the 1940s, 50s, 60s, and 70s caused other "societal policies" to be floated We must remember that the most progressive features of the 1917 Constitution foreshadowed this course of events, even though we will argue that the narrowness of the aspiration has condemned half of the country to "marginalization" within the system.

To test this hypothesis that social development was inspired and implemented largely because of the needs of the emerging industrial order in Mexico, we must examine some general data concerning the pattern of social enhancement in the last 60 years. We are questioning whether the scope, the content, and the intensity of changes in education, health, pension, child care, justice, urban and community development, and nutrition are best seen as measures to modernize the labor force that was needed at any given time in Mexico. Conscious planning would be emphasized by this approach, decisions were made concerning the country's move to industrialization. If the author were an ardent functionalist he might stress the "functional prerequisites" of an industrial order, and see social policy as coming into being for these purposes. The teleological misfortunes of this latter argument must be approached cautiously, but the followers of Cardenas and Aleman were well aware of what was needed for an approach to economic and social modernization. Table I in the opening chapter showed the policy areas and their priority in relation to the transition, the particular type of emphasis involved, and a general description of the practices carried out. Some important dates are shown, as problems of "explanation" demand this.

Social development measures started in the 1930s or shortly before (areas such as public health and primary labor legislation). Broader based pensions were legislated in the early 1940s. The 1950s seemed a bit slower, but the 1960's saw an expansion of benefits to public and private employees (as ISSSTE in 1960) and such added amenities as child care in 1961. 1975 saw enhanced educational plans that tried to pull together the piecemeal programs of the previous years. More labor legislation (1970), pension extensions (1975), further development of CONASUPO, were typical of improvements in the 1970s. About 20% of the Federal budget was aimed at social goals in the 1970s. (See M.S. Grindle, p. 4, or J. Wilkie, 1970.). Some of these areas of social enhancement have more power to reduce the "marginalization" of those who do not as yet share in Mexico's affluence, as in income redistribution and educational areas.

How can we document such a thesis that asserts that the labor and political stability needs of a nation determines the pattern and magnitude of social enhancement? The accomplishment of various health or educational goals serve many purposes, directly and indirectly. The latter qualification may be agreed upon, but the original prioritizing of these aspects of economic development involves a logic and clout that determines many subsequent social events - not the least of which is the rise of what may be called an active as opposed to a passive marginalism. For now, let us just speculate upon what must have been the logic of the planners of the Mexican economic "miracle." We claim that the limited nature of the development goals allowed some fortunate Mexicans to enter the developed sphere and condemned others to active and passive marginalism. With active marginalism the very efforts to improve their lives may trap them in a self- and occasionally systems - reinforced isolation from major social benefits. Later, we will present several types of social reactions to this marginalization process.

Humanitarian Values as the Source of Social Policy

Mexico's history prior to the revolution showed expressions of values that could and did lead to social enhancement. The Spanish crown, the early church, the supporters of Indian culture, the anti-slavery movements, the ardent nationalistic reformers can all be observed as sources of humanitarian and practical values that furthered the patterns of social development of their particular periods. Our question must be succinctly put: Can any particular set of values toward people and society be seen as especially operative in determining 20th century Mexican social policy? For instance, Yankee, middle-class individualism; France's familial orientation, European stress on group well-being versus individual enhancement can be seen as guiding if not determining aspects of those respective policy developments.

The general ideological movements of the late 19th and 20th century in Mexico included values found elsewhere, namely liberalism, socialism, scientism or positivism, anarchism, Social Darwinism, clericalism and anti-clericalism, racialism, and many less comprehensive varieties. In discussions of the "intellectual precursors of the Mexican Revolution," James D. Cockcroft focuses especially upon the liberals of San Luis Potosi, who valued democracy, anti-clericalism, and free enterprise. According to Cockcroft: (p. 5) "By 1903 they were plotting for a violent revolution to overthrow Diaz and introduce profound social reforms." Cockcroft believes that the social goals of the revolution. universal secular education, equal rights for all, etc., have not been achieved in spite of the value precursors and their revolutionary expression in the 1917 Constitution as well. (See p. 6) Perhaps the "Social Darwinism" of the pre-revolutionary period is the "value" that became dominant rather than some more socially enhancing one. Perhaps an effete "positivism" is responsible for the lack of social progress because of its debilitating effects upon social enthusiasm. Particular ideologies are noted as having an effect by Cockcroft, however. European socialism, usually in anarchist forms, is seen as leading to Article 123 of the 1917 Constitution which was "labor's Bill of Rights." The labor strikes against the porifiriato were also seen as being decisive, but not as being sufficient to lead to a permanent revolutionary process. Another source on the powerful "liberalism" in Mexico is Wilfred Hardy Collcott who observes that the horizons of industrialization, the religious competition from Protestantism, and Catholic fractionalism (p. 179) all brought discussion of employment, worker's "vices", "civilizing missions", and institutional supports to the fore. Callcott believes that the Catholic church hierarchy was not a source of reform, at least: "Critics of the church pointed out that most of the important resolutions of the "church" congress died in committee, or were lulled to sleep by long prayers about social justice." Particularly the attack on lay schools was seen as reactionary and part of the anti-revolutionary Sinarquista. Women's and children's rights were also ignored, and only the forces of ideological competition spurred social reform - not the ideas of liberalism or Christianity themselves.

Clearly humanistic values can be seen in several areas, of course. Many of the rural teachers who died for their efforts as well as the work of the Indigenistas, reflect these well.

A Speculative Model of When and How Increased Participation Has Been Achieved

To close this chapter let us diagram (somewhat speculatively) the level of participation in various areas of social development in relationship to some of the probable sources of pressure. Some specific indicators have been used to construct diagram #1. Connecting lines show a mixture of common sense and outright imagination, and the (probably faulty) assumption is that participation of the total population has been more or less steadily upward. Which indicators are used to represent broader areas make this picture subject to bias, but the main pattern is one of low levels of participation in all areas - except diffuse public health areas.

Most Mexicans share little beyond sky, air and sometimes highways, but we do assume an expansion in absolute numbers of participants. Observers of this diagram should note that this is an ongoing effort whose full attainment may be long in coming. Solid, comparable data over time is basically lacking. Some help was given in the Statistical Abstract for Latin America, Wilkie's data on federal social expenditures and Mexican governmental statistics (as from SPP, The National Institute of Geographical Information). The caution must be repeated that only in a few places are these lines anchored in solid data.

In diagram #1 we have plotted seven more specific areas of social development, and a general indicator in the form of percent of the federal budget spent on social development. The latter start on Wilkie's 1970 time series and take government statistics at face value since then. We know that Mexico's social expenditures are relatively and absolutely low. Admittedly various specific indices could have been used to give different pictures of the level of participation. As to the specific areas, pensions only go to a little over a third of all workers, which means only a fourth of the total population (See Carmelo Mesa-Lago and Rose Johnson Spaulding - latter says 27.9% of population in December, 1977, and going down). Education could have been gauged by noting the 18 million Mexican youth now in school versus the 4 million not in school. This would make them look like better providers, however, than the statistic involving the proportion of the population who have ever gone to school. (Spaulding, 1978, p. 297). Our composite graph line consists of a compromise between the 82% of school age children now attending at least the first few years of school, and the less than 20% of adults over 20 years of age who have never had any schooling (See Richard Beesen, in Volume 21 of the Statistical Abstract for Latin America). As to personal health, we use data from the Global plan of the Mexican government (See Levy and Szekely, 1983, pp. 142 & 161). The government itself acknowledged that 18 million (versus 25 million participants) do not have access to modern medical care.

The next line up from the bottom reflects the increased literacy of the Mexican population. The drive for mass literacy in the 1940s, although not as inspired as the approach in Cuba or Nicaragua later on, did bring up the level considerably. In coming up with our level of

DIAGRAM I

PARTICIPATION BY PERIOD

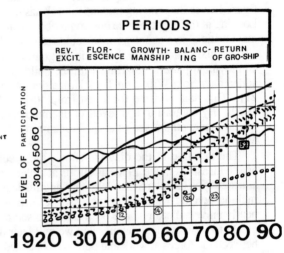

participation here in literacy, we noted a figure of around 77% literate was used by Levy and Szeleky (citing Mexico's S.P.P.). This figure is considerably at variance with ones offered by Richard W. Bessen where the urban population was 67.8% literate but the rural population only attained 32.3%. (The size of the rural population in 1975 was 36 million of 59 million people.) The line we drew for literacy may be optimistically high. Food adequacy has been variously observed in data justifying recent S.A.M. and CONASUPO programs. A figure of about 70% of the population having food adequacy may be argued by people like Ana Marie Flores, May and McLellan, Daniel Acuna, etc., but this figure leaves 30% facing malnutrition, Kuashiorkore or Avitaminosis. Looking at the negative side one could observe an "Asia type pattern of malnutrition" in a country which could feed itself better.

The sixth curve from the top in diagram #1 meant to deal with the employment pattern. Starting with the buildup in industrialization we added data from Wilkie on Total Utilization of Labor (SALA, Volume 21). This data allowed for a just from 40% in 1950 to 70.8% in the 1970s. By contrast to low levels of unemployment (20%) noted by the government, others see over 50% unemployed or underemployed in Mexico.

The last line in the diagram shows the precipitous rise in public health measures in the 1930s as efforts at malaria and yellow fever were attacked (See Gordon Schandel). Our optimistically high curve does not include potable water or unsuccessful efforts to clean urban air, yet nearly universal efforts have been started in some areas. The diagram is meant to show some dynamics and we will later discuss the interaction between the forces at work and outcomes obtained.

CHAPTER IV

A CHRONOLOGY OF THE PAST TWO DECADES

The economy and society of Mexico have always evolved at different rates, in some periods economic change outstripping social change and at other times institutional reforms exceeding the capacity of the economy to finance them. (Clark Reynolds, 1977, page 23)

This chapter will outline the major social policy attainments of the past two decades. Our chosen period, 1972-1992 brackets the sexenios of Echeverria, Portillo, De La Madrid and Salinas. This period represents a roller-coaster ride in terms of economic activity. Hopefully our efforts will be of value in perceiving the trends into the 1990s and beyond.

Using such sources as Nora Hamilton, Judith Adler Hellman, Dale Johnson, Alan Riding, Peter Ward, and David Barkin we can get an accurate picture of this period. While Mexican economic activity has attracted much academic interest (5 times as much in the XVIIth International Congress of LASA in 1992) social outcomes have had less attention (although Greuning, Wilkie, Serron, and Ward have served us well). We do need time series data, as Wilkie presented in 1970 in his book on Mexican Federal expenditures. Table IV here, offers some select highlights of the past two decades. Innovations and incremental gains in various sectors will be discussed in separate chapters. Our overall chronology will try to depict other writer's evaluations of the policies and expenditures, and the motive forces of various governments.

Going back to the regime of Luis Echeverria, Judith Hellman believes that the "populist" programs were finished off by 1974. (See Mexico in Crisis, second edition, 1983, page 205) Echeverria evidently had started a constituency building process with increased social spending in social security, housing, education and health. Many point out that he was trying to overcome his role in the student massacre at Tlateloco in 1968, and that the reformist thrust was also motivated by the continued threat of mass unrest. Hellman notes 160 legislative initiatives in this president's first years. Major attacks from his right wing political flank finally slowed the reformist thrust. As both Hellman and Hamilton observe, the Mexican government and president are only "relatively autonomous" of the national and international bourgeoisie. (Hellman, page 196; Hamilton, The Limits of State Autonomy, 1982, page viii.) No further redistribution was possible for other reasons as well. As Hellman observes:

> Lacking an honest and efficient bureaucracy to collect personal income, luxury, and corporate profit taxes, the government had to continue to rely for its revenue on indirect taxation, which hits the poor harder than any other class and does nothing at all to redistribute wealth.

Still the accomplishments of the Echeverria sexenio included an extension of social security health benefits to 10 million more Mexicans; the construction of over 100,000 housing units; a quadrupling of technical training institutes; a four fold increase in CONASUPO, the national food staples agency; increases in minimum wages nearly up to the level of inflation; and a serious emphasis upon rural reform. The end to this period of reform was due to many things, including what Hellman (page 212) observes about the absence of a sophisticated, social democratic constituency - welcome to the club! Echeverria also faced the assassination of a key assistant, Bonfil, the progressive secretary he had placed in the National Peasant Confederation. The regime ended in chaos, involving inflation, devaluation, explosive rural conditions, threats of military coups, and the flight of the peso.

Echeverria's sexenio gave way to Lopez Portillo in 1976 who moved quickly with The Global Development Plan. Many sets of interests would chip away at this orderly plan for solid economic growth, including the great "peso theft" by which the Mexican government inadvertently created great wealth by underwriting the peso with foreign loans - which allowed the upper and middle classes to exchange pesos for dollars and to profit greatly at the expense of the nation. Hellman (page 227) observes that Portillo seemed willing to cut the freespending "populism" which Echeverria had engaged in, but a powerful union structure had the clout to hold onto its social benefits package. Hellman sees the program as involving ad hoc handouts that functioned as "cooptation", in several regimes. Portillo could only cut public spending by 3% because of internal pressures, and the situation was managed by borrowing 60 billion dollars from abroad! Hamilton in an article ("State-class Alliances and Conflicts: Issues and Actors in the Mexican Economic Crisis", in Latin American Perspectives, Fall, 1984, page 12) observes that the years 1977 to 1981, the core period of the Portillo regime, were ones in which the "petrolization of the development model" occurred. An 8% economic growth surge was achieved each year. Nevertheless, citing Erwin Rodriguez, Hamilton sees increased economic inequality. By 1982, if not sooner, the petro bubble burst, and the international banks were putting together an austerity centered "rescue package." Mexico's lower class was to "bite the bullet" even more desperately, if not the previously high-flying middle classes.

The last three months of the Portillo regime were called the "nationalist interlude" by Hamilton. She notes the demands from the left for nationalization of the banks (which the president did on September 1st of 1982) effective exchange controls and lower interest rates. Portillo had been enraged when one bank sent a third of a billion dollars out of the country in one single day (Hamilton, page 17). Hellman notes that the incoming president, Miguel de la Madrid, did not share much enthusiasm for the bank take-over, and instead favored an "open economy." The trend, however, was at this point toward increased state activism, and the government found that it had become temporary "owner" of many private sector enterprises. De La Madrid did what he could to denationalize the bank take-over by selling shares back into the private economy and to other agencies besides the Federal government. De La Madrid also decontrolled 4,700" non-essential" items (many food items!) which the previous government had sought to control after its biggest devaluation. (Hellman, page 230) And, there were other aspects to austerity! Many thousands of workers would lose their jobs, and real per capita income would take a nose-dive. Protection for many small business people would also disappear. At this point construction on major government projects (like Metro-subways in Mexico City and Monterrey) would be temporarily stopped. Prices on essential food items(from tortillas to eggs to soap) would be allowed to rise, and a great inflation set upon the land that would only be partially compensated by modest level of living increases. Rural areas which were already at the bottom of the benefits barrel, were further degraded when such helpful programs as SAM (Mexican Food System) were dropped for the most part. The costs of all government services and products like petroleum went up sharply, and this complicated both urban and rural living for the hardest hit populations.

Many "subsidies" were dropped or cut, and the personal price of destitution had again increased!

We will give a more thorough description and analysis of these austerity and post austerity developments later on. Let us now describe the general economic and social policy events from early 1982 to the present. Early 1982 seen a number of economic adjustments which might have given hope to something of substance. Facing an inflation rate of 28% and a foreign debt of nearly 50 billion dollars, a variety of fiscal measures were attempted - not all meeting compliance. A "new realism" was to allow certain goods to achieve a true market value. De la Madrid had a plan that was to be fully in place by 1988. It was admitted that there was 100% inflation in the land. A ten point program was to break from the previous irresponsible "financial populism." However, along with a cut in the growth of public spending there would be a stress on jobs via labor intensiveness, an increase in public sector goods, and reinforcement of new norms for public honesty. Labor balked openly by 1984. Other kinds of policies than those relying upon increased expenditure were stressed, for instance decentralization of Mexico city, by giving stimulus to peripheral areas. It also cost little to decentralize health and education facilities and to give some more incentives to saving.

Our Diagram II covering Sexenios and Policies draws upon several students of Mexico's political economy including Thomas Skidmore, Peter Smith, and David Barkin. Just what these supposed swings mean in terms of strategy or fortuity is not clear. De la Madrid was responding to macro-economic events and to management parameters we are dimly aware of. The internal forces dealing with the trade union demands, the needs for stability, and the needs to keep the poorest from total immiseration, are sometimes clear in their intent. Each president must also show a net gain in economic growth, and this may at times be the dominating motivation. In the 1990s the economic growth theme may reoccur, as a reflex response to the lures of "Globalization" and the NAFTA. The latter not quite being a reality or even having an image as of this writing. The situation now (1992) seems one of waiting for a payoff from a source not yet clear! Austerity, reform, modernization and other clichés dominate the policy dialog. "Severe social sacrifices" are no longer called for, but are a lingering specter used to justify the meagerness of benefits. There are still promises followed by phrases like..."If circumstances permit..."

El Pronasol: A Step Toward Social Reconciliation?

There is supposedly a Chinese curse that goes: "May you live in interesting times!" It goes without saying that it will be interesting to see if social solidarity can be achieved given the other, obvious, priorities. The Federal government still has most of the cards as far as budgetary considerations are involved. The individual state's budgets for any spending are up to only 12% of the total and the municipios approach only 5 to 7%. (Mexico: A Country Guide, Edited by Tom Barry, 1992) If government policy is going to promote exports and private investments with its share, and still further the "solaridad" proposals of Pronasol, it will be very interesting.

In describing the "underside of modernization" the staff of the Inter-Hemispheric Education Research Center note the increased problems with wealth distribution and the failure of it to "trickle down." These unbalanced economics have manifest themselves in the areas of housing, nutrition, and health. (page 93) The aggressive approach in the past two decades at "stabilizing development" had helped to keep up the standards for a period. Poverty still prevailed as the lot for most, and the consumer world of shopping malls and modern food markets was not to be for everyone. On the other hand, the "oligarchy", largely in the major cities, the "300" or the real "senate", including old and newly rich, still made major decisions. At various points there was open conflict, and the drama over bank nationalization and the attempts to stem the flow of capital were for real.

All in all the poor seemed to be paying the costs for development (on the backs of this group, say these researchers). This was clearly shown by the fact that wage increases remained well below price increases - thus, squeezing out the resources of the working groups. The results were clear as well. The world bank was quoted as saying that Mexico had (has) one of the "worst profiles of income distribution of any nation on earth." Can social solidarity be achieved when you have a housing deficit of 6 million units, an infant mortality of 36 per 1000, when over half of rural families have no access to safe water, when extreme malnutrition impacts almost 25% of the population and 23% to 43% of the population are below the poverty line? What chance for social peace when 18% of workers are unemployed, by official statistics?

Our effort here is to deal with the issue of affordability as a developing country tries to manage a range of priorities and to achieve social justice at the same time. How much more difficult is the reduction of this deficit during a period of austerity so called? At one time in the U.S. it was estimated that only 13 billion dollars would have been necessary in order to move all of those below the poverty line up to it. One can argue about the merits of the poverty line, and of being a dollar above it, but a finite amount could be said to be involved. Houses, health care, potable water, and even the capital required to create a decent job are definable amounts - even if unobtainable at a given time. Some items are bigger ticket ones than others, and some may take little transfer of funds. Social solidarity may be achieved by much less than the total amounts we will show on the following page; do people accept as legitimate a system based on retrospective perceptions or on prospective beliefs about the achievement of relative social justice?

This 1989 presidential, social welfare program may create social solidarity. According to Barry and Associates (Mexico: A Country Guide, 1992) 50% of public investment in 1990 were via PRONASOL. (See p. 99) As "modernization" proceeds, this program is to keep the popular sectors from being left behind. Our table on the next page, "The Social Deficit: How Affordable Would Closing the Gap Be Or Otherwise" is an attempt to estimate how much the program might have to spend. The area deficits noted are from the Barry volume, and the other figures are meant to give a possible range, keeping in mind that doing nothing will still cost Pesos in terms of social chaos! Striking cuts have been made in the old "safety net". Much distrust exists about who will pay the costs of the new economic policies, or if the damage done is repairable. These figures can be compared to typical, feasible and likely expenditures, and to the improbables of western economic systems up to the year 2000.

Pronasol has been affordable on a one-time basis because of the selling-off of assets like Telmex, although it may have been the franchise rather than the actual capital equipment that had value. Offering short term palliatives on soft moneys may not achieve even the patronage goals, and only divert a few constituencies from "cardenismo." As a kind of "marxist-salinista" or as an elaborate presidential based "charity" it does impact images from within and without the country. Handing out credit, titles to land, scholarships, clinics, help for farmers or schools and electricity will catch the attention of "grass roots" groups. The really dispossessed will have to answer with respect to their participation. Rather we are supposed to have "co-participation" if that is distinct from the old time patronage. The Barry volume may be correct in seeing it as targeted upon Neo-cardenista areas whose loyalty is needed in 1994 and beyond. The concept can go beyond old formulas, of course, and there has always been this element of presidential welfare for the purpose of immediate political gain. It plays well with outside investors eager to see the end of the old "welfare state." There is less "waste" in direct handouts, and the bureaucratic machine is by-passed. Clearly the model might persist and absorb other recurring resources, especially since it rewards the faithful and punishes those who stray. If it absorbs other resources this can be chalked up to the cost of doing business, and a bargain at that from the political point of view. The beneficiaries may be clever enough to keep the process going, as well. Communities in critical political intersections will no doubt sell their loyalty for social services, increased productive capacity, and infrastructure.

As to affordability, most systems are floating their debts, as if they were using credit cards, paying on the installment plan or willing to sell some cherished resource if things came to that point.

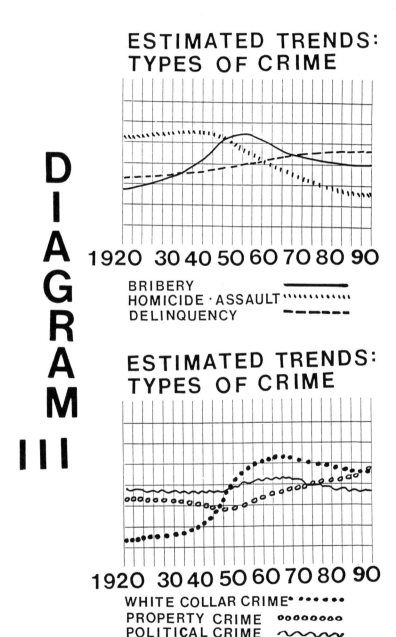

ESTIMATED TRENDS:
TYPES OF CRIME

1920 30 40 50 60 70 80 90

BRIBERY
HOMICIDE · ASSAULT
DELINQUENCY

**D
I
A
G
R
A
M

III**

ESTIMATED TRENDS:
TYPES OF CRIME

1920 30 40 50 60 70 80 90

WHITE COLLAR CRIME
PROPERTY CRIME
POLITICAL CRIME

TABLE IV-A
THE SOCIAL DEFICIT: HOW AFFORDABLE WOULD CLOSING THE GAP BE/OR OTHERWISE?

AREA	HIGH ESTIMATE	LOW ESTIMATE	UNDER PRONASOL	COSTS OF NOT CLOSING THE GAP (SOCIAL CHAOS)
Housing = 6 million unit gap	@ $10,000 = $60 billion gap	@ $5,000 = $30 billion gap	25% of medium estimate (45 bil. = 11.25 bil.)	10% of medium estimate = 4.5 bil
Housing: 40% substandard	@ 6 mil. pesos x 12 mil. units = $24 bil (Ward, 1990, p. 195)	@ 3 mil. pesos x 12 mil. units = $12 bil.	25% of medium estimate of 18 mil. = 4.5 bil.	10% of medium estimate = 1.8 bil.
Access to Health (15% without)	@ 3,000 per = 36 bil. (via market or SSA, COPLAMAR)	@ $1,500 per = $18 bil.	25% of $27 bil. = $7.75 bil. (redistribution would help)	10% of $27 bil. = $2.7 bil. (AIDS a "time bomb?")
Rural Lack of Water = 53%	30% of 80 mil. x $1,000 = $24 bil.	$300 x 24 mil. = $7.2 bil.	25% of 31.2 bil. = $7.8 bil.	10% of 31.2 bil. = $3.1 bil.
30% Under the "Poverty Line"	10 mil. x $40 per week x 52 weeks = 20.8 bil.	$20 per week x 10 mil. x 52 = $10.4 bil.	25% of 15.6 bil. = $3.8 bil.	25% of 15.6 bil. = $3.8 bil. (+crime & unrest!)
Extreme Malnutrition = 15%	$1,000 x 13.5 mil. = 13.5 bil.	$500 x 13.5 mil. = $6.5 bil.	25% of $10 bil. = $2.5 bil.	10% of $10 bil. - $1. bil.
Education = 6 years for 2/3 vs. 8 years for 100%	Up 1/3 = $20. bil.	$10. bil.	25% of 15 bil. - 3.75	25% of 15 bil. = $3.75
Other - corrections, public health, literacy	$30. bil.	$15. bil.	25% of 22.5 bil = $5.6 bil.	10% of $22.5 bil. = $2.25 bil.
Bottom Line	= $228.3 billion	$109.35 billion	$47.01 billion	$22.90 billion

TABLE IV-B
SOCIAL POLICIES AND THIER OUTCOMES: A DECADE & A HALF

EXAMPLES	TRENDS OR COMMENTS
1974 - 160 initiatives (first 3 years) (housing, CONASUPO)	- Deficit financing - Much food imported - Attacks on spending effective
1975 - Rural reform (plan Puebla)	- More technical education (1301 institutes)
1976 - Birth control (vs. income redistribution) - Devaluation crisis	- 10 million more under Social Security - 100,000 more homes
1977 - Portillo moves away from economic reformism	- Shift from "welfare" - Peso supported by loans
1978 - COPLAMAR for depressed areas	- Middle class frantically consuming - "Sacadolares" steal pesos
1979 - World energy plan & "north-south" dialog divert attention	- Internal pressure preserves programs
1980 - S.A.M. established - Plan global Desarrollo - Land reform eneded = production	- Stress on jobs - Plans indicative, not compulsory - Transnational encouraged
1981 - "Informe De Gobierno" admits problems - Mexico city buses nationalized	- Social investments less than 10% of the total
1982 - Pider programs - Arid zones act - Banks nationalized	- Devaluation - February 18 - "Unprecedented austerity"
1983 - MMH attacks "financial populism - Subsidies cut - Judicial "reform"	- Decrim. of abortion beaten - Decebtralization of health, educ. - S.A.M. dismantled
1984 - Nat. Dem. planning system - Segundo Informe = anexo salud	- Under SPP, also Sedue & Coplade in DDF. - Showed 91% IMSS urban areas
1985 - Earthquake changes priorities	
1986 - Renovacion Habitacional Popular	- "Democratic accord" rehoused after Terremoto
1987 - CONAPO (credit for growth rate decline?) - "Econ. Solidarity Pact"	- Demographic transition at work - Parasite decline (social too?) - Inflation cut via stand. of living
1988 - General Health Act - More public libraries	- To "modernize" & decentralize
1989 - Budgetary surplus	- Supposedly used to strengthen Security & CONASUPO

CHAPTER V

SPECIFIC AREAS OF SOCIAL DEVELOPMENT

Some have lavishly praised the Mexican government for its contribution to the economic development of Mexico. Many others have condemned it for allowing the benefits of rapid growth to be so inequitably distributed. (Hansen, 1971, page 4.)

In Mexico and Puerto Rico, for example, a rising (Gini) coefficient did not mean that the income share of the wealthier groups had risen. In fact, it had fallen, with the middle-income groups gaining at the expense of both the lower 60% AND the upper 5%. (Clarence Zuvekas, Jr., 1979, page 282.)

The tendency to emphasize the progressive aspects of Mexican society is also enhanced by the historians' interest in historical differences. But, I believe the importance of these differences has been exaggerated The remarkable thing about Mexico is that, despite its glorious revolution and all the institutional changes associated with it, its class structure and economic organization are all too familiar. (Robert Rhodes, 1970, in Wilber, 1973, page 294.)

Mexico in the early 1980s started a roller coaster ride down from a heady peak of oil revenues and optimistic actions. Previously, for a short moment, it had seemed as if the growthmanship model would be soon fulfilled. Mexico's previous 6% plus growth rate allowed the country to take on some charismatic qualities and also attracted much attention in this hemisphere and abroad - veritable Mexican miracle. Let us look, close up, at some of the materials generated by this attention to better gauge Mexico's rise and decline in the past 6 years, especially as to distributional aspects.

Some Hard Facts, Income Distribution

The British magazine, The Economist, has focused on Mexico's general condition with extensive surveys almost on a regular, three year basis. The Economist's writers, utilizing mostly ILO data, note great unevenness in Mexico's personal development. There appear to be, as we have already alluded to in this volume, great disparities in the distribution of family income. Thus, (April 22, 1978, page 16) "the rich got richer." Paraphrasing this latter report, from 1950 to 1969 the top 20% went from 59.8% of the pie to 64% of the pie. Meanwhile, the lowest 20% from 6.1% in 1950 to $0% in 1969. As a result of this: (See page 16)

> Mexico became the classic dual economy with a modem sector
> small in numbers but rich in money and power, and a traditional
> sector large in numbers but poor and weak.

Apart from an "increasingly" unequal distribution for the poor, which others such as Yotopulos and Nugent document, is not economic life getting better in Mexico for many groups? The Economist notes right off that Mexico's $1,000 (U.S.) GNP per head (page 3) puts Mexico in the middle tier of developing countries. Also the Economist observes that:

> ...the form of development pursued by Mexico since the outbreak of
> the second world war has not improved the living standards of
> perhaps the greater part of the Mexicans by the statistical average of
> 3% or so a year...

This last figure is supposedly meant not to be impressive; that is, the economic level of living for most Mexicans has not dramatically improved - but 33 years would give 100% improvement! It is admittedly hard to decide which statistics to focus upon, so this chapter will examine the economic fates of major groups in the Mexican nation. We will strive for aggregate as well as distributive measures so a more complete picture can emerge. The present author has glimpsed both the tops and bottoms of economic well-being in Mexico, and will try to be aware of the caveat by Darrill Huff, the statistician, that "there are lies, damned lies, and statistics!" We shall also in this chapter look at some of the various explanations for these various outcomes in personal and family income.

The UN-ECLA assigns (1970) a Gini coefficient of 0.53 to Mexico (versus 0.40 for the U.S., and 0.36 for Norway). Although there are a

variety of ways to achieve this measure of income distribution, Mexico
seems to be quite unequal in its distribution. According to Clarence
Zuvekas, (1979, page 280) such measures on Latin American countries
- as opposed to developed countries - are due to the extreme inequality
registered in the upper deciles. (See page 281) Supposedly, there is
less income inequality among the lower half of recipients. Using
Kuznets as a source, these kinds of inequalities are evidently typical of
early phases of capitalist economic development. Clearly, to repeat,
there is great inequality in Mexico. Still we are told, a middle class
with much collective affluence has emerged. Mexico's gilded housing,
numerous automobiles (including large U.S. types), comfortable
amenities, and sumptuous consumption pattern and life style are
apparent in Mexico City and some of the other major cities. Many of
the Capital's major newspapers radiate this affluence - indeed flaunt it!
People's economic choices fit the proliferation in levels of living and
the 1980s consumption explosion. While the lower-middle class may
favor the Gigante stores with their wide array of consumables, the
upper-middle class will probably favor the Liverpool type stores for
their much finer (and status oriented) line of products and sharply higher
prices! The new shopping centers are gorged with products and
customers as any in suburban Chicago or New York City. The 15% of
income receivers below the top 5% have gone from 19.8% of the pie in
1950 to 28% in 1969! This would seem not to be a "middle-class" but
might be an adjunct to a dominant group. It would almost seem as if
cooptation (apart from merit) had been given a statistical description.
These income earners are Mexico's managers, professionals, small
owners, and technicians, as well as its "go-betweens" and legitimators.
Yes, Virginia! there is middling affluence in Mexico as most of
Excelsior's advertisements would reflect. The fine stores on Reforms,
on Insurgentes, in satellite and University city, and in the Zona Rosa
have a considerable clientele. As in U.S. cities, the family desire is for
housing that will match their social aspirations. There are no shortage
of offers for "mas bellas residencias" at "mensualidades" between 10 and
100 million pesos, and at various times in the late 1970s, no shortage
of takers. Such housing comes with tennis club, and horse riding - the
overall imagery is strikingly universal, yet the detail is Mexican.

How shall we best approach the topic of economic levels of living
and their consequences? A breakdown of where money comes from
would initially be in order. Some clear data on income distribution
would be helpful on this important topic. Next a discussion of what it
costs to live well or modestly seems desirable; that is, the implications
of living with certain budgets. Materials on the effects of recent
inflation and peso devaluation's are, of course, essential. Recent studies

of major economic groups would give life to the statistics; and, we can also cover some of the "causes" of poverty - although the author feels that it is a lack of money in the latter case, and need not be obfuscated!

Where Does The Money Come From - And Go To

According to Ifigenia De Navarrete in her excellent summation "Income Distribution in Mexico", (1969, page 133), property income is about 1/3 of the total disposable income; wages and salaries about 30%; agricultural income about 26% and the rest is "mixed" including the self employed. According to De Navarrete, wage earners usually "expand" in a progressive, middle-class economy, but property and money owners were more or less holding their own between 1940 and 1950. The 1950-1980 period saw a substantial expansion here. As a caution, it can be noted that trade, and hence trade profits, may also be undervalued as this category slips out of view of the tax and fiscal process. De Navarrete observes that: "on that evidence, many researchers stated that the inequality of income distribution became more acute and highly adverse to labor..." In order to qualify these perceptions it must be noted that gains or losses depended upon the type of industrial or agricultural work involved. Based on data from the Combined Working Party Study, wage earners in both agricultural and non-agricultural areas declined varyingly from 6 to 27% versus percentage increases for entrepreneurs from 30 to 159%! Taxation was also low or moderate for the latter group, and its standard of living must have risen dramatically, even though De Navarrete offers some cautions on this point. One of her sharper comparisons (See page 141) is that from 1940 to 1950 entrepreneurial rewards increased from 60 to 66% while wage earners fell from 40 to 34% of the total! This would seem to indicate that Miguel Alemán's dictum (1952) that wealth must be created before it could be distributed does apply to the rich. The following may summarize what De Navarrete has to say about distribution and the size of the pie: (page 142)

> Those researchers who protested the unfair distribution of income were right, but so were those who claimed there has been a general rise in the standard of living. An analysis of the data shows that these statements are not contradictory..

De Navarrete senses most of the contradictions herself, as for instance, her perception of the depressing effects of this income distribution upon the economy; the shrinkage of working-class salaries, and the uncertainty of absolute improvements in everyone's lot. Indeed, capitalist dynamics work in strange and mysterious ways! De Navarrete seems to have used the best data available for this early 1950 period, and by using the "combined Mexican Working Party's" data, a 5105 family study of personal income, and some census data, a solid portrait with comparisons were drawn. This portrait did lack the statistical articulation of later analyses done in the 1960s and 1970s with Gini coefficients. Still there are some very instructive comparisons which this early observer noted, including the perception of the average increase from 1950 to 1957 of 23% in real terms while "the lower 20% were worsened in both absolute and relative terms." (Page 166) She notes that the ones who benefited most were the higher VII to X deciles (excluding the top 2.4%). We must ask what some of the consequences of these facts are.

The Cost Of A Good Tortilla

Budgetary studies are recent even in the "developed" countries, much less in Mexico - where there is an apparent avoidance of the issue. There are, however, local studies, and these analysts' general impressions. There are also studies of the impact of specific economic events as Thomas G. Sander's (in May of 1977) who analyzed the effects of the peso devaluation in the previous August. The effects upon the price of food and the general costs of living are evidently very striking. Sanders notes what was happening during this entire period of the first major devaluation: (1977, page 3)

...This was a period in which world petroleum and grain prices jumped sharply upward, and Mexico had to import both. As growth in Agricultural products proceeded at a slower pace than population the government had to import greater quantities of food every year to avoid exacerbating shortages and inflation, which was already unprecedently high...Though Mexico had not serious food shortages ...this happy result was bought...at a price.

More specifically food and basic living commodities took a huge jump in price. Sanders goes on to assess the total impact: (See page 10)

It would seem that the lower, especially the nonunionized classes, have suffered relatively more from inflation than the other groups, since the highest rates occurred in food prices, drinks, tobacco, transportation, clothing and shoes, for which they spend a larger share of their income.

The poor clearly got it in the neck again! The present author's many trips to Mexico, often with his family, between 1967 and 1983 has allowed him to note the differences in peso values over these years - as our food was purchased at local markets and "super-mercados." Prices are stiff in the late 1980s, even on a Yankee Professor's salary.

Equally important is what specific foods people rely on. The price of corn flour at the village level is an important survival matter, as is the cost of beans, oil, leche, spices, pollo and other staples. May and McLellan, a source we will use extensively in our chapter on health and nutrition, note basic peasant and Indian diets as consisting of essentially what many of their parents and ancestors ate. (1973, page 35)

It is estimated that 30% of the Mexicans eat as their ancestors did, deriving 60-80% of their calories from corn and beans. Another 50% of the people are working families in rural areas where most of the dietary resources are produced. Hence, they get a mixed type of diet; in addition to a corn base, bread, pasta, rice, some meat, milk, and eggs are eaten...Finally 20% are sharply influenced by foreign cultures.

May and McLellan note that: "The main meal which is eaten in the afternoon, is based on tortillas as preceded by a soup in which some meat may be present, and followed by beans." May and McLellan observe the lack of protein among the "masses" and the tendency in rural areas to sell such meat to buy higher energy foods. The evident need is for energy now, not body building later! Because we will deal with nutrition and nutrition policy later, we will only note that when corn and beans go up in cost, then there are basically only trade-offs with slow malnutrition. The CONASUPO stores which buy from local producers at levels above the world market and sell at a more reasonable rate to poor (including 50% to the urban poor) consumers helps to keep food coming to Mexican tables. These operations will also be discussed later, but they have been much impacted by recent austerity moves, so much so that only one pasta product is subsidized.

Recent Studies Of The Economic Level of Living In Mexico

As Roger D. Hansen observed in 1971, income distribution (See page 72) in the 1940s (1950s?) was:

...characterized by (1) rapidly rising entrepreneurial incomes, (2) slowly rising per capita wage and salary earnings, and a fall in real wage rates.

Citing the 1960 De Navarrete study we have utilized, Hansen also cites studies by Sturmthal (1955) and by Rosado and Vazquez in 1951. We can also go beyond these studies from the early period of Mexican industrialization. Hansen carries the De Navarrete data to 1963 and we will carry it further, noting as Hansen does the criticisms of such data as that which Raymond Vernon offers.

Yotopoulos and Nugent offer 1969 data in their text on the Economics of Development: Empirical Investigations in 1977 (Chapter 14, "Income distribution, poverty, and Dualism") to indicate that the lowest 40% of income receivers in Mexico gets only 10% of the pie, the middle 40% get 25%, and the top 20% get 64%. It seems that the earlier data noted by De Navarette are indicative of a trend - what ever capitalist apologists say about such data's tentativeness. "Trickle-down" is not working!

Should we view such "trends" and their supposed reversibility according to the Kuznet's interpretation of capitalist development? We can only look to more recent descriptions and hope for an answer to our own questions. Thomas Sanders in reviewing "the contradictions of development" (See Mexico in 1975, page 7) observes that:

> The contradictions in Mexican development are reflected in the contrast between the obvious opulence of the politicians, businessmen, and professionals with the fine houses in Acapulco or the Lomas of Mexico City, and the degrading poverty of the rural and urban lower classes... though national per capita income exceeded $650 in 1970, 72% of those who declared income in the census of that year earned less than $80.00 a month, and nearly 40% earned less than $40.00 a month.

The key reason for the disparities which Sanders discusses is the notion of "marginality" which we will discuss in our theoretical summary. Whereas "businessmen, the middle-employees of government, companies... and unionized worker are the major beneficiaries," other, not so situated marginals have "profited little from the country's progress (see page 7).

We have repeatedly generalized as to whom benefits and who does not from the Mexican economic "miracle." Let us now discuss the general level of living which each major social class experiences. Much data is organized as to rural and urban differences, and in recent years the urban anthropologists have looked at the communities hanging on to the edges (or middle parts) of the major cities. So let us start at the bottom of Mexican economic life, and then move to the silvered towers that coexist with the less privileged communities.

The Really Poor In Mexico: Description And Some "Explanation"

Standards of living in rural Mexico are exceedingly low. Poverty is so typical in the Mexican countryside and in the small villages that any departure from it is striking. (Mosk, The Industrial Revolution in Mexico, 1950, page 204.)

As a whole the data on Shantytown economy reported in this chapter suggest the existence of an economic system that is peculiar to marginality. This system meshes, so to speak, with the urban industrial system since it exists on its waste, inefficiency, and occasional surplus. (Lomnitz, Networks and Marginality, 1977, page 91.)

There have been more descriptions of poverty in Mexico than of the middle classes or of the very affluent. We will review a few of these studies of the former type here.

Larissa Adler Lomnitz notes earlier data by Bataillon and Riviere d'Arc (1973) where 50% of the nation's dwellings had floor space of less than 14 square meters, where the majority had no adequate sanitary facilities, and where a substantial number had only one bed for the family. (Page 91) These descriptions, with all their implied pathos, are like those of the American comedian Jimmy Durante and were such that their idea of a "square meal" was a soda cracker. It is difficult to define extreme poverty, but if you have sat in your car early in the morning and watched a parade of people taking their breakfast from the same cafe garbage can - then you can appreciate that it exists. The reality is, of course, more intense for those being observed in this casual observation. Good citizens of the U.S. of A. were probably not familiar with poverty north of the Rio Grande until the 1960s. The "rediscovery of poverty" came in a variety of forms, not just books about the "invisible Americans." Yankee Americans were evidently ready to be re-introduced to their marginal peoples whether white, native American, Black, Chicano or otherwise. The "affluent society" had bypassed its less connected and geographically isolated members. The political-economic studies of such populations in the 1960s saw these groups as "Internal colonies", "doubly exploited peoples", people who were "culturally deprived", and as victims who were blamed for their own problems. We should first look at the economic circumstances of these peoples at the lowest levels of Mexican society to see what typifies their existence. The sociological notion of "levels" may not suit all tastes because it implies a judgment of either the bottom dwellers or the society - so be it!

In describing the "Internal market" in 1950 Mosk noted the characteristics of the poor in Mexico. (chapter XI.) According to Mosk writing at that point in history, the poor came from the over-populated central plateau; they had suffered there from excessively small land holdings; their worldly resources had subsequently been eroded; there were too many of them; their traditions were probably an obstacle; their diets were amongst the worst in the world; and resettlement would probably not solve their problems. The solutions involving the migration of these populations to the less crowded coastal areas or the more crowded cities (as Mexico city's Netzahualcoyotl area) was also beset with extreme problems. Has this 30 year old description by Mosk much validity today? Are the problems of the very poor less desperate?

Writing about problems attendant to the oil boom and industrialization (New York Times, December 9, 1978, page E 3.) Alan Riding observes the following about the poor and their current experiences:

> In rural hamlets and city slums, inflation totaling more than 50% over the past 3 years has meant a drop in living standards for many people already struggling at a subsistence level. Even such basic products as corn, beans, bread and sugar have risen sharply in price, while milk, eggs and meat are now luxury products for the majority. "Enormous sectors of the population are suffering from hunger, serious hunger," labor leader Angel Olivo Solis told President Lopez Portillo recently.

Riding is referring to Mexico's marginal poor and in this article he notes the Mexican government's hope that by developing big industry this will create jobs in spin-off, labor intensive areas. The likelihood that even these latter jobs will "trickle down" to these marginal poor is debatable - just as it would be if we were discussing the "marginals" in the U.S.

One of the most complete studies of poverty is Mexico's Luis Serron's Scarcity, Exploitation, and Poverty: Malthus and Marx in Mexico (1980). While fascinated by the problems induced by overpopulation, Mexico's dependency ratio and underemployment,

Serron is not a Malthusian. (See pages 75 & 133.) Instead Mexico's poverty is more clearly linked to exploitation and injustice, and he analyzes the attempts of other writers to describe and explain Mexico's poor. Citing Alonso Aguilar, Fernando Carmona, Pablo Gonzales Casanova, and Carlos Tello along with the more lifelike portraits of Oscar Lewis, a vivid picture emerges. Serron's chapter on "The Extent of Poverty in Mexico" is such that we need not repeat his materials here. Serron says, however that "approximately half" of the 1970 population (page 48) are living below or close to the bare subsistence level.

What other studies reflect upon the condition of the current poor in Mexico? Has the rural round of life changed in significant ways? Has the political heritage of Cardenas left us with a cumulative gain for the rural poor? Thomas G. Sanders gives us impressionistic data that things have changed little except for the "opportunity" to migrate to situations more conducive to survival. (See "Migration From the Mixteca Alta," 1975, AUFS.) Right off, Sanders argues that "...a predominantly peasant population can no longer make an adequate living from the land." Small plots, stultified agricultural practices, economic exploitation, inadequate services, low investment, and low skills still prevail. The main cause of out-migration, according to Sanders (page 13) is "the prevalent economic situation in the region." Hence, "even the rich in most towns are poor by developed standards." Violence as a cultural factor is also offered as a reason for migration, but it is secondary to the sheer problems of survival. National culture in any case is seen as diluting or replacing local culture (de-peasantization?) so the set of incentives relating to the modem economies is becoming the norm. Of course, an "escape" door has been opened away from poverty that did not exist until the infrastructure of roads and city "opportunities" came into being - the name of this door is migration. Basically the move into cultural and economic assimilation is an alternative to physical death. Still poverty remains the basic fact of their existence, so let us look at the consequences of this rural to urban migration.

The Federal District Of Mexico As "Pie In The Sky"

The Instituto de Investigaciones Sociales of UNAM has spent much effort studying the migration to the major Mexican cities. (See for instance Munoz, Oliveira, and Stern, 1977.) The cover of one more thorough study shows a migrant pair sleeping on the cobblestones against an urban landscape. But, this volumes' census based data is much less impressionistic, and it is laced with separate studies to determine the total consequences of migration. At this point in history one does not need to be a sociologist or economist in Mexico to "discover" urban poverty. The public dialog and on-the-street perceptions contain enough description for people of any ideological bent to know that festering poverty is widespread. An article in Excelsior (August 14, 1979) notes 5 million marginal people in the Federal District alone. This group according to the article is in varying degrees of desperation and despair. In a city of 18 to 20 million people that is quite a "dualism" compared to the incredible affluence of this great metropolis. We must describe the economic and occupational characteristics of this population which visual observation tells us is a "nation within a nation." The Lomnitz study of marginality (See especially the chapter on "Shantytown Economy", page 64) stresses:

1) Low productivity occupations that utilize obsolete skills (and)
2) nonproductive occupations with little or no skills (and)
3) occupation in low demand.

This emphasis upon occupational deficiency can't be a complete description of poverty or its causes, but it is centrally relevant. By definition, someone with a job (productive or otherwise) who gets a good salary is not "poor". On the other hand, why some jobs pay so little and others so much is not entirely a matter of productivity or even general social value. Based on 1975 data (Secretaria, 1975) one-half million of Mexico City's population were domestics, unaffiliated laborers, etc., and between 3 or 4 million people were economically marginal - or 1/4 of the total. The numbers of the very poor will fluctuate as in the U.S., when they are defined by a variety of criteria. Occupations such as the carrying of water or ice, watchmen, soft drink peddlers, or the "services," typically cannot command high wages, but are functionally productive. Much of Mexico City's life as we know it would come to the proverbial screeching-halt without sanitation workers, road repairers, waiters, housemaids, and carry-it-on-your-person peddlers. The wage structure is a political matter in many ways, not an economic one. These services could, of course, be compensated at a higher level, but minimum wages are widely ignored - or do not cover some of the categories we have discussed. We should look at the labor market in more detail.

Looking at the excellent long-term data in Munuz, Oliveira, and Stern (1977) we see the employment structure changes from 1930 to 1970. Employment in the Federal District has declined for the following occupations: Extracting, farming, textile work, and domestic work. These changes are not surprising. Decided increases have occurred in tourist related activities (Diversions, hotels, and restaurants), metal product manufacturing, construction (although this is down from 1950), and services to the producers (as banking). Occupations for the incoming worker have, hence, dropped or remained constant (as laundry work). It would seem that many new occupational categories would have to be created in order to encompass these recent arrivals, but many are in "service" areas. Much activity still consists of "hustling" in the deviant behavior sense. What was once described as a "queer ladder" of social mobility for the poor in the U.S. also exists in Mexico, and just as corruption exists, doggedly, at upper levels, these forms are seemingly impossible to eliminate. In an effort to understand poverty in Mexico let us look at other treatments of it.

Other Descriptions Of Being Down And Out In Mexico

> Differences in the nature of poverty are also qualitative. That the poor in Latin American live worse than the poor in the United States is a generally accepted fact. (Horowitz, Portes and Ferguson, 1976, page 82.)

There have been:
    1)Anthropological descriptions of poverty,
    2)Psychological descriptions of poverty,
    3)Household economist descriptions of poverty,
    4) Humanist and novelist treatments

The anthropological writers on Mexican poverty include some who have become renowned and well to do in the effort! This first group of analysts includes such writers as Oscar Lewis, Robert Redfield, and Sonia Ruiz Perez. The purpose of the first two was not to describe poverty as such, but to elaborate upon the sociocultural systems in general. Oscar Lewis wrote several later books that touched upon the effects and possible causes of poverty, but one of his best studies of levels of living in descriptive form was the 1951 study <u>Life in a Mexican Village: Tepoztlan Restudied</u> Lewis' chapter on "Wealth differences and levels of Living" actually gives a frequency distribution of the possessions held by villagers in an "economic point scale." (Page 174) Thirty-nine of Tepotzlan's families scored from 100 to 400 points where a cow was worth 3.7 points, a hectacre of private land equaled 7.2 points and an urban house 7.5 points. 119 families had between 39 and 99 points. The bulk of the population (604 families) had between 1 and 39 points. Almost 11 percent had no points - which were, of course, biased toward property or capital possessions. Zero points is really poor, but having 1 to 39 points is rock bottom as well because it is like having malnutrition which even food will not subsequently reverse! Overall, 81% are below 39 points and this structure of wealth graphically resembles the point on a World War I Prussian of officer's helmet. The weighted average of this group, however, could have a house, a plow, a mule, 3 plum trees, and 2 pigs - and that's all. Remember, these resources (animals) may either be eaten, sold, or bred - but in the short run, that's all. According to Lewis' analysis of this data, correlation's of this economics scale with reputed wealth, housing levels, food consumption, and general living styles are generally quite high. Some aspects, like food quality, change more with "modernization" than with income alone.

Lewis notes how many of the "rich" become so. Many it seems got their edge from the chaos accompanying the fighting periods of the revolution after 1910. Hence, some of the newly rich got their start during the hectic days of the revolution when they were able to buy land at low prices from hungry or nearly starved villagers. "Devious methods" were also used, according to Lewis' sources. Also the land division process - which was not ancient - into smaller and smaller successive parcels can lead to "movement down the economic ladder." (Page 178) Envy can come about under such circumstances, according to Lewis, and we have seen the seeds of violence and distrust, which are so disastrous later, emerge here.

A more recent anthropological treatise on poverty is of the professional beggars of San Cristobal Las Casas. (See Beyond Poverty, 1974.) Sonia Ruiz Perez looked closely at a group of beggars in what was described as a "pre-industrial town." The latter town may not have differed from Lewis' Tepoztlan, except for two slightly changing decades of time. Ruiz Perez deals with people whose livelihood is based on begging, most of whom are ambulatory and some of whom are alcoholic. This writer stresses the constant interaction with the other class groups (See, for instance, page 10). A strong patron-client type relationship exists. As to her general description, beggars regularly work their trade in this particular town. The population of practicing beggars can expand during the summer or while fairs are going on. Most beggars seem to have rural backgrounds, and they have come to the towns for economic reasons. They apparently are not urban backsliders. Each relates to a "donor" in a patron-client relationship. Their movement during the days follows the routines of the city moving from commercial to residential sectors, except for the alcoholics. The church is not an area where they tend to gather due to the pressure of the priests to have people give more systematically to charity rather than spontaneously to beggars. There is much more description in this study which could be remembered to the reader, but what can be said about poverty in Mexico based upon its central data?

As a view of poverty Ruiz Perez' anthropological study shows that there are indeed social and cultural phenomenon attached to human poverty - although its core reason remains economic. A pattern of antecedents is related to it, just as in Lewis' Tepoztlan. The poor interact with the rest of us; they also have a pattern of activity which is linked to the common one we all share. It is also clear that the activity constitutes on the whole an economic livelihood, in so far as the average of 10 pesos per day would meet their needs. Much social detail is to be found in such a study and the social functions of the interactions are revealed clearly. The current "institution" of begging does reflect historical change as well. For instance, the church would like to absorb charity in more systematic ways. The present writer, having seen the begging practices in Mexico City - who could avoid them - would have to agree that the pattern could be more variable when the basic setting changes as well. We, thus, have added another pattern to our picture of poverty - one which is probably a minority way of handling financial destitution.   While we will look at our anthropological descriptions of poverty when we discuss "explanations" let us now look briefly at what other disciplines have highlighted about this phenomena in Mexico.

In Erich Fromm's and Michael Maccoby's Social Character in a Mexican Village (1970) we have a relatively recent example of psychological description of Mexican poverty. In a chapter on the "Theory of Character Orientations" we are presented with an explanation and description of poverty stressing aspects of the peasant's psychological or social psychological makeup. This view of Fromm and Maccoby stresses a social loss (of the chance to be productive) prior to the changed psychological constellation which subsequently has its effects. Thus: (page 81)

> When a class has a productive function, like the lower middle class in the 19th century, or the Mexican peasant today, the sado-masochistic admixture seems to be relatively small; when, on the other hand, the class has lost its productive place in the economy, and is slowly being destroyed economically and socially, the sado-masochistic admixture seems to be very high, as for instance among the German lower middle class after 1923 and the poor whites in the American south.

Because most peasants in Mexico have suffered this fate the resultant "authoritarian male" is subsequently more prone to sadistic satisfactions, excessive drinking, passivity as to conditions, unresponsiveness to cultural stimulation, and becoming regressively fixated on their mothers. Such a person is unable to cooperate on the basis of common interests, and even with a common program like in Mexican CONASUPO they remain distrustful and ineffective. (See pages 211-212.) There is also an "avoidance of success" (see page 220), and rowdiness, an inability to use culture creatively for development purposes or personal satisfaction, (page 224) and the on-going character formation continues to contribute to the gap between the rich and the poor. (page 231) We will deal with the explanatory aspects of this formulation below, but many people feel that it describes the persisting aspects of Mexican peasant poverty. It is useful in helping to point out that the "depeasantization" of the rural Mexican as industrialization proceeds need not have immediate, positive effects. A macro-economic strategy for the country which ignores the psychological qualities set in motion will create more problems for adequate social development down the road.

Readers of our present volume may be aware of the variety of studies of how much it takes to live modestly or well put out by the U.S. bureaus of Labor and H.E.W. Nitty-gritty analysis both of what people consume and need for various levels of living are not readily available for Mexico or the U.S. Frank Tannenbaum's description of those who participated in the "parochial versus the national market," (1960, page 173) gives us a general picture of how people live in rural Mexico.

> In fact, for the rural folk the economy represents an ancient design upon which modern innovations have made little impression. Most of the people live much as they did at the time of the conquest; they use primitive tools, till the soil in a manner little changed in hundreds of years...live in adobe or reed huts without windows, furniture, or covered flooring, and subsist on the rim of the modern world.

While this description was from the late 1940s, many live somewhat in this fashion in the early 1980s! Food is still raised at home; furniture is hand wrought as is clothing in many instances; and a non-pecuniary economy continues. Any detailing of poverty at the actual levels of household consumption would still have to see it as absolute as opposed to being "relative" as might be the case in much of the U.S. Indeed, every aspect of personal consumption that is described would show these stigmata of poverty. While we will spend considerable time on nutrition later, let us take a look at an early study by a Mexican-American team under the sponsorship of the Rockefeller Foundation and reported upon by May and McLellan (1972, page 38.) The sample studied included two groups of poverty struck in Mexico City, two groups of Indians (Otomi and Tarascan), and some villagers from a small village in Guanajuato. These people had diets based "upon environmental food availability supported by tradition," (page 39) and the conclusion was that "in spite of some deficiencies, the pattern of nutrition of these groups was surprisingly sound." The question that is asked, however, has to do with how well the nutrition of these groups will be with "nutritional acculturation" and reliance upon subsequent financial resources. Indeed, animal protein was already scarce in 1940, and may become an impossible food resource. Household studies could also focus upon housing, clothing, conditions of sanitation, and even more "luxurious" aspects of living. Deficiencies are usually what are documented.

Luis Serron has made an attempt to observe the level of amenities obtainable by the poor in Mexico; for instance, in the area of housing. Citing studies by Mario O'Farril and Perez Bugarin from Revista de Economia he notes that food needs eliminate money that could help purchase housing. In 1960 only 1/5th of the population (see page 92) would be able to purchase a house with the basic amenities of sanitation, livability, and security. (Based on the private market). Crowding becomes the result of the unmet need, but having any viable means of shelter for the poor seems often a more pressing question. Many writers can, thus, judge the consequences of Mexico's poverty in terms of the amenities of a decent life. Next let us turn to the most qualitative of approaches, via the humanities.

The humanist's view of poverty in Mexico is a necessary compliment to that of the social scientist, and in some ways it is a more realistic portrait. It is hard to imagine a country with a more vital production of literature, poetry, films and graphic arts to represent its native and peasant population and their predicaments. The Indian has been strikingly portrayed in a body of classical writings in the 20th century as by Gregorio Lopez y Fuentes' El Indio in the 1930s. Whether these groups are depicted as a metaphor for "mother Mexico" (just as in the corresponding literature and art in late 19th century Russia) is not immediately apparent. Poverty is, however, clearly manifest in descriptive and potentially explanatory terms. More writing is to be found depicting the long suffering peasantry, than the recent, urban migrants; but the latter group is becoming represented in a new genre that probably began in the 1930s. Well exemplifying the urban poor and their "crunch" is the 1950 film <u>Los Olvidados</u> written and produced by Luis Bunuel, who has become a greatly honored artist. Socioeconomic factors loom large as content and rationale in these works.

Of those who depicted rural poverty, the most clearly is Mauricio Magdaleno whose works were said to show how the poor suffered the most "under the yoke of the ruling class." (See <u>Mexico,</u> 1973, page 280.) The list of Mexican humanists who have demonstrated the highest levels of social consciousness is longer than we have time for here - they have not been an irresponsible group! Mariano Azuela, Margarita Paz Paredes, Jose Revualtas, Carlos Fuentes, Carlos Gonzalez, Andres Molina Enriquez, Wistano Luis Orozco, and Luis Cabrera are a few of the names representing progressive work in poetry, literature, and film. And, who could pass this topic without mentioning the works of the muralists whose world-class efforts will give eternal cogent in those artists with "third world" orientations. What are the images of poverty in these works?

Largely the misery and poverty depicted in this literature is one that is seen as having been inflicted by the greed of ruling groups. The latter group are not all cut in the hacendado image, but may represent the middle class, especially those who desire reactionary control in order to achieve their particularistic and selfish ends. The Revolution is seen as being betrayed by these groups, and although the chief world view is not overtly Marxist, it represents a critical and moralistic realism. The poor are not seen as especially noble, but rather as human in their struggles for dignity and survival. The environment caused by the Porfirionismo and the "eternal return," early and late, is seen as being overwhelming to the people who are its unknowing and unwilling objects. Much of the tragic imagery of writers like Octavio paz is nurtured in the light of this realism, which coexists with an escapist romanticism of earlier origins.

Varieties of "Explanations of Poverty in Mexico

Many of the descriptive attempts discussed above are also attempts to show the causes of poverty, in Mexico and elsewhere, and also to justify the phenomenon in some cases. Some of these explanations also demand societal transformation or reform at some level. This list is probably not exhaustive, but is meant to further the discussion.

1) Poverty as "marginality
2) Poverty as "culture" or sub-culture

3) Poverty as a result of "internal colonialism"
4) Poverty as poorly developed human capital, and
5) Poverty as exploited labor

Larissa Adler Lomnitz has written an intensive study of life in a Mexican "shantytown." Poverty is seen as being integral to the situation of marginality; to quote Lomnitz: (See page 91)

Marginality may be seen as a combination of cultural, economic and social characteristics pertaining to a specific economic niche, which is interstitially related to urban, industrial economy.

It is worth going further with the excellent description of poverty as dependent marginality which Lomnitz gives. Ms. Lomnitz discusses the scavenging orientation of this poverty, where jobs are taken almost at random. "The use of waste materials can become a way of life." (page 91) These street vendors, unskilled workers, service personnel, and scavengers are characterized by economic insecurity that existing social networks (or political clout?) can not remedy. For Lomnitz, ten years are seen as being necessary in moving from a "rural-type marginality to an urban-type marginality." However, if we read Lomnitz correctly, marginality is becoming a permanent feature not a transitional one. (See page 207.) Poverty becomes totally integrated in the national economy, but according to Lomnitz, new survival tactics do emerge. There is a transformation from rural "individualism" or familialism to new forms of mutual assistance and cooperation (See page 211). The survival value of the latter is stressed in these circumstances - it is their most active behavior, and one that is lacking in non-marginals. What is the value of this approach as an "explanation?"
Lomnitz clearly indicates that marginality is a cause of subsequent events; consider the following: (page 209)

Since marginals are barred from full membership in the urban industrial economy they have had to build their own economic system.

Social "resources of the marginals are (then) converted into economic security." (page 208) And, from the point of the "urban economy, although marginality may be said to represent a 'surplus population'...it performs important though perhaps as yet unrecognized social functions." (page 208) It seems that Lomnitz does not want totally to be put into the category of explanations involving exploited labor, but the stress on "marginality" remains clear, in any case. But, we must go a little further for her full views. Lomnitz notes that "the rise of an urban middle class in Latin America is greatly indebted to cheap labor and services provided by marginals..." She could have easily qualified for our last category of explanation stressing exploitation with this modification! Even if poverty arrangements or survival arrangements involve saving social responses we must not allow metaphors to obscure the total process. A stress on the philosophy of cooperation by the poor is different from the more socially pessimistic Social Freudianism of Fromm and Maccoby, but their goals may not be too different. In Lomnitz, much of the continuing grief comes from the sorting out of class arrangements, as when she notes that the proletariat industrial workers become an elite which is moving rapidly away from these marginals due to the political economy of Mexico in the 1960s and 1970s. In any case, Lomnitz gives us an elaborate view of the social responses to being "marginal" to the industrial order. It may be a view that obscures some of the basic issues. In the next perspective, the culture of poverty metaphor is casually linked with the desperation of the lower orders. Another kind of obscuritanism may be involved there.

Let us look at Oscar Lewis' work and the so-called "culture of poverty." As a thoroughly criticized concept in the late 1970s the notion is still given currency by those who choose to "blame the victim." Somewhat like the "adjustments" made in Lomnitz's shantytown, poverty is seen as becoming self-perpetuating due to psychological and social adaptations. Pessimism, short-run hedonism, and other self-defeating behaviors are said to depict the peasants which Lewis characterizes. Based on the criticisms leveled by the Valentines, William Ryan, Seymour Parker, and others, (including Lewis' own recanting) we would have to weigh acceptance of these ideas carefully. It must be true that many people have experiences that subsequently incapacitate them; one can become one's own worst enemy, it seems. Does not the villager or the shantytown citizen have their own "cultures", or at least make compromising adaptations

The "culture of poverty" idea as "theory" takes poverty out of the realm of political-economy and gives peculiar power to some social-psychological variables. It, in fact, ignores social class, social structure and the human struggle for a better life through the limited institutional frameworks available to them. Nor was the original poverty or its dual-opponent, affluence, explained by such behaviors and attitudes. Kliner and Parker observe that such adaptations to extreme poverty are in fact realistic, understandable, and common human short-run phenomenon; and the poor act in a positive sense to avoid mental stress, mental illness and other forms of individual destruction. To believe that your "ship is going to come in," despite the fact that you are impoverished, old, minority and ill is to invite personality dissolution! Such short-run survival tactics that may arise from the predicaments of poverty are not "cultural." Oscar Lewis may well have been stressing the absence of class consciousness, but his persona-non-grata status in Mexico may not have otherwise been deserved! Levels of living are determined by too many other substantial factors without pointing the finger at the attitudes and short-run adjustments of the poor to their predicament.

Many writers who stress political powerlessness see poverty as a matter of "internal colonialism," despite its unlikeness to earlier patterns of colonial domination. As an analogy based on 19th century colonialism some have looked at the so-called separate groups who have been placed at political, cultural, or territorial disadvantage. The economic connection to the larger society is not stressed, and, indeed, the motivation for the enforced separation (if such really exists) is not clear.

One of the writers using the internal colonial model for Mexico is Pablo Gonzalez Casanova. (See Democracy in Mexico, 1965.) Casanova is trying to explain the isolation of the Indian and the exclusion of up to 70% of the population from the main benefits of Mexican society. There is much appeal in this analogy because of the extreme hurt which the poor experience, and the lack of understanding as to why such hardship exists. Clearly the poor are left out of the benefits, but they are not really separated from the economy. (A problem which marginality theory has as well.) The poor including many Indians have the fruits of their labor drawn into the system as Lomnitz notes above. The poor may not be in a literal "colony", but they seem to be in an exploitive relationship to the means of production and unable to participate fully.

A more recent utilization of the internal colonial analogy for Mexico is offered by Peter Smith. (See Labyrinths of Power, 1979, page 49.) Smith, however, discusses the lack of access in terms of the concept of "limited pluralism" which is one in "which access to the competition is sharply restricted." Mostly the limitation is observed for political competition, but citing Casanova, Smith lays the full model out: (See page 53)

> Various factors underlie the situation (of passive acceptance versus mobilization:). One is the size of what Gonzalez Casanova calls the "marginal" population, perhaps 50 to 70% of the total, including many Indians...The dedication is simple enough: This is the most socially and economically deprived portion of Mexican society, it

cannot mount effective demands on the system, ergo the system does not have to confront any basic challenges from those who have the most to gain from structural change.

Smith notes the lack of effective organizations, and, hence, the "low degree of mobilization." Apathy is the result of this situation of powerlessness according to Smith. Contrary to the exclusionary features of the model, and for what excesses Brazil and others have practiced, Mexico includes those groups who become "mobilized." Forced or coopted inclusion of groups runs contrary to the internal colonial model's precepts to some extent, but for a description of the immobilized poor who are outside of the benefits system it has some value. Stability of the government's power base (and hence reward system) seems to be more important as a political-economic process than does exclusion or separation. Even South Africa's classical internal colonies need two models (little and big Apartheid) to handle the kinds of denial of access and the kinds of economic integration and exploitation. So with Mexico there may be denials of access in some ways, but the main thrust is to integrate the groups to the greater benefit of the system - as it is now constituted. The internal colonial model does not work well when the groups are of similar ethnic backgrounds, either. Perhaps the poverty is best seen as a result of the meagerness of the pay-off for all those who are only exploitatively integrated into the system. Some may use the I-C model to stress solutions to political integration, and others may use it to avoid the language of the left and of Marxism.

Are the poor in their predicament because they have poorly developed personal resources? Our problem in answering this question comes from the diverse nature of the poor and the lack of data about their varied circumstances. This type of an explanation is similar to the "culture of poverty" types of theorizing because it looks at qualities of the poor themselves, rather than at the structure of power and privilege in the total society. Do all the people who have a reasonable level of education, skill, or health possess adequate jobs; or in fact are there not other barriers? If only personal resources were needed it would seem to be relatively easy for the country's political leaders and business men to end poverty for many, as most jobs do not require that much training - even medical corpsmen can be trained in 90 days! Also one suspects that requisite levels of motivation are to be found amongst the poor, and a greater problem is to find scarce jobs in the capital intensive work sectors. Because we will be dealing with human capital issues in our theoretical chapters we will not go further here.

Marxist theories of poverty as applied to Mexico have the problem that people marginal to a system can not be directly exploited by that system - as for instance, a well integrated worker could. There is little "surplus value" outside of the capital intensive areas, but, of course, the petite bourgeoisie are taking their rake-off of the water, ice, periodicals, soda pop, scavenged materials, and curbside foods offered by the poorer peddlers! How should we view Marxist theory's relevance for Mexico's poor?

Pablo Gonzalez Casanova, whose work we have noted in other parts of this essay, says that Mexico is "pre-capitalist" (page 159, 1970) and "the domination of the bourgeoisie is not fully organized" (see page 163). Casanova does note that the "pre-capitalist latifundism has practically disappeared" (see page 162) but that "class opposition has been obscured" by the transition from rural living to proletarian status in urban areas (see page 163). This is the kind of logic which Casanova calls the "Marxian analysis." Despite the lack of a full development of capitalism the theory may explain poverty by showing how reform, and, hence, an end to poverty, might be achieved. Even though an "anti-imperialist, nationalist" struggle may obscure class struggle it can help to explain the lack of reform and the reduction of poverty. The left is, thus, to join in the "anti-imperialist, nationalist" struggle while capitalism and democracy precede apace.

A less ambiguous statement about how classic forms of exploitation maintain poverty is offered by Roger Bartra whose analysis of poverty in Mexico has "led him to conclude that a revolutionary class alliance should be formed between the urban proletariat and the rural masses." (See "The Influence of Marxist Structuralism on the Intellectual Left in Latin America," by Richard Harris, 1979, page 71.) Bartra aims to exclude the rural petty bourgeoisie and the national (liberal?) bourgeoisie from the alliances that could be formed, although as Harris notes, this structural analysis runs contrary to that offered by the Communist Party of Mexico (the PSUM) which stresses an alliance that tries to establish "a broad, anti-imperialist" front. Apart from the dialectics offered by these writers, does exploitation create poverty or help to maintain it? If we are to believe writers such as de Oca and Susan Eckstein (whom we dealt with in the first chapter) the answer would be that the middle and upper classes conspire to keep reform on poverty issues from occurring. The original poverty may be from the destruction of the latifundium and the substitution of capitalist agriculture; the persistence of urban and rural poverty comes from the machinations of the dominant classes at the present time as resources which are necessary for the poor's advancement are denied. To paraphrase from de Oca about the nature of the struggles (see page 54 in

Reyna and Winert, 1977):

> Many of the so-called "peasant struggles have really been struggles
> of an agricultural proletariat for proletarian, not peasant demands.

What Montes de Oca says about rural struggles, Eckstein repeats
concerning the urban poor and their situation. (See page 43 in Reyna &
Weinert.)

> The State's support of its urban poor seems to enhance its ability to
> allocate certain material resources to other interests besides capital,
> while informal forces enable the government to act against the basic
> interests of the urban poor.

To Eckstein then, the "small propertied urban poor ... are becoming
an important social base for the conservative, pro-capital regime."
Eckstein is really discussing political exploitation, as the poor
supposedly offer their acceptance of the "legitimacy" of the system in
exchange for crumbs off the affluent table. Apart from the varied
ideological assumptions of Gonzalez Casanova, Roger Bartra, and
Montes de Oca and Susan Eckstein, can not we get a definitive answer
about who is getting what - and at who's expense?

In dealing with data on "Income Distribution in Mexico" Ifigenia
M. De Navarrete (in Mexico's Recent Economic Growth, 1970, page
137) we may have an early, partial answer to the previous question.
The level of profits seems to have jumped from 27% in 1940 to 41% in
1950. At the same time the level of income of rural farmers did not
increase, nor did that of urban workers. Many more people who had
migrated in this decade were now living at urban worker's constant - or
declining? - levels however. This is the kind of overall analysis which
we will eventually need so that we can judge the causes of poverty or of
relative affluence.

Luis Serron who, as we noted above, follows Marxian arguments
and cites one way in which poverty or unemployment can come out of
increased productivity (page 177).

> On the exploitation side of the question, there is some evidence that
> increasing productivity are making for job attrition and
> displacement. Fisher reports a 29 per cent decrease in employment
> in textiles coupled with a 177 per cent increase in the value of
> textile production.

Hence, poverty can come out of the process of capital accumulation, and, of production increases. Over one million jobs disappeared as a result of increases in productivity in agriculture, service and manufacturing areas. Let us now turn to materials on the economic circumstances of the middle class.

The Mexican Middle Class: Its Economic Base and Consequent Lifestyle

...the middle class is taken as that group of the population whose share of income is in proportion to its size, so that 1 percent of the population receives 1 percent of the income or an income equal to the average... (Ifigenia de Navarrete, 1970, page 170).

Some of the benefactors of Mexico's industrialization in the 1950s and 1960s with the tremendous bureaucratic expansion and the rush of foreign investments and tourism were an enlarged middle class. This well educated, healthy, and lavished-upon group constitutes about 22% of the population as of early 1980. The genealogical background of this group is mestizo, but with a decided European tint in their presence and being. Their father's occupations were also often middle class or white collar, at least until the past decade, when more blue collar fathers made an appearance. More than one-half of this group is in Mexico City, with 3/4 being in the largest four metropolitan areas. The wives are probably quite homogeneous as are the male bread winners, and they do not represent a cross-section of the Mexican population. After age 25 the preponderance of their wives are also no longer "economically active" and so the middle class status (except for 15 to 20%) is based on the husband's salary. (See Dorothy Place's "Female Employment in Mexico and Demographic Transition," ASA paper, September, 1979, page 5.)

In any case, the incomes of this middle group places it between the 70% of the population with only 1/4 to 1/2 of their income, and the decidedly more affluent 10% who have incomes from 2 to 10 times higher than those in the "middle class." It seems that the overall income structure is somewhat, geometrically tri-modal, but skewed incredibly in terms of pesos and property toward the upper end. Yet a middle class, by many indicators as well as by definition exists in Mexico. The Mexican economy needed such a creation! This middle class group may also have been the chief recipient of the social development benefits to date; witness its consumer habits. As a group it seems to have gained in short run at the expense of upper and lower class groups, if we are to believe data collected by Clarence Zuvekas ("Income Distribution in Latin America: A Survey of Recent Research," Milwaukee: Center for Latin America, 1975). This can be inspected. Supposedly the middle classes have gained their economic position by drawing from the resources of the lower 60% and the upper 5%, but with such minimal tax or fiscal control over the top 5% of wealth holders these data may be disputed in the latter instance. Many national economic and development policies may in fact have aided this expanding middle class, and the move away from agrarian reform in the 1950s as well as modest assistance to the very poor were coincidental with greater prosperity for the "middle class." It seems that government policy as much as the "free working of the market" created the social fabric of the 1950-1960 period. To quote the 1960 Mexico handbook put out by the foreign exchange bank:

...When that policy is considered as a whole, it is obvious that throughout the last 30 years the combined effects of state intervention in economic life and the operation of factors primarily connected with the development of private capital have wrought great changes in the nation's economic and social structure.

It was claimed that Mateos administration (1958-64) "raised the standard of living of the farm folk;" increased consumer goods; and developed the country in such a way that the "fixed income sector of the population would not be harmed nor the problem of the unequal distribution of wealth aggravated." Specific social policies as free text books, new school rooms, more public housing, (as for example "Unidad Independencia") were as much the basis for shoring up a new middle (lower?) class as for redistribution to the real lower orders, it seems. Here are some descriptions of the processes leading to the emergence of this newly enlarged "middle class." T.R. Fehrenbach notes the expansion of this group around 1950 (page 614):

The total national product rose sharply after 1946, and wages rose with production. There was a corresponding rise in living standards for the urban population. The entrepreneurs and the middle class benefited most but if "labor" were defined as urban, unionized proletariat, including organized workers from factories, shops and restaurants, Mexican labor kept pace with other sectors.

Fehrenbach is saying that only a small portion of the laboring classes were able to stay parallel with these other groups. What are the specific factors that have contributed to this middle class emergence?

Bo Anderson and James Cockcroft (in Horowitz, page 369) observe how public welfare policies contributed to this middle class emergence:

> For the urban workers low-cost housing, subsidized staple foods, and a federally determined minimum wage level (it varies from state to state) are among the welfare policies. The middle class, especially that sector which consists of government employees, also has available low-cost housing, cheap vacation plans and other benefits.

But not all analysts stress the strength of the middle group. Susan Eckstein (in The Poverty of Revolution, 1977, page 196) is not sure that the middle class is doing well in the market place. In describing consumer habits Ms. Eckstein comes up with a different perspective about the middle class' status in the general economy:

> Since only about 10% of them (the total sample) have savings, most of them are dependent on credit buying, making purchases all the more costly.... The lifestyle of the "middle" and upper classes, the advertisements of the mass-media, and the persuasion of door-to-door salesmen all seem to induce them to consume beyond their ability to pay.

A relatively marginal existence is seemingly described for the "middle class" if consumer power is utilized as the criteria. Yet, this middle class is seen as having an initial edge, while the lower class is plagued by lack of access to good-paying, secure jobs and the benefits associated with this (see page 206). In this perspective Ms. Eckstein comes closer to Gonzalez Casanova who sees the social structure as having a very advantaged upper 35% versus the down-and-out 65%.

Access to the sectors of economic and political action have other advantages. The opportunities that characterize the middle class have special qualities that should be noted. Roger Hansen discusses the political avenue to financial affluence via corruption (1971, page 178):

> The better-educated members of the Mexican middle class who choose to follow government careers have increasingly entered the political system through the civil service, while their less-educated counter parts often enter via lower-echelon elective offices under PRI sponsorship. Through whatever route ... the ambitious Mexican who rises to the top of the political bureaucratic heap ... rarely needs more than six years to accumulate sufficient capital to retire for life.

Such are some of the opportunities for improving upon middle class security and status! It seems that some periods allowed this avenue of mobility more than did others. The expansive Alemanist philosophy provided for an economic opportunism in government as well as in business. An Economist article on Mexico in 1978, even in the face of this corruption, was moved to write the following:

> Many members of the Mexican middle class are nice enough to feel today rather ashamed of their privileges. A congress of Mexican economists in April, 1976 did a unique thing for a congress of economists: they all agreed that the old model of development had failed. Earlier governments, they argued, had fallen into the trap of encouraging industry by over-favoring industrialists. So as not to disturb the precious confidence of the captains of industry, tax reforms had to be delayed ... the corrupt trade unions had (to be) manipulated ... into accepting wage increases far lower than the increases in worker's productivity ... food prices were kept low, so the peasants in the country became under-capitalized and condemned to subsistence on the poverty line. (The Economist, April 22, 1978 - Survey 16).

Thus, the bottom line concerning the middle class is that it is smaller than in the U.S. or other industrial orders. It is a privileged group that has benefited from government policies. It has also helped itself when the opportunity has arisen. They live well; but may be burying themselves in their greed. They must be conscious of their position in the whole structure of Mexican society and culture. Their political consciousness occasionally is manifest as well. Consumerism has probably engulfed them more than shame, and they have been increasingly pitted against other conscious groups in competition for rewards.

The Good Life in Mexico: The Wealthy and Their Lifestyles

> The disproportionate investment power of the conspicuous consumer in Latin America is made clear even when class-income distribution in Mexico is compared with several non-Latin American sample countries. (Peter Ranis, Five Latin American Nations, 1971, page 290).

> The data illustrate the greater inequality with which scarce resources are distributed in Latin America. Whereas in the United States the

richest 5% of the population appropriates 16% of the total income, available figures in Latin America range from 18% (Uruguay) to 36% (Brazil and Honduras), with most countries doubling that U.S. figure. (Mexico=29%) (From Portes and Ferguson in Horowitz, 1977, page 82.)

...In supporting these public works projects they emphasize their own public spirited, "cooperative" attitude in order to make the case that they are using their wealth for community benefit....In fact, they justify their leadership by organizing the others only for projects which promise profit for themselves, and they are the first to withdraw from the institutionalized cooperatives. (George Foster, quoted by Fromm and Maccoby on the richer peasant, page 207).

As a result the feminists, many of them university graduates from wealthy families, have begun working closely with leftist opposition parties. Earlier this month they presented Congress with a bill calling for the legalization of abortion. (Alan Riding, "Mexican Feminists Seek to Tackle Broad Social Problems," New York Times, December 2, 1979, page 10).

As in the United States the wealthy in Mexico have a certain invisibility. It took the Ferdinand Lundberges, William Domhoffs, Cleveland Amorys, and the like to reveal their socio-economic outlines and substance in the U.S. We still are not sure how much social fantasy is involved in their depiction. Let us try, from available sources, to describe this group in the Mexican setting.

Ifigenia de Navarrete, in a source we have noted before, observes that the top 5% of income holders in Mexico receives from 29 to 37% of all personal income. This she admits is a conservative figure of net worth because it does not include the ownership of assets and the accumulation thereof. Much income does not come under scrutiny, we are led to believe. Brothers and Solis in their volume on Mexican Financial Development (1966, page 101) observe the character of Mexican business activity which is such that it might obscure a realistic picture of wealth:

First, most Mexican-owned business enterprises are closely held family or group concerns which are reluctant to turn to outside financing because of the loss of secrecy, diminution of control, and the sharing of profits that would be involved.

We use this quote to show that wealth may be a difficult condition to diagnose with great accuracy. Clearly in Mexico we have a group of native financiers and entrepreneurs who have become enormously wealthy since World War II. Property ownership still constitutes a good share of this total as well; including agricultural ownership. Nor is this group heavily taxed although there has been some attempts at making the tax structure more "progressive" in 1971 and especially in 1972 "Tax Reforms." (See Mexico, 1973, Banco Nacional de Comercio Exterior, page 211.)

The basic objective of the 1972 reforms was to lighten the tax burden of the low-income strata, for which reason rates were raised at the other end of the scale, introducing a system that taxes a person's total income, regardless of whether it is earned or not, so that he pays according to his real capacity.

The law, however, continued to give tax exempt status to the sale (and profit therefrom) of land owned more than 10 years. According to this source (page 212):

Rates on personal income up to 300,000 pesos annually were left unchanged; but on higher income up to 1.5 million pesos, the tax rate became progressively steeper, reaching a maximum of 42% instead of the previous 35%.

Luxury taxes were increased as well, but these may have been aimed at the tourist, rather than the affluent Mexican consumers. The reforms seemed to involve a measure of progressivism, protection of special interests, and token exemptions (as on cheap tobacco).

Apart from its obvious financial security how can we describe the qualities of life amongst the very well to do? Their housing is said to be some of the most attractive real estate in the world, and its decoration takes from the best of European, American, and Mexican craftsmen. Shopping trips to the U.S. return nearly 1/3 of the money which many more U.S. tourists lavish on Mexican delights! Much travel is made abroad for educational, medical, social and consumer reasons. Flights to Houston, Miami, Dallas, or to New York can be for any of the above reasons. Newspapers have a great display of advertisements offering European flights on a grand scale. But not all of the wealth is offered as conspicuous consumption. There are different styles in the display of wealth within Mexico, but much of the manner in which wealth has a public presentation differs greatly from the United States.

Prosperous residential settings may exist in the ancient walled, courtyard pattern, thus, not presenting the level of affluence to the total community. Houses like this exist in all cities, and whether you are taking of Coyoacan in south Mexico City, the Las Palmas area in Cuernavaca, or the lava gardens area their display is much different than parts of North American cities and elite housing. (It is true that the "compounds" of Hyannisport, Palm Springs, the tree secluded estates along Green Bay Road north of Chicago, or hill-perched Beverly Hills are relatively inaccessible.) Nor are large automobiles the common form of display that one sees by banks in Chicago, New York or Philadelphia. Instead small and powerful European or Japanese cars are more common - the latter more in keeping with courtyard parking. The housing and garden areas, well terraced and planted, might be too ostentatious for <u>Better Homes and Gardens</u>, but might be reflected in coffee table design or architecture books north of the border. Dress styles are functional, graceful, but their basic affluence does not let style overwhelm the persona of the wearer. Nor do the well-to-do walk in public areas; they emerge inside of buildings where the action is to take place. They are more likely to be visible in the recesses of financial, cultural or decision making institutions. There is less of the "if-you've-got-it, flaunt it" demeanor that the U.S. public has become used to; they are more at ease or, perhaps, more cautious. Contact with the public, and many of the very well-to-do have positions with public responsibilities, does not draw attention to their wealth or power. This is not merely the avoidance-of-jealousy behavior described by outside anthropologists who study village Mexico. It is also what lower-middle class Americans would describe as "class" behavior, whether affected or not. Perhaps, European styles of being born-to-wealth are what have been emulated over the past 3 decades. Even the servants of such families move with a strong, quick sense of belonging in these settings. Lobby workers, gardeners, delivery people are not exceptions. Unless one is invited to their homes because of some tangential mutualism, the only glimpse into the courtyards would be when they are being freshened up with broom and hose in the morning. Eat your heart out otherwise!

Menno Vellinger has described the bourgeoisie at the top of Monterrey's Class structure. About 50 families dominate this city and about 300 dominate the whole state with its industry based wealth. Some of the groups (as associated with Cuauthemoc and Fundidura) represent "traditional" families of wealth. Newer wealth came from the import-substitution policies after World War II, but the families are closely knit and can make a "common front" when their interests are threatened. Economically they have diversified and even invested abroad. The families have· turned some of the·works over to professionals, in order to pursue leisure activities it seems. The professionals may then be integrated into the social community in a way which William Domhoff described in the U.S. of A. This group described by Vellinger represents "the most advances ... toward the creation of a national bourgeoisie.

Basically, the rich in Mexico, as elsewhere, were much helped by public policies. Wayne Cornelius in describing the political economy of Mexico (Mexican Studies, Volume 1, Number 1, Winter, 1985, page 83) notes the lavish subsidies to industrial producers. What happened to this largesse? Much of Mexico's capital ("at least 22 billion in saving and investment capital") fled the country during the Crisis of 1981-82. The great "peso theft" also allowed the rich to use an artificially supported peso to buy dollars - meanwhile the foreign loans to allow this drove the country into a pit. These "Saco Dolares" or "dollar looters" made off with approximately 75 billion dollars to Texas, European and other banks and also through foreign real estate investments (see Hellman, Mexico in Crisis, 2nd Edition, 1983, page 222). Efforts at repatriation of this money have largely been unsuccessful according to Cornelius (1985, page 95). The flight of so much money may have actually changed the social structure of Mexico; but the effects of a migration of the rich have not been well studied.

How Do The Big Events Impact Income Distribution In Mexico

Things are in the saddle, and they are riding hombes y mujers.

By looking at major economic events in the past 60 years we may be able to relate to this question. Substantial income redistribution will not come by legislative or probably even by executive action. Major processes will be involved in the future as in the past. Table V displays a sample of the processes that have shaped income up to this point. Fluctuations in national needs and policies have had decisive effects upon income distribution, and will continue to do so. The likelihood is that such events of the magnitude of the Import Substitution Policy, the run on Petro dollars, the crunch of IMF-type austerity, and the improbabilities of the upcoming NAFTA policies have and will have more class differentiation. On the other hand such events as land redistribution, the "balancing" of the revolution, and the hoped for 600,000 new jobs (what kind?) via the NAFTA may lead to more equity if not equality. What does change such indicators as the Gini coefficient? A free trade deal will have effects beyond any current

TABLE V
EVENTS IMPACTING MEXICAN INCOME DISTRIBUTION, 1930-1990S

EVENT OR PROCESS	GROUPS IMPACTED	NATURE OF IMPACT
Land Redistribution (1930-1940s)	- Land Owners - Middle Peasant Groups	Continued Issues of Productivity (but helped integration)
Import Substitution Development (1050-1960)	- Business Groups Able to Take Advantage of Market - Worker Elites	Protected Inefficiency Great Profits For Some
"Balancing" of the Revolution (1960-1970s)	- Emerging Middle Classes - Youth	Benefits Spread (but tracked, as with education)
Petrolization of the Economy	- The Very Wealthy - New Urban Working Groups	Peso Supported Abroad, Consumer Paradise (for "saco dolares")
Austerity (1980-1990s)	- Urban & Rural Poor - Recent Middle Classes	Subsidies Cut Capital Extorts Benefits
N.A.F.T.A. & Beyond	- Businesses With Right Link to Markets - 600,000 New Job Holders	- Greater Equalization (if have good relationship to emerging markets) - Less Redistribution Outside of Market & Its Political Appendiges

abilities to predict as to the distribution, even the aggregate impacts are problematic. Certainly jobs will be impacted, and an initial" boom" may have a longer term, net impact. But, what has been the long term impact of the border assembly plants a decade later? The maquiladores have had a mixed impact on the lives of those involved, but probably have not greatly altered income distribution.

Upcoming economic-related events - from over the horizon - may only give us more of the same. Fluctuations in the "global economy", the world price of oil, the labor policies of the trading partners, resurgent political movements, U.S. policy petruberations, or just luck in one form or another will have their due. New fortunes will be made within Mexican parameters, which might serve aggregate ends, and which may even "trickle down" to use that quaint notion. Most older processes will not reoccur in the same forms, but there can be policy decisions that augment previous outcomes. No economic policy is neutral with respect to income distribution or redistribution. Many leveling policies (home ownership? - not necessarily so says Ward, 1990) as opposed to differentiation policies are easy to spot at the offset, but some which augment class differences masquerade as general improvement policies. This is a truism everywhere.

Part of our problem with income distribution and its measurement is that services can improve life quality which after all is the issue. By starting our analysis with income matters we may see if our remaining areas of social development restore the balance left by this very skewed distribution system. The "Revolution" did offset many inequities, but the real economic life of Mexico or any other country is otherwise. The "real" economic parameters of Mexico include such elements as the "informal economy", the general winking at laws and policies otherwise promoting equity, the local cicaques with their stranglehold on everything from vice to garbage dumps, and the general grind of transactions that get to the best of people with little to start with. Income redistribution occurs in the latter by muscle if not by extortion and deception - more than by contract or exchange on a level playing field. Measurement of improvement is difficult, but it can not be obtained by counting the number of television aerials or nature of the automobiles driven.

The income pie and the wealth pie could be cut differently without raising the issue of affordability. Capitalism constantly raises the latter issue, but grudgingly allows for redistribution in order to accomplish other ends. The economy can grow without the impoverishment of the lower half or two-thirds, and healthy human capital can substitute for cheap capital sucked out of the unfortunates by price or wage maneuvers.

Pronasol, the presidentially focused "welfare" program after 1989, will probably not alter income distribution. Some have hopes that the particular form can be modified down the line so that it amounts to an income redistribution mechanism or channel. At present its goals are ostentatiously political in its display of benefits for the loyal communities. Services and community resources are typically not counted as income or wealth, and this is open to dispute.

The Health of the Mexican People

> At the turn of the century it was a considerable achievement in Mexico merely to live to become an adult. (Gordon Schendel, 1968, page 108.)

> We are speaking of societies in which, at any given time, a third of the children may have diarrhea and more than that may be malnourished. Their lives are saturated with the causes - poverty, crowding, ignorance, poor ventilation, filth, flies. (John Bryant, Health and the Developing World, 1969, page 39.)

> In general, affiliates (of IMSS, ISSSTE, PEMEX, MNR, & and the ministries of the Navy and Defense) have received better medical attention, as seen from the fact that some indicators rose faster than did the number of persons covered: for example, clinical analyses advanced by 34.4% between 1970 and 1972... (Mexico, 1973, page 244.)

The life expectancy of Mexican citizens has climbed steadily in the 20th century until it is nearly 70 years of age. Gordon Schendel is full of praise for this accomplishment in public health and medicine: (Schendel, page 129)

> In no field has Mexico's progressiveness been better demonstrated - or have its achievements been more substantial and even spectacular - than in the field of public health. And particularly in the field of rural public health.

In observing that the life expectation at the turn of the century was only, roughly 26 years, Schendel notes that there have been problems. For instance, there have been problems of professionalism versus the curanderos and Brunjos or witches. There have been severe problems of rural hygiene (especially attacked since President Cardenas). There have been problems with contaminated food and water, for instance, endemic diarrhea killed nearly 70,000 a year in the 1950s. There has been the "war" on Malnutrition (centering upon anemia, goiter, tuberculosis, etc.). There have been the attempts to improve human environments (as with better housing); and the attempted eradication of tropical diseases (mostly in the tierra caliente). These problem areas have clearly led to humane achievements, as well as to agonizing gaps. Schendel's volume basically discusses the early campaigns for public health, with some references to later clinical achievements, and although overly optimistic (based on other materials we will review in this chapter) the work helps to document these initial achievements. We will also contrast it with more recent sources, as the work of Daniel Acuna. For his part, Schendel tells us of specific campaigns to remedy tragic sources of illness and death. Schendel's volume tells of battles with witches (who accused the government health teams of stealing blood!) and also of battles to reduce contact with scorpions and rabid animals. Poverty is not ignored as a cause of this misery, even though he seems to stress personal ignorance as the linkage between the person and the health menace. How shall we view this positive assessment of health accomplishments, and this theory about the causes of ill-health?

May and McLellan (whose research for the U.S. Army we will review in our section on nutrition) are less inclined to stress ignorance than they are government policy. Hence: (See The Ecology of Malnutrition in Mexico and Central America, 1972, page 45)

As it is now, the subsistence or semi-subsistence areas do not produce enough of the right kind of food to keep their population healthy and active, while the agribusiness areas produce too much, encouraged as they are by the policy of price supports.

Thus, there exists a variety of views about the remaining rural and urban concerns with health. Government policy seems to be more implicated in the May and McLellan volume where rural and semi-rural areas are seen as having 3 to 8 times the nutrition linked disease as urban areas have. (See Table 16, page 62.)

Our first paragraph in this chapter have discussed the accomplishments by Mexico and the work that remains to be completed. Should we emphasize the conditions and policies associated with the former or the latter? Rather than either of these options, we will first trace health progress in the last 100 years or so, including a profile of typical illness and health patterns as seen by writers in ethno-medicine, epidemiology, and demography. Next, we will look at government and private efforts to effect this pattern, especially public health and medical practice since the late 19th century. Remaining health needs including policy modifications or additions will then be discussed. Finally, a model depicting the main institutional and Epidemiological elements in the health area will be sketched.

100 Years of Health and Illness in Mexico

What has the health-disease pattern been like in Mexico over the last 100 years or so? What do we know about the changing patterns of morbidity, and how has social policy played a role? What sources do we have about the pattern of illness? Obviously there are several kinds of data we can refer to regarding early health and illness patterns. Anthropologists have an ethnomedical literature which is more closely related to cultural practices used to deter or buffer illness, rather than to descriptions of the physical patterns of illness themselves. There is a tradition with this latter approach to stress the irrational aspects of people's approaches to illness. There are additionally the epidemiological materials which public health personnel have gathered from field or clinic. Here the concern goes beyond incidence and prevalence data into causes and "vectors." Lastly, for our purposes, there exist demographic data on mortality rates, morbidity, population fluctuations and population composition. All of these sources can be combined to enhance our picture of the health-disease pattern which social development and economic development would have to cope with in Mexico.

The ethnomedical literature on Mexico includes at least (according to Michael Logan, 1973) the writings of: Currier, 1966; Foster, 1967; Ingham, 1970; Lewis, 1960; W. Madsen, 1955; Redfield and Park, 1940, and Mak, 1959. Most of these studies dwell upon the peculiarities of the cultural-medical approach and they tell us little about patterns of health or illness. We must face the fact that much social science effort has little direct application to human problems or the attempt to be constructive through social policy efforts. In this literature there is much fascination with the humorial medicine and the "hot" and "cold" treatments by native populations in Mexico and Guatemala. All that these studies can offer to the person interested in practice or policy about disease is to caution sensitivity - if they are on the front lines of dispensing treatment. The latter is, of course, no small matter, but it is not our concern here. But the more "action" oriented social science could be of assistance to national planners, but, then, these writers are "scientific" in their ultimate orientation. The literature on mental health may be of more assistance because the behaviors studied at least can be evaluated in terms of social goals. The ethnomedical literature on mental illness has been summarized by Arei

Kiev and others, and, it has focused on such behaviors or fears associated with the complexes of human action named "susto", "mal ojo", and "evil eye" - with the latter complex being something which 30 year old Gringos will remember from "L'L ABNER", and such. This culturally-psychiatrically oriented literature has also typically focused upon the role of the native practitioner as potential competitor to the western-trained doctor. The efforts of the curandero to alter outcomes are traced in detail - being even more appreciative of the rituals involved than the practitioner might be! We probably can get a glimpse of patterns of illness and illness behavior from this literature, however, that might reflect what was typical 100 years ago or very remote areas today. We might ask ourselves if we consult this literature, what supportive or interventionistic policies and strategies would help the lives of the peoples concerned. However, just as economic policies can become more "realistic", it is probably true that social policies that ignore "evil winds", "black magic", and "hot and cold", or the "evil eye" would not be more realistic when dealing with rural medical offerings.

This ethnomedical literature does offer a view of the actual pattern of physical and mental problems, however. One might assume a similar pattern, or worse, 100 years ago. It is not too speculative to assume mortality rates of 60 to 80 per 1000; a life expectancy of around 22 years; high infant mortality rates approaching 50% (in Whetten's Rural Mexico, 1948, page 330, it showed an infant death rate of 223.1 per 1000 in 1922!); high rates of infectious diseases as causes of death; and less concern for the chronic disorders. Physical injuries would be common as these develop from work related accidents, aggression, and the general unsafeness of life. Based on this anthropological literature the common disorders in Mexico in 1870 (both urban and rural) would have included intestinal parasites, dysentery, diarrhea from a variety of sources, pneumonia, arthritis, skin infections, bronchitis, childhood diseases such as measles, and social psychological disorders such as "susto." (See Carrusco, 1960; Clark, 1959: Foster, 1953; Gillin, 1948; Guileras Holmes, 1969; etc., this list is from O'Neil and Selby, 1968). The latter disorder is characterized by listless and depressed behavior and a variety of somatic complaints. Because of the cruel residues of the hacienda system it is likely that the nutritionally related diseases not current (See May and McLellan, 1972, page 42)) were at least as prevalent a century ago. The latter would have included Kwashiorkor or protein deficiency; nutritional anemia with low blood iron; goiter or iodine deficiency; hyperkeratosis or avitarninosis; and pellagra or vitamin-niacin deficiency. Malaria, consumption, cholera and hepatitis were grim-reapers, and background malnutrition and diarrhea would push one of these or pneumonia up front. Such awesome diseases as yellow fever, typhoid fever, tetanus, schistosomiasis and hookworm should not be forgotten either. Much of Mexico, especially the tropical areas, would have been what Weisbrod and others have called "Insalubrious."

Using a combination of epidemiological and demographic data Whetten in 1948 covered health and mortality in Mexico during the first 40 years of the twentieth century. (See Whetten, Rural Mexico, Chapter XIV.) Between 1922 and 1943 the infant death rate is seen as dropping from 223.1 to 117.0, although Whetten warns of changed methods of record keeping in the early 1930s. Clearly the pattern was changing, as the Rockefeller Foundation and others worked on such killers as yellow fever, malaria, and hookworm after 1918. Evidently the country had settled down enough after 1920 so that reasonable statistics were possible. The overall death rate seemed to drop from about 25 per 1000 in 1922 to about 20 per 1000 in 1944 - the U.S. was about half the latter figure in the early 1940s. By the 1940s the main listed causes of death were diarrhea and enteritis (20% of all deaths), pneumonia (15% of all deaths), malaria (6% of all deaths), and violence or accidents for about 5% of all deaths. Some of the gruesome public health menaces had been conquered by Mexican public health programs, with the assurance of international agencies. By the late 1930s there were sophisticated public health programs based on cooperation between the School of Medicine of the UNAM, the Department of Public Health, and other institutions as the National Polytechnical Institute. One such internal agency that went right to the core of the remaining public health concerns was the Bureau of Rural Hygiene and Social Medicine. Some of the ejidos benefited by an extension of modern clinical medicine during this period as well. The great endemic diseases, except for those associated with bad drinking water, were considerably reduced during the 1930s and 1940s. The statistical data being collected also showed what remained.

The United Nation's Demographic Yearbook uses what demographic data the country of Mexico passes along - not that full cooperation is not achieved. This kind of data, as is more fully displayed in such sources within Mexico as what Direccion General de Estadistica offers, gives modern social planners the scientific basis for their policies. From the 1977 Demographic Yearbook (pages 426-27) we can see that enteritis and diarrhea (rate = 87.5), pneumonia (rate = 90.1), and accidents (rate = 67.4) are still big killers. Such sources of mortality as heart disease and cancer are increasing, however, as the life expectancy and living style approximate that of the U.S. of A. "Modern living" will also have its due! But many of Mexico's traditional problems are resistant to change it seems as well. Comparisons are always fraught with danger, and may be our chief forms of ignorance - but Cuba's pattern shows greatly lessened enteritis (rate = 18.2) and pneumonia (rate = 39.1) showing that health policies can have great effects. It may not be safe to assume that Cuba started with the same handicaps in the health areas, and the differences in the motor vehicle rates (Mexico's 67.4 versus Cuba's 12.1) reveals nothing except fewer cars and fewer mountain roads for Cuba! Mexico's overall death rate of 755.9 does not compare generally or very well with Cuba's 622.5 per 100,000, nor Panama's 520.7, nor Puerto Rico's 611.1; although Guatemala's 1261.5 may give an indication of Mexico's achievements. The choice to use these comparisons are the readers!

Based on demographic data we see a population with a tremendous increase in life expectancy, a substantial reduction in infant mortality (although some feel that it could be considerably lowered), and an altered list of causes of death. Horacio Labastida (in "Programacion Social", 1966 & 1978), lists some of the remaining problems based on the current demographic-medical picture:(See page 191 in Bases Para la Planeacion Economica y Social de Mexico, 1978.) There is a need for the following:

Salud. El programa nacional de salud y su expresion a traves de los servicios de sanidad local y rural; los centros de salud y las unidades medicas moviles. La preparacion del personal de sanid asd: medicos, enfermeras y auxiliares. Los requisitos y fascilizacion de los preparados farmaceuticos. El saneamiento ambiental. Las medidas de higine preventiva y social: education sanitaria del publico a traves de las activadedes profesionales, las escuelas, la accion social, la difusion de material docente y la comunidad. Higiene mater-no-infantil: ninos en edad preescolary   escolar, la atencion dental de los ninos.

Specifically as to remaining public health problems, the quote goes on:

Prevencion y lucha contra las enfermedades transmisibles: paludismo, treponematosis, tuberculosis, viruela, fiebre arnarilla, tifo, difteria, tracoma, etc.

By concentration on causes of deaths demographers and epidemiologists converge to a considerable extent. Some of the statistics produced are worth a thousand words, as the following summary of a comparison produced by John Bryant. MD.., of the

Rockefeller Foundation in his book Health and the Developing World (1969, page 38). Using materials from the Pan American Health Organization, Bryant observes that while deaths from diarrhea have declined for several age groups for El Salvador, they have not declined significantly for Columbia and Guatemala - nor significantly for Mexico. The latter was especially true, based on this presentation for those under one year of age in Mexico, although there had been progress for other age groups in Mexico. Guatemala's record seemed actually to be worsening between 1952 and 1964.

Much of the demographer's attention has been glued to the problems of population increases in recent decades; and this is understandable considering the funding sources and motives. Since the third world has rejected "over-population" as a supposed cause of "under-development" (as has the Rockefeller Foundation!) there may be a return to the more basic, internal problems which demographers can document and developers can work on. With a mortality rate of 9.7 in 1970, Mexico was making progress that deserved to be documented - so that further improvements can be forthcoming.

Daniel Lopez Acuna in his volume La Salud Desigual En Mexico has 80 tables and charts with health and demographic statistics from 1971 to 1979. This is one of the best recent survey of health resources, planning and effects available. Stressing problems of organization, coordination, and elimination of barriers to access, training of professional and financing, this volume is a must for those who want a more complete health picture. Recent plans for the extension of the health services are also included (see page 213) and the insufficiencies of the present system are dealt with realistically. This volume also contains international comparisons that place Mexico (as of 1967-77) about one half the way between high level services (Yugoslavia, Israel, Canada) and the depths of countries like Iran and the Philippines. We will look at some of Acuna's data later. Our second part of this chapter will try to document how the attack on these health problems took place

Public Health in Mexico: A Continuing Challenge

The eradication of contagious diseases and epidemics has been one of the chief tasks of the federal government and its various agencies in the field. They have been outstandingly successful, totally eradicating various diseases...such as carbuco, encephalitis, aphthous stomatitis, estronglilordiasis staphylococcus infections, linforranuloma typhus, and others... Despite the above mentioned achievements, the incidence of other diseases grew in the same period. The number of cases of influenza per 100,000 inhabitants rose from 65.1 to 116.2; dysentery, 47.1 to 101.9; malaria. 33.2 to 93.5; amoebic typhus, 13.9 to 18.8. The timely discovery of these increases will make it easier to intensify the eradicaiton campaigns in the areas where epidemics occur. (Source = Mexico, 1973, page 240; Note that the period in point here was from 1967 to 1971.)

The mark of a developing country is the ability to mobilize its resources in order to achieve its own ends, and in this regard Mexico is doing exactly that. This section will look at that mobilization and also evaluate its achievements - keeping in mind that few health utopias have been achieved anywhere in the world.

According to William P. Tucker (The Mexican Government Today, 1957, page 337) "the health function has long been recognized in Mexican government." The greatest modern thrust took place under a move to set up federal health offices in all states of Mexico during 1926-7. A combined Ministry of Health and Welfare set up in 1943 reinforced the federal impact on health matters, avoiding the debilitating decentralization or multi-centeredness found in the U.S. The main policy thrust comes by the federal application of the "Sanitary Code" which has evolved since the revolutionary period. This code was not completely realized because "restricted budgets and other limiting factors have often caused performance to fall short of declared policy and goals." (See page 340 in Tucker, 1957.) What needed to be done?

One of the best descriptions of the early problems and the attempts to mobilize health resources is to be found in Ernest Gruening's Mexico and Its Heritage (1934). To paraphrase from this source we see the following:

> While for a small urban minority, physicians, asepsis, and foreign-owned drug stores have existed for a generation, pre-conquest practices prevail among the masses to whom civilization has brought some of its diseases, but few of its cures.

Gruening cites a 1916 book "Hygiene in Mexico" which is an indictment of health practices under Diaz, and it spells out a death rate in Mexico City that is "nearly treble the average mortality coefficient of American cities having similar populations." (See page 533.) (See original work by Alberto J. Pani.) Gruening's model of causation concerning ill health is worth quoting at length. (See page 534.) Gruening quote:

The unhealthiness of the Mexican people is due to a variety of causes which in this day may be reduced to heading of "social": Under the caste system the little modified in four centuries, its serfs, living often no better than animals, could scarcely cope with disease. But aside from sheer destitution, a definite heritage of bad habits nullified available assets for good health.

Gruening goes on to note "ignorance of ventilation" at all levels, the lack of bodily cleanliness (where the Aztec temazcalli or steam bath has disappeared), noxious drinking water, (and its replacement with potable alcohol!) and the quality and character of their diets. Gruening is livid in noting that: "The most detrimental factor in that diet is the caustic CHILE" which, he believed led to "the extraordinary preponderance of gastro-intestinal ailments." (page 542) Generally, Gruening stresses "bad habits" although "serfdom", "foreign drug stores" and poverty are implicated. His total prescription involves the following however: (See page 550)

Restoration of health in Mexico likewise depends on far more than the utmost efforts of even the best conducted government reconstruction. It depends on achieving a higher economic level, higher standards of living; on a commercial and industrial revival; it depends on the discarding of deep-rooted habits and the formation of others - in short on education, it depends on housing, irrigation, communications; it depends on national prosperity.

Gruening notes (Page 544) that "...the first determined attack on Mexican ill health came with the Calles administration" where only neglect had existed under Diaz. Federal appropriations were multiplied 20 fold, sanitation regulations were enforced, and there were "sanitary brigades" sent out after specific epidemics. Separate drives were made against spinal meningitis, bubonic plague, cholera, hookworm, and small pox. As Gruening notes "5 million persons were innoculated in 2 years" (page 546) and dispensaries spread out from the cities. Much health propaganda was used, as more people than Gruening stressed ignorance as one of the main causes. Indeed, even in the cities there were campaigns against inoculation, and, in Morelos, mothers ran into the mountains with their children to avoid them! Still the basic effort "to hygienize the nation" went forward. We must remember our own swine flu side effects before we completely dismiss these reactions, however, as medicine is to iatrogenesis as holiness is to doubt.

Both Whetten and Tucker describe the specific governmental efforts of the 1930s, as Gruening's work only goes up to about 1927.

Whetten in Rural Mexico (1948, page 346) observes the 1936 plan involving the UNAM and the federal Department of Public Health to train more physicians for rural areas. The purposes were to decentralize the availability of medical services, and to enhance the doctor's training by allowing "him" to practice before they had their degrees. In order to better achieve the goals, however, there was established a unique practice of demanding "a dissertation on the social economic, and health problems of the community into which "he is sent." The latter did not seem to be an empty requirement, as an advisory committee had to pass it before the final medical exam could be taken. This was a well conceived program, and deserving of application elsewhere. The activities of the pre-degreed doctor were focused on four areas: health education (even working through the schools), preventative medicine (as via vaccinations and providing potable water), curative medicine (as full fledged physician), and scientific investigation (centering on how to do good without much funding!)

Another program described by Whetten for this period (1936-43) had to do with cooperation between the federal Department of Public Health and the ejidos. Under the "Bureau of Rural Hygiene and Social Medicine" a "cooperative" arrangement to supply medical and sanitary services was developed. Unfortunately a pattern that we still see with respect to funding developed in this service oriented program. (Whetten, p 349.)

> The service is designed as a co-operative arrangement in which the ejiditarios are expected eventually to shoulder a fair share of expenditures involved. With certain exceptions, the bureau has tended to shy away from communities that give little evidence to share the responsibility for financial support. Unfortunately, as we shall see later, this inability probably applies to the majority of the villages in Mexico.

> Whether the motives for this approach are a set of incentives to the poorest groups to get "their act together"; or are a primitive "triage" arrangement where the attempt is to save the strongest; or are just a form of reactionary economics is not clear. What are the services that were offered? (page 350.)

> The service usually consists of a physician, a midwife, a nurse, a pharmacist and a sanitary officer, who are located in a central village and work out into the surrounding pueblitos.

Much of the extension activities of this service were educational. With resources so thin, the effort of these emergency out-reach services was merely to set a good example. Whetten goes on to describe the activities that went from these central villages out into the hinterland:(page 350)

> The work of this unit resembles that of a charitable organization wherein only a few of its more critical cases are given attention and where an attempt is made to demonstrate a few of the more elementary rules of health.

The effort seemed oriented to impacting the traditional approach to health problems, and to motivate the communities to mobilize their resources toward this model being offered at least to some communities. If the Ejido had no money for shares in its bank, or indeed no bank, than it would have been unlikely to receive assistance. In any case, the statistics regarding support are interesting: By 1940 there were 121 agencies in operation, "of which 97 were being supported entirely by the bureau and 24 were co-operatively supported." The total number tended to decline in the early 1940s, but more were "co-operatively supported." These health agencies were also very concentrated, with 45% being in one area, the Laguna region. (See page 352.) This effort seems to have been, ultimately, a demonstration project.   The percentages contributed by the bureau or the Ejidatarios varied considerably in the other agencies around the nation. (See page 353.) Whetten stresses that "an important beginning has been made" (page 354), and the effort of the late 1940s was to build hospitals in regional areas, and 20 of an anticipated 58 were constructed by July 1946.

William Tucker's treatment of this period is shorter but described the rationale of this period more clearly. It seems there were three types of arrangements between the Bureau (or servicio) and the local region. The first type of "arrangement" involved attempts merely of preventing or controlling contagious diseases. The second was a more elaborate service where the community could pay part of the costs, and its services were aimed at individuals. The third type existed where the Ejido was in a commercial farming area, and the cost sharing was about equal. In this latter instance, a hospital and a fuller range of services was available. Tucker also notes the cooperative efforts with the United States, where the chief medical officer was a non-Mexican. Three large health centers, at Boca del Rio, Ciudad Juarez, and Xochimilco, were set up. Much effort at controlling venereal disease and malaria are to be found in these settings.

It is clear that the early development of health resources could have taken other forms, and more resources could have been switched from other priorities. Yet, progress was being made against public health menaces. A more comprehensive structure, though somewhat disarticulated was also being built. Mexico, 1968, put out by the Banco Nacional de Comercio Exterior, observes the plethora of agencies involved in health services: (page 352)

> The institutions mainly concerned with public health (and social security) are the Ministry of Health and Welfare (Secretaria de Salubridad y Asistencia), the Mexican Institute of Social Security (Instituto Mexicano del Seguro Social), the State Employees Institute of Social Services (Instituto de Seguridad y Servicios Sociales de los Trabajadores al Servicio del Estado), the National Institute of Child Protection (Instituto Nacional de Proteccion a la Infancia), the Mexican Institution for Child Welfare (Institucion Mexicana de Asistenciaa la Ninez), and others.

This official government source notes one of the crowning achievements of this early period as was accomplished by the National Commission for the Eradication of Malaria, which brought the death rate from this disease down to 0.01 per thousand in 1967. Admittedly the principal causes of death remained pneumonia, certain childhood deaths (related to malnutrition and impure water), and gastroenteritis. A superstructure for a concerted attack was supposedly available by the late 1960s, but let us see how this came about. In the first decades Mexico extended a rather empty structure after the revolutionary dust settled. It was, however, open to cooperation with external sources, and has continued so. With an increased rural orientation and a national atmosphere of uniting the country, some demonstration and experimental approaches to public health and clinical medicine were undertaken. The effort was to see how local resources could be established, and an educational impact was very central to the efforts. The results may be less than effective however.

Bryant (see page 71) discusses an anonymous Latin American country where "little is to be gained by naming the country." Let us see if it resembles Mexico in any way. Bryant says of his unnamed country that "the system for delivering health care is fragmented and of limited effectiveness, and the system of medical education is antiquated, under-financed and out of touch with the needs of the country." In this mythical country health services are administered mainly through 3 ministerial departments: social assistance, social security, and public health, but also by other governmental and non-governmental organizations. There is "limited cooperation"; they fail to develop priorities; and "overall, an uncertainty of domain leads to duplication of services in some areas and absence of services in others." As a result of this pattern: (See page 72)

> A municipal dispensary, a tuberculosis clinic, and a hospital may be located in the same community but operate under separate authority and with separate policies, none accepting responsibility for health in the comprehensive sense.

The very critical, but abstract portrait continues, and apart from the fact that is also reminds the present author of the U. S. of A., it nevertheless represents a failure to correctly mobilize existing resources!

> Again and again, in dispensaries and hospitals, physicians seem to lack many of the elements essential to the practice of modern medicine. Their understanding of disease processes is inadequate to help them make even relatively simple clinical decisions.

Educational programs and health needs in this country do not meet. Budgets are typically too small, and many people are not covered by this mediocre system. Well Virginia, this system probably does not specifically represent Mexico; but it reflects problems that any developing system would have to deal with. Let us look at a variety of current sources that can help us evaluate Mexico's efforts at health mobilization. We have, of course, discussed both public and clinical approaches here as the two have developed together - but in uncoordinated ways.

Some Current Assessments: Health and Its Costs

With many public health menaces in retreat, the problem of individual, clinical medicine comes to the fore. Extrapolating from the 1970 data in <u>Mexico</u>, 1973 we would estimate almost 200,000 persons employed in medical services, about which 80% are government employees and the remainder are in the private sector. There are nearly 40,000 doctors, of which about 30,000 are government-employed, part or full time. The breakdown of the total would include over 1/4th (60,000?) being in administrative or related activities, about 50,000 being nurses or specialized aides, and the next highest category being paramedics (12,000). Again extending our 1970 information, we might assume that about 60,000 of the 200,000 total persons are employed by IMSS, who employ about 12,000 doctors, 18,000 nurses, 1000 midwives, 7,000 paramedic personnel, and 16,000 administrative types. Much of the medical activity is probably still centered in Mexico City, just as it was in 1970 when 42% of the doctors were there! The poorest states of Chiapas, Guanajuato, Guerrerro, Oaxaca, Quintana Roo, Tlaxcala, and Zacatecas probably still have the least access to the country's medical resources.

But, we can offer more recent data concerning the extensions of medical services in Mexico. Daniel Lopez Acuna in his 1979 article "Salud y Seguridad social: Problemas recientes y Alternativas" has the following to offer concerning the expansion in the 1970's. Ward (page 157) says that the latter should not be underestimated for both rich and poor as far as usage is concerned. Red Cross and Green Cross institutions are an additional sector, but may be included in the "private" one. (Another error in classification impacting social services?) ISSSTE probably is in closest proximity to its clientele, because government employees tend to be so concentrated.

Ward's concern is largely for the residents of irregular settlements and the treatments they obtain. He is surprised at the number who have recourse to the private sector even though they may have access to the government services. Convenience may dictate this contradiction of use, and a wider geographical distribution of services is advocated (page 165). Popular protest, Ward feels, would correct this maldistribution, but the state effectively stonewalls these urges by offering minimal services in a deal that you can't refuse. Dissent is also diverted.

> Currently the state can afford to offer the bare minimum without fear of generating strong protest. In addition, it has created a range of one-off "trouble-shooting" institutions which appear to make concessions or provide relief where it is required. (1990, page 167)

As with Hansen, Peter Smith, Susan Purcell, and others Ward sees that "largess from above" helps to head off "any serious movement toward social change." Additional manipulation, divide and conquer and channeling of unsightly responses completes the pattern leading to acquiescence. Ultimately it is the conservativism of the poor (Their "damned wantlessness?") that defeats improvement according to Ward and some other observers. The concessions given take all the steam out of possible revolt scenarios. The range of repressive strategies takes us well beyond simple cooptation. Paradoxically, most are "satisfied" with services received from IMSS, SSA, and so forth. Health services seemingly reflect the pattern found in other areas where minimal offerings are reinforced, and protest stifled.

Tom Barry's edited <u>Mexico: A Country Guide</u> also stresses inequities in the health care system of Mexico. There are other problems, however, as the two level illness situation of having both third world infections, also the chronic illness pattern of more developed countries. Mexico additionally has the second highest incidence of AIDS in Latin America (Barry, 1992, page 234). Granted that the problems of inaccurate statistics about such touchy subjects as cholera, measles, AIDS, and malnutrition, these remain as publicly recognized problem areas in Mexico and abroad. Why should one be cursed with third world infections, and chronic illnesses, and modern, elusive epidemics?

As an active, interventionist state, Mexico has approached health-illness situations with the same vigor as it has toward education and social security. Despite improvements in longevity, total death rate, and such areas as public health, there are still 10s of thousands of preventable deaths every year. There are shortages of health facilities and personnel and certainly, maldistribution. (50% too many doctors in Mexico City, versus outside areas) When will Oaxaca and Chiapas get their due? Infant mortality in the latter areas is three times the national average. The programmatic cuts of up to 50% in the 1980s can not bode well for these areas even if the left hand of government in the form of Pronasol helps them out, at least since 1989. The 900+ deaths from measles in 1989 in the southern highlands was more than a simple embarrassment. The background of malnutrition would be more of an horrendous indicator of insufficiency. Polio, typhus, and cholera hover close by as well. We are not referring here to ancient history, but the living present, here in the early 1990s. The air and the water are still problematic: the desirable food supply skewed away from marginal areas; medical prevention and important clinical forms unavailable as well.

To talk of policy as a choice is to ignore the money issue, and affordability is the name of the game. Good health care costs a lot of money, but not as much as is lavished in the United states appeasing the health-medical powers that be. The boom periods in Mexico have seen an extension in service to many in rural areas via IMSS-COPLAMAR, and the retrenchment has only been modestly supplemented by Pronasol. Clearly pesos make for much of "policy." Our concern for affordability is legitimate, but the relationship to the actual meeting of human needs becomes more complex. Let us examine several case studies for a closer look at the policy and affordability issues. These are current health issues that will take us, unfortunately, into the 21st century. No doubt that a spate of manuscripts are being prepared to lay on the doorstep of the new century - and it would have been nice not to claim that these health concerns would still be around.

Our table shows 7 or so case studies (chronic illnesses could be further elaborated). These illnesses cover in one way or another all regional, class, age and cultural groups in Mexico. All lives will be impacted by them, and demands for policy and financial inputs will be made. Some are being dealt with up front, like malnutrition, air pollution (in Mexico City), and chronic illnesses; and some seem to be getting less attention (AIDS measles, and junk food). Some of these health-illness areas will demand much financial assistance, as AIDS, the necessary environmental cleanup, and chronic illnesses. Others like systematic immunization for measles and telling Grupo Bimbo to improve the nutrition value of its offerings would be more affordable. It may not be easy to tell numbers of multinational corporations like soda pop vendors to put vitamins into their product, but the savings in healthy popular diets may be such that NOT changing diets is UNaffordable! Tom Barry's Mexico: A Country Guide has only two photographs, these on the lead page of articles about such matters as foreign influences which allow a sweet young child her liquids from a cola bottle. Let us discuss each of these case studies for their policy-affordability issues.

AIDS as an Illustrative Case Study

It is not something that I would describe as a major problem, "said the director of the National Council for the Prevention and Control of AIDS, Dr. Carlos del Rio, "but there is clearly a potential problem. (Tim Golden, New York Times News Service, The News, March 9, 1992, page 2.)

Tim Golden's article hints at the denial concerning AIDS as a serious problem, perhaps this denial coming from two countries in need of policy initiatives. The policy-public denial is only outdone by the cultural denial on the Mexican side of the border as well as in the United States. Is the situation noted in the quote above one of only pre-policy concern? Tim Golden's article goes on to quote the head of the AIDS program in the state of Michoacan who says: (page 4, The News) "The uproar will come later, in a future not so distant." One of the points of the article has to do with the transmission via migrants whose patterns of behavior were changed by that border crossing, but who go back to an unaware community. Much of policy making fails because the situation involved is beyond its field of efficacy. How can we stop lonely, single migrants with money from meeting their sexual

TABLE VI
CURRENT CASE STUDIES IN VARIOUS HEALTH AREAS: PROBLEM & POLICY OPTIONS

HEALTH PROBLEM	POLICIES IN PLACE	NEEDED INITIATIVES	COMMENTS
AIDS ("second highest incidence in Latin America)	ConaSIDA educates but pressures are great to deny problem.	Must acknowledge the problem, Catholic Church must back off, educate public and doctors.	Two countries are involved in control. Outcome will be unaffordable!
Malnutrition (up to 90% of children in some communities)	Many subsidies via INPI, SAM, CONASUPO, COPLAMAR, PRONASOL.	More outreach in poorer states like Oaxaca, Chiapas. Don't run subsidized food thru multinationals.	PROSASOL may focus diverted funds; too much stress on political loyalty.
Industrial Pollutants (as in Maquiladores)	Border communities have few regulations.	Need an OSHA with teeth. The NAFTA may bring it about, but this is problematic.	Affects community, not just workers. Regulais is not expensive, but opposite is built in.
Junk Food (that fails to give adequate nutrition)	Not much, only support for a watch dog which barks.	Political will would have to take on all of the big guys on the block.	Need ways to make the traditional diet more appealing? Take after Grupo Bimbo, etc.
Persistence of diseases like measles and cholera	Old public health efforts have diminished.	Must acknowledge the problem. Restore cuts in doctors who are obligated for 'servicio-social' in rural areas.	Illnesses are indicators of failed systems. Improvements may be more costly than immunization.
Chronic illness; CHD, cancer, etc.	Not much food residues, air standards are shaping up in Metro areas; some education as to diets.	Need a cancer register, more social epidemiology.	Lifestyles and diets can be changed. Reduction, finally, is most affordable route.

or other needs? How can we stop them from returning across the border? Will even a saturation education campaign reduce the incidence of infection? How can cultural attitudes be modified amongst potential victims, their social groups, and the attendant medical community? The lag in public attitudes and in policy making was noted in a book entitled, "And the band played on..." This delay is likely to be the case in Mexico regarding AIDS being included in the process of finding adequate treatment. Barry's volume discussing "Health hazards multiply" (page 236,1992) uses 1990 data to come up with 3,944 AIDS cases and a probable 200,000 to 400,000 HIV positives. Yes, epidemiologists have computed a probable rate of "multiplication." Barry claims that after an initially aggressive start the government agency responsible, ConaSIDA, was shackled by the Catholic church and other forces, probably monetary in form. This case study is not meant to declare that a health concern is beyond responsiveness to the policy process, but it is not like iodizing salt in order to stop goiters - which took long enough to accomplish several decades ago!

If our solution is cost-involved or one of hyper-unaffordability, AIDS will be a difficult one. Even hospices for the dying with a little support and some palliatives costs more than the communities have at their disposal. The long term intensity of adequate treatment matches cancer treatment as a drain on medical resources as we know, and AIDS has this built-in (potential?) multiplier impact. Mexico will not be able to isolate the problem like island Cuba is attempting. The main issue may be the standard of care in such a manifest illness, or it may be the cost of treatment of people who are only as yet HIV positive, but not yet full-blown immune deficient.

There are many related issues such as the isolation of patients in some form of testing or quarantine process. There are social issues regarding treatment of people in their respective communities, and of the obligation of those communities to support medical treatment. A form of sanctioned quarantine falls into the policy sphere, but social ostracism is mostly beyond policy and resides in cultural values not easily manipulated except through educational campaigns. How much official ignoring of the related problems is not yet clear, of course - there certainly has been benign neglect or worse in other places than Mexico. The tainted blood incident in France comes easily to mind at this point. AIDS treatment probably will not occur substantially in the private sector, even as Mexico's private medical service may be expanding. The costs of care, personal or clinical-pharmaceutical can not be borne by those affected. A public policy approach is likely one way or another, and this implies that cultural and social matters will have to be confronted. The cultural reaction vis GRID or Gay Related

Immuno-Deficiency (Deficit Immunitario Relacionado Con los Homosexuales) will only slowly be modified by policy driven approaches. Without stereotyping, hopefully, in a culture that sorts out "machismo" and "marianismo" in a serious fashion we might expect difficulties via perception of the medical problems that may be sexually induced. We will now turn to a case study (malnutrition) that is mostly policy-money responsive. (No culture yet observed obfuscates the need for adequate nutrition, except that found in the "safety net" type of Gringo psychology!)

Malnutrition and Related Ill Health Conditions

> Between 1981 and 1987, for instance, there was a sharp decline in per capita consumption of such important foods as fresh milk (21.8%) and corn (10.3%). Per capita consumption of beef, pork, and fish declined even more. (Health and welfare, in Barry, originally from "El estigma de la desnutricion", DEMOS, #3, 1990, by Jose Luis Calva)

The decline in food availability will be less dramatic as to nutrition as foods are substituted for those which have been economically outpriced. The culture of diets is real and has an impact on basic nutrition, apart from economic resources. However, the forces at work with respect to adequate nutrition are, by and large, economic. People seasonally change food choices in much of the world, but this is almost always for economic reasons as well. The previous moneys spent on SAM and CONASUPO and on their nutrition programs was based on a policy choice in a finite world pitting one possible expenditure against another in the real world. The clear choice of supporting by credit, tax, and trade policies foods for export rather than for supporting basic, domestic foods seems to be a macro-economic choice. By not funding the infrastructure needed for one food type (as to irrigation or transportation) as opposed to another is one of political-economy. As conservatives often declare, some problems do not improve when we "throw money at them", but nutrition tends to be money-responsive. Lunches for children via INPI improve nutrition levels, thresholds of malnutrition related to measles, pneumonia, or gastroenteritis deaths are all to well correlated with expenditures. They are Peso responsive. A modern market for food has emerged, and it is cash and carry from the checkout areas. There are few subsidized staples remaining as of 1992, perhaps only rice and some beans outside of the CONASUPO stores. Alternative programs like food stamps and commodity exchange have not caught on in Mexico. Briefly what are the health implications of these shortcomings?

Avitaminosis, Kwashiorcore, and specific deficiencies like pellegra are accompanied by drastically reduced resistance to what's going around - especially for children. The causes of death may be measles or gastro enteritis on the record, but they have to do with malnutrition on the bottom line. With horrendous infant mortality the implications are clear enough. What is the policy, political-economic background of this food deficiency?

Barry and colleagues in reflecting on the "structure of the economy" note how government agricultural policies attempted to stimulate new growth by eliminating price lids for many products. The idea was to stimulate the planting of basic grains. (page 164) Low prices supposedly were the cause of limited supply for domestic needs. The export market soared on the other hand, thus, also limiting domestic supplies. Fruits and vegetables along with coffee went north of the border. So did beer which could have drained the domestic supplies of barley and other food grains. The role of foreign firms and Mexican government policy with respect to credit, technical assistance, and subsidies could be discussed at length, especially as to how domestic supplies and costs are impacted. (See Barry, pages 165-169). Lack of internal effective demand (no pesos!) must be dealt with by changes in income distribution - Mexican citizens need more financial strength. Henry Ford knew this in Gringo land because for the economy to work, workers and others needed money to buy the products of the economy.

Food policy in Mexico was well studied since the 1930s by outsiders and nationals. As a post-World War II version, the American Field Service raised questions 25 years ago about this policy area. Merilee Grindle's study of the bureaucratic-political aspects of CONASUPO highlighted the relationship of food policy to the larger dynamics. Recently (1990) Aida Mostkoff and Enrique Ochoa discussed the supply of basic grains from 1925 until 1986. Is Mexico the victim of world markets or its own internal version of self-immolation? Is the issue one where self sufficiency was damaged by exportation of cash crops? Mostkoff and Ochoa say that it is "more complex" than the latter would indicate. We must define food shortage and food crisis they proclaim, but does not a high prevalence of malnutrition do that? Or is the issue one of distribution? Or policy failure? Or of demand problems centering upon consumer preferences?

David Barkin's recent attempt to define Distorted Development spends much effort on the topic of "The end to food self-sufficiency." (Chapter 2, page 11) Internationalization supposedly has increased Mexico's problems of rural development and food distribution. Reorganization of resources for the export market and for animal foods impoverished the domestic supplies creating food dependency. Far off markets tend to do this, and only a radical, new departure involving a "war economy" with labor intensive activities would rescue the food situation. (See "An end to the food Crisis", page 132) A real price increase in food via an import substitution policy for food would seem to do the trick. The chain of logic allowing for "substantial investments by U.S. agribusiness interests" and "looking to Mexico to replace domestic production" seems fanciful. Yet, some drastic change is needed to halt the dynamic decline in domestic food supply and the food import-substitution approach may well be it. After SAM was ended in 1982 there have been few replacements that would support the small scale producers. Meanwhile, many million more have fallen into poverty because of this austerity, and because they can not afford food from expensive providers. Barkin details the decline in food availability in notes supporting his second chapter, and there is little need to reproduce it totally here. Food costs tended to assume the international price, and having lived in Mexico off and on since the late 1960s, this seems obvious. SAM had many critics in the agricultural and in the transnational sectors, and nationalists seen it as an open door to multinational intrusion. Brad Miller notes that when the government gave the transnationals a substantial tax credit then SAM was forced to abandon its attempts at regulation of food advertising. (Page 31, Progressive, February, 1991) SAM may have been too costly as a rescue package, and the adaptation of the international style of marketing in Mexico further deteriorated food availability and affordability. The production of animal foods (red hybrid sorghums which are unfit for humans) cut further into domestic supplies. More technical knowledge and credit in the right places, as for the ejidos may help a reversal as well. The previous, new class of wealthy farmers typically got more assistance. Barkin sites two 1988 works on nutrition (Livas and Miranda Merida and also Centro de Ecopesarrollo) as some of the most recent available. Let us turn to another case study stressing an environmental hazard.

Industrial Pollutants

> Throughout the country the conflicts between productive demands
> and the health of workers and neighbors are becoming more apparent
> as researchers delve into these issues. (Distorted Development, page
> 48)

Barkin writing in the late 1980s and early 1990s suggests that the research knowledge is progressing slowly. A triple incidence of low birth weights is a possible indicator of toxic work conditions for women and men in the assembly plants. Run-away plants now are free from back home regulations - often minimal in the first place. The border workplace is also free of accident prevention, perhaps. The agricultural work setting is, no doubt, exposed to more hazards in the form of fertilizers, pesticides, and dangerous machinery. Water and air resources are additionally impacted in health-deleterious ways. To add to the deterioration there are U.S. based toxic disposal companies doing their thing across the border. The assumption seems certain that the impact is massive, and we must ask what are the health policy implications.

Our discussion could focus on the zootic epidemiology of pollution related illness, the affordability of various remedies or the political resistance to be overcome in the policy process. Our major focus has been on affordability and this is an area where costs are considerable if suitable policy is not forthcoming. Passing along costs is not the way to make profits even when the economy is in an early stage of development. Both capitalist and socialist economies have largely ignored the externalities reflected in spill-over pollutants, and to do so does not reflect the true costs of production. Should not the processes involved be taxed in order to pay for these health and social costs down the line? Such risk insurance may not reduce the illnesses initially, but can cover subsequent damages amongst workers and community members. The pressures to keep the border industries highly profitable will no doubt overcome work place rules, and the pressure to carry through with the NAFTA will intensify these pressures. The border environments are deteriorating in many ways based on the author's personal observation. Processo, an authoritative and courageous Mexican magazine, often has articles on the industrial toxins in border industries. (See "Media docena de Empresas de Tijuana en guerra por la basura", by Geraldo Alba, #792, January 6, 1992). Campaigns to reduce the toxic and hazardous work situations are there in incipient form, but only totally obnoxious conditions are approached. The policy making problem of any noxious circumstance is the time frame in which effective argument can be established - witness the asbestos and nuclear cases in the U.S. The epidemiology of industrial related illnesses can bolster policy making when causes can be established that are direct, timely, unequivocal and unique. The additional problem is that causes of such illnesses are not well known (as lung or bladder cancer) and differential outcomes of exposure are more common than one on one causation. Aggregate statistics and variance of risks are sufficient for scientific criteria of a linkage, but may not be for legal action. Alternative approaches to improvement could be worker organization, community action, economic action such as boycotting, and indirect action (as via increased insurance rates if workers or community members sued successfully). Again we have a variety of policy circumstances associated with different illnesses, and a single model for policy intervention would be hard to substantiate.

Junk Food as a Health Policy Arena

> The promotion of Coke, Pepsi, Doritos, Kool Aid and the like persuades people to give up inexpensive native diets for more costly and less nutritious food. ("Pass the froot loops, por favor", Progressive, February, 1991, page 30)

Many horror stories could be offered about low nutrition foods, fast to otherwise. The hard sell to children of "froot loops" and Jello products may be only part of the situation. As Brad Miller notes in the above quote: (page 30)

> Mexican nationalists have been trying to break the government-corporative television connection.

The National Consumer Institute faults this connection for having "failed to provide an adequate nutrition-education program." "Coke adds Life" and dental cavities, and malnutrition related illnesses. What are the policy-health problems apart from those discussed under malnutrition generally?

Basically political hegemony is maintained by the "connection" that Brad Miller details. We are not just referring to Snickers, cupcakes, Ruffles, Sabritas, or snacks, but to the very basis for national political power. Complaint is like asking a dragon that is devouring you to change his brand of toothpaste. It is clear that Mexican nationalists, who ever they are, have a broader agenda of concerns than children's diets - but they may be on the attack here for their own strategic reasons.

Other Illnesses - Other Policy Scenarios

Health issues are not mere issues of disease vectors and medical patch jobs; they rattle every cage in the land and finally resonate everywhere. The previous issue of children's nutrition involves the multinational corporations, the very development plan, and every knuckle in the power apparatus. To note Brad Miller again: "The companies invest here, buy their basic products on the Mexican market at a very low price, use cheap labor for production and packaging, and then sell their unnutritious product at an inflated price." (page 32) Big, profitable deals are made at every level, and the results include the ruin of the small farmer, the robbing of national nutrition, and the twisting of the law to accommodate various export, land, employer, and corporate interest. What about other illnesses?

Chronic illnesses are increasing with longevity and with life long epidemiological chains. Prevention seems minimal except for inadvertent cases, as where vitamin C may head off the pernicious effects of certain food preservatives. Given the difficulties of prevention on a systematic basis (yet educational campaigns against AIDS, for instance, will make a difference.) the resultant medical paradigm will be an expensive one for cancer, again as a for-instance. The system of health care can rule out expensive C-scan technology for the public hospitals, the number of hysterectomies, angiograms, gall bladder operations and so forth can be wisely cut. Research can be focused rather than pan spectrum. Condoms can be passed out at clinics. Mental disease, so called, can be medicated - as in the "modern" systems. Costs can be controlled in many ways - including rationing of elective surgery. Patients can be shunted into the private market, or across the border to Houston or elsewhere. When the author taught medical sociology it stressed that illness and health were social matters, and best approached from the broader perspective - including the economic and political context. If one fails to see this broader context, then the analysis is part of the problem!

Social Security in Mexico

> Mexico's social security system and its origins in the constitution of 1917, as regards labor and social security, the authors of the constitution drew up a set of protective laws which have served as an example for labor legislation in other Latin American countries. (Mexico, 1973, page 238.)

> On the expenditure side of the equation, we have already noted that the concentration of public sector funds in infrastructure investments left little for those social expenditures which might have directly raised lower-class standards of living. Public-sector investments in all the social welfare fields as a percentage of total public investment averaged less than 15% a year during the period from 1935 to 1960; only in the late 1950s did the figure rise above 13%. (Roger Hansen, 1971, page 85.)

The first old age, invalidity, and death benefit laws in Mexico were passed and implemented in the years 1942 to 1944, although wishful legislation covering specific groups preceded this by 3 decades. The Mexican Social Security Institute (IMSS) was founded in 1943 as an agency to administer social insurance for white and blue collar workers. In a U.S. document "Social Security Programs Throughout the World, 1977" Mexico's IMSS is seen (page 161) as administering its program through both regional and local boards. Generally its ultimate supervision comes under the Ministry of Labor and Social Welfare. This Institute operates its own clinics, hospitals, pharmacies, and rehabilitation centers as well. As we shall see, the IMSS has a broadly defined mission even if it does not cover the majority of the population. The most important things to say now about the Social Security system as first envisioned was that it was to be a multiple contribution system to which workers and government each gave 25% and the employers the remainder. The system was initially aimed at industrial workers and only very few agricultural laborers - just some sugar cane workers. The benefits of participation were seen as extending "from cradle to the grave," and as described by one very positive source included:

> ...prenatal, obstetrical, and postnatal care; all needed medical, surgical, hospital, and pharmaceutical services for every type of illness or accident; pediatric attention; preventative medicine; benefits for chronic invalidism; and finally, old-age pensions, burial expenses, and survivors benefits. (Gordon Schendel, 1968, page 252-3.)

These impressive services tended to center on the Federal district and some larger cities until just fairly recently. Mostly the middle and lower-middle classes were the recipients of this very elaborate system, which according to Schendel included, besides clinics and hospitals, such amenities as: "primary schools, supermarkets, movie theaters, an outdoor theater for amateur productions, billiard rooms, bowling alleys, basketball courts, swimming pools, and numerous play areas for children." Indeed, a self-contained way of life was being offered - for members at least.

While no one could fault the social security system for comprehensiveness, there seem to be many who do not benefit. Only selected groups have been favored, even to date. Industrial employees, members of selected cooperatives, some small farmers and small business-personnel, self-employed workers, domestic workers, the military and a few others are all that have been covered. There are also a variety of ways in which funds for specific groups are arrived at, especially the cooperatives, which have had to accept quite diverse arrangements in order to participate. As to individual qualifying conditions, based on our H.E.W., 1977 source, 500 weeks of contribution are required for the old-age pension, and 150 weeks for invalidity or survivor's pensions. The cash benefits run about 35 to 45% of the previous 5 year average salary, with 150 pesos per month as the minimum pension (about $50 today). The maximum pension equals 100% of earnings, if 2,000 weeks of contributions have been made - the latter favoring a select group of workers. Widows would receive 50% of their spouse's salary and orphans 20%. Some interesting benefits include Christmas bonuses, marriage grants, and layettes. Health provisions started under the 1943 law and were augmented in 1973. Work injury provisions have been separate since the 1969 laws.

There are more agencies than IMSS which are dispensing social security and social insurance type functions. ISSSTE, Pemex, FFCC, SDN, and SMN are additional agencies which we could discuss. Based on a table in Daniel Lopez Acuna's "Salud, Seguridad Social Y Nutricion" (In Mexico, Hoy, 1979, page 177) we see that these various programs at best cover 36% of the 1976 working population (see page 199). IMSS in 1976 alone accounted for 26.8% of the total working population. Many are not covered as of 1980, and at minimal, 60% of the total population must look to their own resources for old age survival - as opposed to 84% in 1965. As we noted above Mexico has essentially the lowest amount of government revenues available for such programs as social security in the whole Western hemisphere! (See Hansen, page 86.) That any social policy would get adequately funded under this low level of national commitment is surprising. The benefits and services involved in social security are most centrally directed on making the labor force fit for the tasks of industrialization - it is hard to describe their nature or their scope on any other basis and be as consistent in your interpretation. Let us see if this preliminary interpretation stands up after we have successfully looked at historical, current, and projected materials concerning social security.

Historical and Recent Materials on Social Security in Mexico

It should be pointed out that in many respects Social Security in Mexico has exceeded the levels reached in countries of greater economic potential and with more experience in this field (President of Mexico, September 1st, 1962).

In order to understand how social security has developed in Mexico we could use James W. Wilkie's views of Mexico's political development (page xxiv, 1970). Wilkie says that many observers stress that President Cardenas' social policy sacrificed economic growth for social enhancement, could times be otherwise? The move toward social security in the subsequent Camacho regime supposedly had similar values, but then we are told that President Aleman sacrificed social enhancement in favor of economic growth in the time period from 1947 to 1952. Also, after President Lopez Mateos from 1959 to 1964 a balance was struck between economic and social growth. In the latter period of what was called by some the "balanced revolution," we are said to be making steady progress in both areas. Hence, social security, or education, or health, etc., would see progressive development on a more equal basis to economic growth. Can we accept these scenarios as adequately reflecting the real events and gains? Actually, the growth of any of these social enhancement areas would follow the priorities and perceptions of the regimes as they respond to national needs. We can well imagine the humanistic and pragmatic reasons for the initial implementation of Seguridad Social in the 1940s, but the actual expansion seemed linked to national priorities of industrialization and economic growth. Also, when the system needed more even-handedness - lest revolution occur - then Mateos "balanced" the economic surge with a move from roughly 8% participation to about 16% in 6 years. A rise in the rural areas from about 4% to over 11% was also dramatic, and gave the Mexican government the propaganda victories it needed internally and externally. Mexico was taking care of its "underdogs," and they would be loyal during this period of emergence from decades of economic isolation. Let us look at some studies of how social security was viewed during this supposedly emergent period.

Two of the government reports available on social security and social development in general in the 1960s stressed the positive side of the total picture. A report of the Mexican government on "Economic and Social Development in Mexico" in October of 1962 distributed through the Organization of American States stressed the 610,000 new participants in IMSS and the 1,700,000 working participants and 5,000,000 potential beneficiaries. (See Document #32, page 12.) The development of ISSSTE for 600,000 civil service workers was also noted. Those millions who were not enrolled were not mentioned! Only the "cradle to the grave" qualities (from "layettes to burial expenses") were stressed. Another report was given indirectly through a Canadian group, the Canadian Institute for Public Affairs, which noted the "socialistic life span" approach to "medicare" which in 1965 covered 6,686,000 or 16% of the total working population. By this time, since government employees, railroad workers, the Armed forces and a few other groups had their own pension and medicare program and it was stated (wrongly?) that "one in four Mexicans have medicare and social security." (see page 8) In this report, which was dished out by Mexican government officials to the Canadian visitors, 10 million people were seen as being covered with an additional 20 million to receive benefits in a then expected 1966 act. Actually, the anticipated procurement of $291,000,000 for this latter expansion was never fully realized Indeed, no anticipated budget in the social security area has ever been completely realized - many have not been substantially completed because of the conservativism of administration.

This latter Canadian report also observed whom was not participating. Thus: (page 8)

> Still not covered are employers, professional workers, taxi drivers, domestic workers, most peasant farmers, and those in special industries, like fishing.

The latter groups were very large in fact, and many general workers and non-workers were also excluded. This 1966 report listed the social benefits as including: "Medical facilities, short term financial benefits (loans?), provisions for dependents, social service centers, social and youth centers, vacation facilities, and housing estates." Indeed, the concept of IMSS was a many-splendored thing for all who could participate.

The medical model to be utilized by IMSS was the family system used by others as British in their health service. Serious illnesses were to be referred to the various seven modern medical centers in the Federal District with many thousand bed capacities for each. Costs were to be met by the 3-way funding pattern noted above, and by the "investment and property returns" which the Institute was involved with. Thus, the costs of administration were in line with its current projected income except for the standing debt incurred by its building program. As a much more comprehensive report the overall problems of IMSS were noted. These were (see page 9) problems of financing, providing remote facilities, and problems of general administration. One of the financial problems had to do with the omnipresent peasantry where other population sectors would have to pay the costs for small farmers who had no employers, but whose work benefited all most assuredly. Most importantly, attitudes were changing about who would finance these services for the groups not participating in a visible, political sense.

By the mid-1960s, according to Charles Cumberland (Mexico, The

Struggle for Modernity, 1968, page 323)

> ...at long last the leaders of the Mexican nation had come to realize that the greatest natural resource available to any society is its people...

Noting the improvements in general health (most of which occurred before IMSS) Cumberland is elated by these social gains. Less positively inclined toward Mexico's social enhancement including its social security efforts is Roger D. Hansen, whom we have already cited. (page 85.)

> ...the Mexican government did gradually extend the coverage of such public services as free education, social security, health and welfare services, and housing, food and transportation subsidies. But what most foreign commentators who praise such achievements have failed to note is the extremely limited nature of these efforts when measured against total public-sector expenditures, GNP, or against similar efforts in other Latin American countries.

Hansen notes Howard Cline and Robert Scott as those who "extol the virtue of Mexican social expenditures." (See page 85.) As evidence of Mexico's total unprogressiveness Hansen observes that by comparison to Mexico's coverage of 6.1% of the total and 18.9% of the workers, Argentina covers 24.9% and 66.3% respectively. Chile (21.8% and 67.4%) and Brazil, Peru, and Venezuela are also relatively more progressive in the Social Security areas. Thus, Hansen notes (page 86)

> By either measurement - as a proportion of total population or of those economically active - the Mexican efforts to extend Social Security coverage have fallen behind those of major Latin American neighbors whether relatively rich (Argentina) or poor (Brazil or Peru), relatively industrialized or agrarian.

Let us look at some more recent views of the process.

If nothing else happened in the mid and late 1970s a generation of great, global Mexican analysts came to an end. The Greunings, Simpsons, Clines, Scotts, Padgetts, etc., gave way to two new groups: first the Mexican students of their own society - what could be better! And, secondly, the new breed of Gringo (or outside) observers. The former group includes social analysts such as Gonzalez Casanova, Daniel Acuna, Enrique Forescano, Arturo Warman, Rudolfo

Stavenhagen, David Ibarra, and Arnoldo Verdugo. The latter group includes such as Eric Wolf, Roger Hansen, Martin Needler, P. Smith, Alan Riding, Susan Eckstein, C. L. Kreps and C. Kuykendall, and Carmelo Mesa-Lago. Whether Mexico's dynamics in the 3rd decade of its industrialization are too complex for the globalist or not, there seems to be no shortage of critical analysts. Some of the former group like Dr. Stavenhagen had received part of their education in the U.S. as well. For both groups the level of analysis has become very sophisticated - witness the excellent compendiums like Mexico, Hoy, 1979 and El Perfil de Mexico en 1980. The Mexico .Hoy volume contains up-to-date articles on health, social security and nutrition by Acuna and by Adolfo Chavez. The new views of welfare, including social security, stress the conflicts of values and interests and are becoming soundly fact oriented. The 1950s and 1960s saw a transition period with global essays by the new writers, but an empirical bent has been added to these descriptive or theoretically oriented writings. National statistics, concerning who gets what, are becoming available through government, university, agency and even business sources. These statistics can reveal the real workings of implicit or explicit policies and decisions.

As to explicit policies, social security was updated by laws in 1975. The reasons for the most current legislation were administrative, financial, and also extend the system to some extent. Sickness and maternity policy had been altered in 1973. But aside from these kinds of descriptive observations the new kinds of social analysts ask "who get what out of the system?"

One of the 90's writers, Carmelo Mesa-Lago, a Cuban, assumes that the: "evolution (of social security) has taken place in a piecemeal fashion through pressure groups that base their power on four main sources; weapons and coercion, politico-administrative control, the market, (and) unionization and violence." (page 228) Mesa-Lago notes that social security has become "stratified along occupational lines" and has become a "regressive factor in income distribution." He sees four periods in the evolution of the system: (page 229) 1) 1900-1925 = state laws on occupations, 2) 1925-1942 = mostly federal groups covered, 3) 1943-1953 = specific white and blue collar workers covered, 4) 1953-1973 = agricultural groups and self-employed, plus reorganization for various groups. Mesa-Lago probably over stresses the strictly political factors that lead to coverage for a specific group. He seems to neglect factors having to do with the rise of the particular form of economy that came about in Mexico, and the roles played by each group in this evolution. It is true that the political clout of each of these groups that are included in social security increases somewhat proportionately to their economic importance - but political clout is too broadly described by Mesa-Lago to be of much help in our theorizing about why social development takes place as it does in that country. Certainly the fact that most of the social security benefits were lavished only in the Federal District as late as 1942 would seem to stress the political basis for the system, but a closer look at what groups got benefits and in what years reveals less certain political-military clout than centrality to the developing economic infrastructure. Hence: (page 232)

1904-1928	Salaried Industrial Workers are included.
1925, 26, 28	Civil Servants, Military and Teachers.
1931, 35	Petroleum and Industrial Workers.
1936-38, 41	Railroad and Electrical Workers.
1943	Blue Collar and White Collar Workers.
1955, 59, 63, 79	Rural Wage Earners

Mesa-Lago's "bases of power" theory about their inclusion seems less relevant than the importance, in sequence, of these economic groups to the evolving system. Teachers, for instance, had little clout or administrative control from any point of view, but it is true that parts of the military were an early recipient of benefits. The total list of legislative inclusions should be consulted by the reader. (Contemporary Mexico) Mesa-Lago's list of inducers also includes the "worker" and that may be a "base of power," but again this seems too diffuse to account for the pattern of social development in this area This kind of approach is ultimately what we need for our concerns, however.

Mesa-Lago's perception of the work yet to be done is also instructive. A footnote at the end of his article (owing to the timing of the publication and the new President's pronouncements) notes President Echeverria's admission that only 1/4th of the population was covered, and many "marginal groups were in urgent need." (page 25S) Mesa-Lago notes paradoxically that:

> In contrast with this attitude concerning extension, the law
> immediately raised the amount of several benefits for those already
> insured, and introduced day-care centers for the urban-insured, to be
> implemented immediately and financed entirely by the employers.

While we can read this proposition as, "to those that have, shall be given," and the "pressure bases" may be still as Mesa-Lago implies, the clear aim towards the most productive, modern sector seems to support our contention about the treatment of <u>needed</u> human capital. It is, of course, a narrow view of human capital that is held in the Mexican system, and labor redundancy seems to be one of the factors that keeps a more progressive view from emerging.

Let us spend some more time describing the total social security system itself before we go on with our theoretical model of why the system developed as it did. This next section relies heavily on Mexican government sources, and may be more up-beat than the system deserves. The authors own feeling is that an excellent example has been set near the core of Mexican society - and it eventually will have truly revolutionary effects, given adequate integration into the system.

A Description of the Apparatus Itself

> Properly speaking few Latin American countries have welfare
> systems at all (with the exception of Cuba...) and most would more
> accurately be described as limited social insurance states, although
> Chile, Costa Rica and Uruguay do have policies that go beyond
> social insurance. (James Malloy, 1985, page 29.)

In describing all new world pension-benefits programs, it is safe to say that they do not compare with European or socialist progressivism. New world systems, including the United States social security, are less generous if not regressive in their impact. Perhaps the values and political ideologies in the New World were the basis for this regressivity. Louis Hartz notes that the point of departure from Europe led to several "fragments," and that "Feudal fragments" were established in Latin America. The "bourgeois fragment" affected the U.S. and English Canada, and only Australia in the overseas areas was affected by the "radical fragment" from working class Europe.

There is more to the making of Mexico's social security system than these political-class values, however. It is clear that the "social minimum" concepts of European systems did not get established in Latin America. Nor, did Lord Beveridge's universalism. Neither did the social redistributionist ideas spawned in other old world settings. The United States also has a limited social insurance system, backwardly financed, and suffering from an additional means tested "welfare" system. It is true that an "institutional" approach to social security did arise in most new world settings as the industrial push made families and the private market insufficient. Thus, public programs seen as a "right rather than a gratuity" emerged, but they were not universally granted and they remained residual in their impact. Also, most new world systems suffered from the general "crisis" of the political economies of the states in which they resided, and continuously get shaken by systems crises. Carmelo Mesa-Lago sees progressivity in Latin American systems for their relative earliness, and their occasional health insurance, and family allowances. (1985, page 1) The United States of America lacks most of these features, and is limited to a few risks. Yet only 11 to 37% of the Economically Active Population are covered in Latin American countries, according to Mesa-Lago (1985, page 5). So what may we say specifically of Mexico?

A Description of the Social Security Apparatus in Mexico

The Mexican national Foreign Trade Bank has put out periodic volumes descriptive of the general economic and cultural life of the country. Six volumes in the developmental years between 1960 and 1974 carry materials on the social security system and its health, housing, and general service spin-offs. As an official, public bank aimed at promoting foreign trade the materials are meant to impress the trading partner or potential user of Mexican labor. While we have discussed how the social security system emerged out of historical factors involving political pressures and the needs for a viable economy, these next few pages will focus more on its general functioning.

The 1968 volume in this series, Mexico, 1968, was written with the Olympiad visitor in mind. It stressed the long history of the social security function in Mexico going back to the "laws of the Indies" in the early colonial period. The modern beginnings in Article 123 (sections xxxi and xxix) of the 1917 constitution are noted as well as the 1929 revisions and the broad 1943 implementation. Agencies associated with social security (as IMSS, PEMEX, ISSSTE, etc.) have grown tremendously as to budgets and number of personnel. The 1968 stress concerning the total program is upon such items as: Public health, the extension of pension benefits, the increase in personal health services, the movement toward rural coverage, and the augmenting of various auxiliary services. In most cases, these published data stress the extension of services in recent years, not the number of people who are not yet covered. The 1968 volume does mention, however, that the services are not universal (page 355). Since the 1940s blue collar and white collar workers are treated about equally, and constitute about 80% of the total who are insured. (See Mesa-Lago, page 235.) Those left out of the system, both rural and urban, can opt for a form of voluntary insurance - but few do. Most of those left out, are rural populations, and as few as 8% of the local populations are covered in some South Pacific states. While only 1/4th of the total population of the country benefit, Mesa-Lago observes that the rest of the Mexican nation pay for it with their taxes and higher consumer costs (page 249). In the Mexico, 1968 volume the urban bias of the Mexican system is also treated as a positive factor. Indeed, a well supported labor population is what this volume wants to stress. Actually as to whom the system benefits most, Mesa-Lago states that IMSS bureaucrat's salaries went up so much in the 1960s that the system represents "an income redistribution from insured to administrators." Payment for the system is, as noted above, based on funds from the worker, employer, and the state. Direct taxes are not involved in the building of the basic fund.

The original IMSS system of the 1940s was augmented by the ISSSTE (Instituto de Seguridad y Servicios Sociales de los Trabajadores la Servicio del Estado) in 1960. The increase of Federal government employees and the enhanced public sector in general is stressed in this volume. A broad range of services, going from sickness benefits, educational programs, to home loans are noted in the 1968 volume - with an amazing proportion of its total budget going for loans. The provision of cultural supports for its members (including arts and craft classes) is a hallmark character of these programs as well.

The remainder of the 1968 volume stressed housing which was noted as being "one of the most urgent problems confronting the country." According to the data presented, 5.1 of a total 6.4 million families live in only one or two room houses. The government's response in the form of the National Housing Finance Plan has to do with the channeling of public and private funds. ISSSTE is also involved as a housing broker.

By 1973 it is obvious that the extension of services was proceeding apace. An overall total of 156 thousand people were involved in health services in 1970, for instance. These service personnel constituted almost three-fourths of all health personnel in the country. Victories in public health are again noted with many (rare?) diseases being eliminated. The urban advantages with respect to the availability of medical services (as to doctors, etc.) is also noted as continuing. Most striking is the IMSS medical achievement of 44 million consultations in 1972. Near universality is alluded to, but some rural gaps in coverage are admitted. There may be some exaggeration here, and the fact that non-workers are not even covered is ignored. But, the 19% increase in medical consultations in 2 years is impressive. The breadth of support services of IMSS (including athletics, handicrafts, and even vacation services) is again emphasized. The 1973 volume covers the parallel services of PEMEX, the National Railways (FNM) in more detail than the 1968 version. Much more is written about housing programs in 1973, and, indeed, there has been much government activity here. Our coverage of housing policy can be briefly summarized here: Impressive numbers of houses have been built, but 70% still live in inadequate housing. One change that seems quite progressive is toward more comprehensive community planning into which these individual units have to fit.

Concerning major features of Mexico's various social security systems, the following seem true. First there are unique elements, although universality is not achieved (or sought?). Demographics will alter the finances of the system just as ups and downs in Mexico's economic fate have done in the past. More working persons are living longer thanks to their original advantages, and they will claim more of the existing pie. The "politics of incorporation" as James Malloy calls them (1985, page 43) are clearly involved. The Mexican approach seems aimed mostly at the economically and politically active!

As to the financing of Mexico's biggest program IMSS, Peter Thullen (in Mesa-Lago, 1985, page 169) notes a "surplus." This surplus resulted from low expenditures as assets, income and expenditures are "kept below real value." Much of these surpluses are actually reinvested in medical infrastructure. Given this measured approach, a "crisis" is put off because there is a large surplus - due to under returns to the contributing population. No immediate "crisis" is seen, but Thullen raises questions of "Socio-economic adequacy," legal aspects concerning investment policies, and the cost of their general and medical expenditures (1985, page 173). This "underadjustment of pension values" supposedly has put off a financial crisis until the year 2022.

Perhaps one should note the innovativeness spawned by the above reallocation of "surplus" funds. There seems to have been an effort to "implement...a wider social solidarity" (see Giovanni Tanburi, in Mesa-Lago, 1985, page 76) through medical services. This has resulted in such innovative cooperation as the IMSS-COPLAMAR program in Mexico with its stress on primary health care. By using a "scaled premium system" the 6 percent contribution rate has generated a "surplus" which has been allocated to other needs. The effort clearly is to preserve social peace with the moneys generated by Mexico's largest social benefits program. Let us now relate what descriptive materials we have arrived at to our more general, theoretical concerns.

A Closer Fit Than We Might Suspect

We have noted in this chapter that some groups of workers could from early decades claim modest insurance provisions, if not full-fledged pensions. When a more complete social security system started in the 1940s it most assuredly coincided with the beginnings of economic "growth acceleration." (See Lloyd Reynolds, Image and Reality in Economic Development, 1977, page 266.) Groups seemed to be "let into" the benefits system as they performed vital functions for the nation in terms of the economic infrastructure, political processes (as of stabilization or of allocation), or of actual production itself. Carmelo Mesa-Lago's perception that "muscle" was involved in the actual process leading up to the procuring of benefits status need not trouble us. His model is more diffuse than our own, it would seem. The antecedent conditions he uses hardly omit any key processes. It seems likely that a relatively high level of consciousness about where the social security benefits should be allocated is involved in Mexico - rather than aimless muscle of groups coming from out-of-the-blue who push themselves into the benefits circle. If Mesa-Lago means essentially the same things as we do under such rubrics as the "market" or "government concessions" then we are not so far apart.

Let us look at the problem of what determines social development from another vantage point, this having to do with one might expect if there were a modicum of rational action and autonomy in the system. If we were to construct a chronological diagram with points representing the early budding of industrial activity, or of a political-national revolution with great aspirations for development, or of a period of instability and institution building and the need to integrate disparate parts - especially rural one, or of the final consolidations necessary for industrialization, or of the struggle for a "balanced" formula for growth - economic and social, and the final surges toward a mature economy, then the concessions of social security, health or education we have witnessed would make good sense. We are not saying that there was some "functional necessity" which would legitimate these patterns of social development, or that the political pressures are presumptuous or inconsequential. It may take the pressure of organized groups which became effective in the work areas, in order to make themselves even more efficacious to the rise in productivity.

Nor is the formula for the attainment of social development merely one of labor scarcity, because most of the groups who have gotten to the benefits circle in Mexico have not really been that scarce. Some writers like Turner and Jackson (Economics Journal, Dec., 1970, pages 827-49) also assume, at least on a world-wide basis, that we will have "unlimited labor forever." The point being that workers, teachers, the military, etc., can be replaced, if we are willing to let the function to be performed lag somewhat. In any case, we can admit the cogency or many other perspectives about the basis and motivation for social development. We will again in this volume look at the competing theories about the determiners of the extent and scope of social development. Undoubtedly, the six year term (as having to do with the break between the Cardenas and the Camacho regimes, for instance) had something to do with the timing of social security. The Mexican "Revolutionary Family" as a power elite would also have to be taken into account, and it seems clear that this elite was trying to avoid the more potent radicalism of Toledano in the late 1930s and early 40s. They were also being pushed to achieve these more moderate goals - just as the ADA Democrats in the U.S. felt that they had to purge the more radical Henry Wallace supporters. No doubt that we could go through our whole list of alternative explanations and make a plausible case for the periodicity we find in social security. However both its positive attainment in enlisting specific groups, and its slow progress in "marginal" areas of economic productivity - seen narrowly - lead us to other explanations.

Can the System Afford Expansion?

> Although Mexico has expanded population coverage, it has done so much less than Costa Rica, Cuba, Chile, and Uruguay. In addition, benefits and entitlement conditions in Mexico are more restricted than in these countries. (Ascent to Bankruptcy, Page 165, 1989.)

Carmelo Mesa-Lago's 1989 book details the problems of systems expansion or contraction in 6 nations. This author notes that as of 1983, 42% are covered by pensions and 60% by health benefits. (He observes a lag in the data, which as of this writing faces the same problem.) In Mexico the extended cost is low at 2 to 3% of GDP, and he believes that Mexico "could have done better." (p. 143) Given the type of funding, recent economic crises have lessened their surplus. The health expenditures (especially centered on maternity expenses) have been a drain on IMSS, ISSSTE and SSA total funds. Previous qualities that helped the "surplus" to build up, were according to Mesa-Lago were the unified aspects of the services, their recency in demographic and calendar terms, and the meagerness of coverages allowed.

To answer our question about extension one must ask why can't the universalization or approaches to it be attempted if different types of funding were achieved. The sheer inadequacy of services available makes the extension of health services problematic on a universalistic basis, even when most of the nation's resources are so oriented. What about pension extension? It is already automatic if one has a job, either via IMSS or ISSSTE, etc. Another helpful aspect would involve the reduction of administrative costs, which are amongst the highest. (Page

165 in Mesa-Lago) Should health expenses be separated in order to preserve the integrity of pension funds? Can the system afford the notion of "social solidarity" which allows expansion of IMSS via COPLAMAR? Mesa-Lago observes how the latter does favor an extension:

> Mexico has gone beyond the expansion limits of the Bismarckian social Insurance model because of social solidarity and the IMSS-COPLAMAR programs, which have notably expanded the health coverage of the total population. (1989, page 152)

What has led to the philosophy o f social solidarity is a separate topic except that it deals with the pressures and the attempts to handle them. The real parameters may be philosophical, rather than with economic affordability. Yet the system will be sorely tested economically by such challenges as the AIDS virus which is being carried back and forth across the border.

Mesa-Lago stresses that Mexico has managed to add "the modern rural sector" and, thus, approach the "pioneer countries." The Bismarckian social insurance system with attention to separate risks, coverage (largely) of the urban employed, three part contributions (state, employer and employee), and contributions equaling payouts can be bypassed by true social security systems. Philosophy and some affordability are what have moved Mexico beyond the minimalistic Bismarckian concept. A need to incorporate sectors that can otherwise raise hell may have something to do with it also. In the real world these are issues of affordability per se, as Mesa-Lago's concern with Bankruptcy shows. The oil boom in the late 1970s had allowed an expansion (up to 4.7% of GDP), and only another boom will supposedly allow for an expansion along social solidarity lines. This may be the bottom line for the big ticket items, except the case study of Mexico shows that a philosophy can take on a life of its own.

Nutrition: An Area of Uncertain Progress

> The National Solidarity Program (Pronasol) reports that more than half of the deaths of children under four are related to malnutrition; in rural areas only one in four children under four have normal height and weight. (Mexico: A country guide, Edited by Tom Barry, 1992, page 235)

> As it is now, the subsistence or semi-subsistence areas (in Mexico) do not produce enough of the right kind of food to keep their

populations healthy and active, while the agribusiness areas produce too much, encouraged as they are by the policy of price supports. (May and McLellan, in <u>The Ecology of Malnutrition in Mexico and Central America,</u> 1972, page 45.)

Mind blowing discussions have taken place as to whether wheat, corn or beans (or some combination) are perfect, adequate or unsuitable diets for the Mexican people. We shall in this chapter look at the concerns for an adequate diet for the Mexican people, but also we will focus on problems of distribution, allocations, and resultant patterns of nutrition. The objective will be to assess the nutritional adequacy of food and diet patterns as of the mid to late 1980s. The health implications of these patterns will also be assessed based on Mexican and comparable studies. Finally the nutritional pattern will be related to our central theoretical concerns having to do with the motive forces leading to human sufficiency and adequacy in the various areas

Concerns for the Adequacy of the Mexican Diet

The U.S. Area Handbook for Mexico offers a short description of the Mexican diet: 2,600 calories and 72 grams of protein were seen as being the average in 1969. However, this source also cites United Nations data in that decade which indicated that "half or more of the population suffered from some degree of malnutrition" (See page 40). This largely rural problem existed even though an estimated 30% of produced food perished in the fields.

Much of the problem with protein, for instance, was seen variously by different analysts. Some stressed inadequate distribution, others stressed poverty. The U.S. Area Handbook stated that the protein deficiency was due to "dietary choice," where fish, milk, eggs and meat were not preferred, and were "not prepared." Relatively more fruit, sugar, and garden vegetables were utilized with corn and beans being the basic and chosen food - especially for the poor. The various tortilla, taco, enchilada vehicles allow many other traditional foods to be consumed as well. This source over stresses cultural preferences, perhaps, especially as urbanization occurs, and we can clearly see the changes in diet. As a beverage, for instance, pulque the cactus beer has given way to European type beers. The latter drinks have become increasingly expensive for the villagers, and cheaper varieties have been produced locally or brought up from the Yucatan. And, whether nutritional acculturation is good or bad, it has occurred, and the preferences have also been transformed. In any case, malnutrition is noted in this and other sources, as the following. Ana Maria Flores in her study, La Magnitude del Hombre En Mexico, concluded: (1973, page 70)

En el ano de 1970, un 14/5% de la poblacion de Mexico sufio hambre. La desnutricion se provoco debido a que la dieta nacional tuvo deficits, del 12 al 25 por ciento en numero de calorias per capita.

There are many numerical estimates of the extent of the nutrition problem, but let us look at some of the dietary specifics. We must ask why there are such deficiencies in a land of obvious plenty. Clearly droughts as in the Sonoran-Sinola "breadbasket" as in 1977, can have their disastrous effects, but what is the more normal situation.

Food consumption in Mexico as elsewhere is clearly linked to the economic circumstances of the individual, and to a lesser extent the geographic and cultural regions they reside in or came from. A well-to-do peasant or villager may buy goat or sheep meat and other high protein sources at village markets or carnicerias. Also fruit and vegetables of good or better quality can be found easily with cash on market days or otherwise. Some policies and market incentives in recent years have clearly improved food distribution, consumption and adequacy, but other federal policies continue to be an important factor retarding these matters as well. Some areas obviously have better opportunities for adequacy than others do. Probably the Federal district has the least nutritional or dietary problems, except for the shantytowns described by writers like Lomnitz. In medium-sized towns, as the relatively prosperous Cuernavaca which the author is most familiar with, 2 or 3 levels of food consumption clearly exist with the top levels utilizing the Yankee-type super mercados, the middle groups utilizing these and local markets and vendors, and the bottom group eking out more traditional, low cost, high starch diets. A United Nations source (Social change and development policy in Latin America, 1970), observes that food expenditures are heavily impacted in the urban migration process by economic trade-offs and nutritional acculturation. Hence, (page 265) "the family diet is thus likely to deteriorate even if the family income rises." Money alone may not be the complete answer.

The locus of the most severe nutritional problems is discussed by May and McLelland. Citing large scale surveys, which we will review below, they state: "...as usual, the preschool child was the main (not only) victim of malnutrition" (page 42). Based on these surveys of up to 20,000 individual cases, they project over one-third of a million children in Mexico with the protein and calorie deficiencies, kwashiorkor and marasmus. One study of childrens' diets and nutritional status at Fresno, a poor suburb of Guadalajara, found the following:

33.5% had signs of 1st degree malnutrition
10.0% had signs of 2nd degree malnutrition
and, .77% had signs of 3rd degree malnutrition.

The causes were seen as being the high dietary proportion of corn and beans which were also seen as being deficient in quantity and quality as to protein. Inadequate riboflavin, niacin, and ascorbic acid also were found in this sample, but more pervasive shortcomings were found in other studies cited. For instance, Zubiran and A. Chavez found caloric deficiencies all over Mexico, and even protein levels were deficient in better supported urban areas (see page 37). Other surveys (Flores, page 16; Schendel, page 188; Adolfo Chavez, page 228) see the effects of maldistribution as being more broadly spread in the age structure. The pattern of the results from these surveys indicates that maldistribution and its consequences must be addressed. May and McLelland state unequivocally that the problem is one of distribution:

The preceding pages indicate that Mexico is self-sufficient in all the basic food it needs. Hence, the problem of keeping its population in a satisfactory state of health and nutrition is contingent upon adequate distribution of food, education and income.

Many kinds of foods do not yet (as of the late 1970s) go through rural distribution systems, but the spread of the CONASUPO units may remedy this for those who can buy from the area stores or mobile units. Mexico has the food, it clearly has not found the will to solve the remaining distributional problems. Our United Nations source, Social change and social development policy in Latin America, (page 18-9) notes that Mexico has the fourth highest per capita food production index in Latin America after Venezuela, Uruguay and Guatemala. The varied geographical environments of Mexico allow great productivity even from limited tillable acres, but then the problems begin: "...wide gaps between producer and consumer and their wastefulness in terms of high proportions of foodstuffs spoiled before reaching the consumer" (page 265). Cheryl Christensen in her article on "world hunger, a structural approach"; observes (pages 186 in Hopkins and Puchalia's The Global Political Economy of Food) that Mexico devotes less than one-third of its cereals land to export crops (cotton and coffee), and hence, should as a nation, tend toward self sufficiency. Citing the need for new marketing systems brings us to the Mexican government efforts to avoid these distributional and price difficulties as with the CONASUPO programs.

Merilee S. Grindle's study of CONASUPO (Bureaucrats, Politicians, and Peasants in Mexico, 1977) deals mostly with the career aspects of such a policy area. However, she describes the functions of this state agency with respect to the pricing and availability of food. The Compania Nacional de Subsistencias Populares, SA, or the National Staples Products company and its many subsidiaries have, since 1965 and before, tried to regulate the basic commodity market, increase the income of poor farmers, and allow lower income Mexicans to acquire basic commodities. (see page 19 in Grindle) Specifically, such activities as selling subsidized milk (including infant formulas), moving corn flour supplies to tortilla factories, marketing wheat flour products, operating retail outlets (Diconsa), and providing construction materials and farm supplies. Nearly 5,000 retail outlets and 1250 rural warehouses are involved in these distributional activities. The CONASUPO program started in the conservative Ordaz administration and blossomed in the more "redistributive" Echeverria period. Even though massive pressures were common, the CONASUPO stores helped to regulate the prices of basic foods and also to stabilize nutritional access throughout the country. "People's Drug Stores" which were planned to provide low cost medicine met too much pressure from the largely transnational pharmaceutical industry, and they failed to materialize during this period in which CONASUPO otherwise expanded. CONASUPOs activities, as support prices, became more of a policy to assist rural development than to benefit the urban consumer. (see page 90) CONASUPOs thrust was to break the hold of the middleman or intermediaries, unaffectionately called the "coyotes."

The author and his professional homemaker wife engaged in comparative shopping in Mexico City and found that the CONASUPERS were less expensive on many products - if not across the board. But there are solid studies of the nutritional situation in Mexico, so let us look at some of those sources. Then, let us look at the policy attempts in this area of nutritional adequacy and the ramifications for our attempts to understand the motive forces for social development.

A Sample of Major Studies of Nutritional Adequacy in Mexico

There are several recent kinds of studies of nutrition, diets, and adequacy in Mexico. Clinical studies of nutritional problems have been carried out by The Hospital de la Nutricion. (See May and McLelland, page 42.) Schendel (1968) notes in his chapter on "Moving in on Malnutrition" the earlier work by Dr. Salvadore Zubiran at the National Institute of Nutritional Diseases. These various studies are dietary investigations that start with historical references and then come up to date with caloric surveys. There are also sophisticated biochemical analyses of typical diets as well. One of the latter according to Schendel pointed out that the typical 64 grams of protein are basically from corn, and are lacking in amino acids - namely, "tryptophe, methionine, lysine, threonine, and sometimes...valine" (page 179). Schendel notes that the outsider's caricature of the siesta-taking peasant captures, instead of indolence, the "ill segment of the population." Schendel observes how these illnesses sap the efforts at economic development as well, and he lists anemia, pellagra, stunting, urinary lithiasis (from the lime in too many tortillas), goiter, and T.B. as debilitating consequences of malnutrition.

Of course, there have also been surveys and subsequent health crusades by Mexico's Public Health Department. The latter, for instance, made a strong attack on goiter which is common in the iodine free volcanic areas of Mexico. There followed a spasmodic attempt to iodize the salt of the nation, which had less success in backward areas. Perhaps, this episode could be seen as a more typical outcome of the policy implementation process in Mexico. Backwardness could be stressed, but later, in fact more decisive policy application eliminated the problem in all but the more remote areas. Let us look at another survey of nutritional matters.

Wilkie's poverty index utilized available dietary information from the various national censuses, data from the 1940 general census, the Compendio Estadistico of 1950, and the resume of the census of 1960 to get the changing proportion of wheat and corn-bean eaters. The assumption was that:

> The traditional complex of foods is notorious for being deficient in animal protein, fats, vitamins, and for supplying an overabundance of carbohydrates and vegetable protein. This complex tends to cause acidosis, high blood pressure, anemia, inadequate growth, lack of energy, weak resistance and premature old age.

Wilkie's prescription is to integrate modern, high protein foods (milk, meat, eggs, fish, fowl, and wheat flour) with the traditional diets. Wilkie, using data from a study by Butterworth ("A Study of the Urbanization Process"), sees migration to the cities as improving the diet...at least by the typical addition of beans of various kinds. Only 5.6% of those in the Federal District ate tortillas versus 60.8% in nearby Queretero state.

Based on the list of nutritional studies in this volume, it seems clear that we have more nutritional data than in 1948 when Whetten wrote: (page 304) "The diets of rural Mexico have never been adequately studied." Corn and wheat have now been well analyzed for their body building - or reducing effects. The consequences of not having the milk, meat, egg, fish components have also been studied. For those populations who have access to the modern protein complex via CONASUPO or commercial stores the break with traditional body types and diets has been made. No longer should the corn-beans-chile diets or the atole gruels stunt the life of Mexico's populations. There were, of course, foods in the traditional diets that made their contributions to nutritional adequacy, as from Whetten some examples: (page 313)

* Malva, a wild spinach-like food, high in vitamins A and C and iron,
* Charal, little dried fishes, good for protein and calcium,
* Questo de tuna, from the prickly pear, with iron and vitamin C,
* Pulque, or fermented maguey cactus, high in vitamin C,
*Gusanos, or small cactus grubs that are fried to no great nutritive gain!

This list of traditional foods was supposedly the basis for an argument that a "U.S. type diet" need not be adopted, and, indeed, there are many problems associated with the latter. The Whetten data were from the National Institute on Nutrition and especially from Rene Cravioto's "Consumption of typical Mexican Foods" (*Journal of Nutrition,* XIX, Number 5, May, 1945, page 327). The Rockefeller study of 1945, despite "signs of abject poverty" found "little evidence of malnutrition." What a remarkable convergence of data supporting inaction in rural areas! There is a naive naturalism, often found in cultural anthropology, that worships what cultural solutions people have arrived at in order to survive, but it does not mean that nutritional adequacy for modern purposes has been achieved or even that a reasonable standard has been arrived at for the traditional group. How would we deal with goiter, for instance, unless the groups found fat necks sexually attractive or somehow functional elsewhere!

Now the latter are remarkable results, and without doubting their data we could question their representativeness. Some peasants and Indians, doubtlessly, have achieved "balanced" diets, but the timing of these conclusions at the threshold period of industrialization seemed to free up national resources away from that task. Actually the Otomi Indians were not the issue, but rather the numerous other peasant and Indian groups who were not so well "adjusted (through) centuries (of) food habits." Meanwhile, "attempts .to change would be a mistake until economic and social conditions can be improved and something really better subsisted." Hopefully all other things would remain the same for these people as well. (See page 314 for the quote.) Still the "balanced" Otomi were 700 calories short, and this data (page 316 of Whetten) showed less protein by 10%, less riboflavin by 125% and less niacin by 25%. No one would have argued that we should rush into these situations with "Wonder bread" or McDonald Burgers, but one wonders if the situation should have been treated to such benign neglect.

The Policy Paradigm for Nutrition in Mexico

Let us consolidate these diffuse materials and discuss the nutritional policies that have emerged in Mexico in relationship to our concerns.

One must remember that much of the fervent constitution making was an attempt to secure land and food for the Mexican people. The ending of peonage after the latifundistas were defeated meant that even more basic problems, those of human survival, had to be confronted. Government efforts prior to the 1930s were able to help only a few workers, a few soldiers,, and some children; but one must also remember the level of open turmoil before this. The world-wide depression, although sparing much of Mexico, did effect food potential, and much of the back and forth activity over land "reform" kept food potential from being realized as well. Later, too much of some export crop, as sugar from Sinaloa, would be produced instead of other consumables. Even a considerable amount of rice from Michoacan was sent out of the country, and much of the coffee from Chiapas, the less-than-edible cotton from Torreon, and the sisal from the Yucatan made for a very thin soup! (See Fire and Blood, page 589.) Exports dominated in the period of nation building, and a firm foundation for food production and distribution was not accomplished. Small farmers typically grew only subsistence levels of corn and sometimes beans. Neither, did the ejidos produce the food that was needed, according, at least, to the historian T. H. Fehrenbach.

Fehrenbech discusses the "economic failure of the Ejido system" where 5 million people gave little back to the country in terms of food surpluses. Thus, (page 592):

The Ejido population comprised 42% of all Mexicans employed in Agriculture. But, the Ejidatarios produced only 19% - at best - of the cattle, fowl and honey and their relative production of staple crops like corn and above all cash crops for export, was so disastrously low that Cardenas' administration deliberately concealed the figures by refusing to calculate them.

This interpretation fails to appreciate the purposes and activities of the ejidos during this period, but it may be that national food supplies were not greatly elevated by this ejido policy. Perhaps failing commodity prices had more to do with Ejido "failures" than their faulty conception. And, one must remember the shortages of credit that characterized their efforts.

The 1940s saw a focusing on rural populations, but actually few viable programs were offered to assure self sufficiency. By the 1950s the country's problems in terms of supply shortage caused the investment in new production of old food stuffs, and the enhancing of new sources, as fish. High protein sources were evidently favored. Many activities centered on more efficient distribution of food stuffs, culminating in the CONASUPO structure of the 1960s. In the 1960s school lunch programs extended from pilot to mass pilot to mass levels as well. The logic of better products, and better distribution, and more rational food economics extended into the 1970s - except for areas like pharmaceuticals - where powerful interests prohibited this extension.

Some of the more recent attempts at solving food-nutrition problems include SAM (The Mexican Food System) which was set up in 1980 but dismantled in favor of other programs in 1983. Basically SAM (according to Levy and Szekely):

Aimed to establish a formula for sharing risks between the government and the peasantry in order to reach certain production goals for maize, beans and other products. The government committed itself to providing the peasant with fertilizer, seeds and other inputs at very low prices; it promised to see that products would be bought at established prices; and it guaranteed a minimum income in the event that the crop is lost because of a natural disaster.

Levy and Szekely also note the policy change <u>away from land</u> redistribution where the peasant allows his land to be used by neighboring large landowners. The goal is to achieve higher food productivity, but it represents an end to the more radical concept of rural equalization. This Agricultural Development Act of 1981 evidently is still on the books, but as we noted SAM was scrapped in 1983. The new National Food Commission attempts to deal with the contradictions and lack of muscle in the SAM program. Much food is still imported and passes by the food stuffs destined for the markets north of the border. Meanwhile great nutritional problems remain. As of December of 1988 the "hunger problems" is being addressed again. The "newly created National Food Program" will spearhead the attempts to end hunger (<u>The News,</u> December 10, 1988, page 3). Pointing to the "economic crisis" this presentation by two top secretaries ignores the implications of previous policy decisions. The inclusion of the secretary of fisheries harkens back to the 1950s, but for several reasons has not advanced apace. Citing budgetary, land management and coordinating resources a note of pessimism is struck from the beginning!

We have seen food policy in its broad context and have seen the real moves to improve popular nutrition as being very recent. Many of the improvements merely involved facing up to the issue, as with the elimination of goiter by dietary additions. Other improvements were more costly if not radical in scope, as with school lunches or the dislodging of commercial intermediaries. The lateness and tenuousness of genuine food availability programs tells us something about the motive forces involved. These motives seem to have less to do with humanitarianism or with the forces of popular pressure (unless there are government responses to the unrest in Mexico's northwest). The governments typical <u>particularizing of dissent</u> seems to be less in evidence in the CONASUPO distribution schemes, but it seems that the latter switched from price lowering competition to a program which seems to essentially be a sop to rural, small producers who were in need of capital which they would get nowhere else.

There is much good food in Mexico, if one has the pesos. And, the culinary level matches any in the world. However, the summary of nutritionally oriented policies on page 125 seems to indicate that the food has been aimed at specific populations and has missed others. There has been great improvement in food products, as with corn and wheat. Remedies for specific deficiencies have been obtained. There has also been an improvement of distribution, and in the producer's return.

TABLE VII
POLICY EFFORTS (From 1934 To The Present)
TO REMOVE MALNUTRITION IN MEXICO
(Drawn From Robert Jackman's Politics & Social Equity)

YEAR(S)	POLICY	STRUCT. INVOLVED	# OF AGENCIES/ PEOPLE COVERED
1934-40	Redistribution of land to the Ejidos	Ejido supports via land, credit, etc.	750,000 (Fehrenbach, p. 591)
1945	Cooperation with International agencies	As the Rockefeller agency	
1950	Modernize corn and tortilla production	MICONSA	1 production unit
1950s	Improve corn varieties	Agricultural Dept.	
1960s	Utilize fish supplies better	Educational Programs	Training for 1000 students
1961	Free school breakfasts/lunches	INPI, Nat. Child Care Institute	From 80,000 to 3 million by 1964
1961	Modernize milk production	LICONSA	2 production units, 365 sales units
1963	End Goiter	Iodize all salt via Mateos declaration	90% of the population
1965	Better food distribution	CONASUPO	2/3 of the society?
1968	Modernize wheat production	TRICONSA	Low income consumers & Government. Institutions
1973	Spread sales centers	DICONSA	70% of the population?
1975	Distribute pasta and oils	ICONSA	5,000 personnel and 2,5000 outlets in 1975
1980-1983	Promote more food production	S.A.M.	10-20 million peasant producers?
1988	Eliminate hunger, 17,000 new stores, 105 new milk centers	The National Food Program	25% of population in poverty
1989	Targeting of groups	PRONASOL	What ever redistributed moneys & political necessities allowed

The Nutritional Budget as of the 1990s

An inventory of Mexican diets and nutritional well-being as of the early 1990s will show an improvement over May and McClelland's portrayal from the late 1960s. Improvements will be correlated positively with improved income status to be sure, and some to increased market sophistication. Some may argue that improvements would be due to a more complete nutritional acculturation and "modernization", but that remains to be argued. Harkening back to the Rockefeller studies when peasant diets were examined for their adequacy we have been treated to a number of visions of this adequacy or its opposite. Without arguing about whether a real improvement has taken place in this age of soda pop and cosmic twinkies, how much control over diets do people have, and what kind of policy issue is nutrition?

Many programs like CONASUPO and SAM have impacted Mexican diets. Liconsa and its related programs, school lunch efforts, anti-goiter programs and potable water activities have improved the picture as have regulation of pure food laws, better farm to market expediting, and even the super-mercados and "fast food" chains. Mexico still remains a bonanza of fresh fruits and vegetables what ever issues of sanitariness and chemical residues persist. So it is elsewhere. No doubt the strong points of modern food marketing contains the major draw backs as well. What are the big issues in the nutritional area now?

Large scale production of food for export with subsequent need to import basics must be high on the list of problems. The withdrawal of subsidies on innumerable food products during the "austerity" years grossly impacted the poor half or Mexico's population. Kwashiorkore, a-vitaminosis, and general protein deficiency for children and others are major deficits to be overcome. The actual quality of food is suspect and this refers to nutritional values as well as an absence of toxins - given the large scale use of herbicides and pesticides. With many excellent programs now in decline, it is also sad that the better-off groups claim so much of what is offered under the heading of food policies. As to the status of these issues, unless there is widespread starvation, there seems to be little response potential compared to other issues. They remain on the agenda, but malnutrition is a more silent issue as Robert Coles observed in his U.S. writings. In the 1960s the issue of malnutrition did help to mobilize student radicals who were very verbal about its wide spread existence. (See Ernesto Olivera, 1975) We are talking about motivations for social policy and a sense of injustice, even when another group is involved that wants to justify their own actions and positions.

The timing of nutritionally related programs (land reform in the 1930s, school meals in the 1960s, and thereafter CONASUPO, MICONSA, and SAM in the 1970s) shows the relationship to development and increased prosperity. The lingering quality of malnutrition is a mobilizing issue at a time when middle class reasons for their conscious political action are being sought. Even allies amongst the great unwashed and starving would be of help! Nutritional adequacy is also a measure of the progress of the system as a whole if policy makers want to really use it.

The Mexican Educational Enterprise

It is unmistakable that the school is paramount and supreme in Mexican life today. (George Kneller, 1973, page 28)

A history of Mexican education would reflect upon much lavishing of personal resources and some considerable disposal of public funds as well. George Fredericks Kneller notes a list of current strengths and weaknesses, which we will paraphrase in order to orient our readers to these particulars. (See page 226.) The tangible results:

include strong education for citizenship; a strong vocational program; much emphasis upon self provision; an expansion of elementary education; the qualitative improvement of public education, a recent stress on student participation; and an increasing budget. As for deficiencies, large classes; too much competition; and distrustful school officials; inadequate statistical reporting; and insufficient educational materials are involved. (The Education of the Mexican Nation, 1973)

Harsher, less "balanced" analyses of the educational system can be found. Critics observe the rural inequalities, the lack of universality with respect to application, the tremendous "drop-out" rates, the inaccessibility to higher education, the minuscule budgets available for all levels, and the continued repression aimed at higher education.

How has the current system evolved - what ever its status and quality? Can we point to specific milestones that will help us to understand the current situation? In brief, Kneller notes the Aztec's understanding of child development, the Spanish-Indian fusion through religious education, the sincere attempts to rescue the Indian cultures from feelings of inferiority, the socialist aspirations of the 20th century, and the inexorable demands of recent high-tech industrialization. Specific events in the battle for educational

TABLE VIII
RELATIVE COSTS OF DIFFERENT EDUCATIONAL FORMATS IN MEXICO

PERIOD	FORMAT	COSTS	CONFLICTS/ PROBLEMS	PROGRESS
1900-1910	Elite preparation	High per student	European oriented?	Some practical knowledge
1910-1922	Only in monasteries, some conservatories	"	"	"
1922-1942	Socialist education, 'Casa del Peublos', university isolated	Rise in public expenditure	Native content not universally appreciated	Education seen as a right; needs also perceived
1942-1960	Aleman's educational recession, slow expansion of base	Lowest in Americas	Drop outs, low professionalism, graduates unemployed	Short on technicians, too many lawyers
1960-1980	Coordinate higher education, more technical education	1.4% of GNP	Bypassed many in rural/urban areas, UNAM overwhelmed	Some rural catch-up, more Vo-Techs
1980-1995	"Reform" (NYT, May 21, 1992), broader base, more "professionalism", tuition deregulation= higher fees	Improved expenditure	Technocratic solution favors middle class, teachers versus the "system", quality of instruction	More balance between levels, new contracts to reward teaching, the NAFTA may stimulate

fulfillment included the war on illiteracy in the 1930s, the "Emergency Law" of 1945 which escalated that war, and the progressive educational enhancements having to do with vocational and higher education in recent years. But there is an earlier set of precedents which the reader must be aware of.

A Short History of Mexican Education

There is no shortage of historic events that the proud Mexican nationalist could point to. The specific founding of schools like San Francisco Elementary School in 1523 gave popular education very early beginnings. Educational trends of course were tied to cultural ones, and although a rigid scholasticism pervaded the middle centuries, the Jesuit's classical studies supposedly eased the tightness of the educational noose a bit. The political revolutions of he 1800s, according to Kneller led to high "educational aspiration" even though they were available only to the few. Nineteenth century education, however, became "obligatory, free, and lay." Mostly Kneller's history notes conflicts of sentiments with finances, however. Again, education reflected the cultural ethos, and the nationalistic goals of the last century fostered a particular focus that is better described as "statist," rather than popular. By 1891 schools were made "free" and compulsory, as well as increasingly secularized. Rural schools were bypassed and neglected by those applications until the 20th century, where change occurred somewhat faster. Momentous events in the society would, of course, be reflected in education. The revolution of 1910, shortly followed by the Carranza victories allowed for the education oriented articles of the great constitution of 1917, namely numbers 3 and 130. These articles mandated that education would be a Federal activity and the articulators clearly struck at religious schools.

Kneller notes the specific impact of one article, number 123 on the children of workers. Indeed, these were momentous sentiments, but reliance on the states led to the failure to mobilize sufficient resources. Yet even some of the conservatives now favored educational enhancement., according to Kneller. (See page 45) Some belatedly realized that an "educated, consuming proletariat" contributed to the well-being of the well-to-do more than merely ignorant, inexpensive labor would. And, rural education got more attention after 1923 from the "cultural missions" in the form of the "casa del pueblos." Yet, the Escuela rural made itself, if we are to take the word of Emilio Portes Gill, one of the teacher-statesman of Mexico.

And in the ascendant march of the Mexican social movement, in 1920, rural schools made their appearances as a product of the revolution itself. No one, no teacher, had proclaimed the rural schools as the Revolution itself did. Some few revolutionary school masters were ones who discovered the formula of the rural school, constituting the foundation of the present proletarian school. Rural schools arose spontaneously, no intellectual person of any rank made any suggestions as to how they should function; it was the rural teachers who built the system up, the peasants themselves who planned this new school... (See the Mexican Schools and the Peasantry, 1936, page 16.)

Kneller's good history of Mexican education notes the main perspectives between 1921 and 1946, and beyond. Other sources on this period of emergence in Mexican education include Marjorie Johnston, Clark C. Gill (both writing for H.E.W.), Emilio Portes Gil (just cited), George Sanchez, Goodwin Watson, George Booth, and more recently such as Charles Nash Myers, who traces educational development against its broader background. These sources cite people and events that must be comprehended by the reader; we have just so much to work with at this point. Such personal figures as Jose Vasconcelos, who was connected with the emergence of higher education in the 1920s, is seen as contributing action-oriented leadership toward "forging a fatherland" through education. Besides, nationalistic achievements in the 1920s, there was also the start of adequate teacher training operations. The practice of itinerant schools began to carry practical education to the very remotest of the hinterlands. Another important figure was Elena Torres who was a leadership person in the "cultural missions" period, helping to bring the "houses of the people" to their natural heirs. Also, who could forget the epic contribution of the world-class muralists who captured the revolutionary spirit of their times. By this sponsorship, the ministry of education reflected the Mexican people's coming-into-their-own-times. Indeed, the murals of Rivera, Siqueiros, and Orozco represent universal education in its ultimate sense.

Besides, what we note above as to the popular surge, an educational bureaucracy was growing. Much as in the U.S. of the 1920s, a movement became less focused; it seems that capitalist societies, especially, create "professional managers" to interpret and implement people's needs. The latter process was at least an antidote to archaic church forms of education which muddled up the human problems which could have more readily been approached by secular education. To understand even more salient issues than those of church and state we must view the emergence of socialist educational precepts between 1935 and 1941. George Booth (1941) tries to show how and why this socialist school of Mexican education developed. Booth's book was written, partly, to explain this emerging form of education to inquisitive Yankee neighbors - many of whom were foaming at the mouth. Booth noted that the legal basis for this apparent departure was somewhat as follows: Article 3 of the 1917 constitution, as revised in Queretaro in October of 1933 set out to avoid divisive individualism, and to stress instead the "socialization of the group" (page 7). The Queretaro conference to interpret Article 3 tried to remove education from both the church and from "professional educators," and, also, the "education imparted by the states shall be a socialistic one..."

The principles of socialist education can be paraphrased from Booth to show both what the reaction was against and also the more positive elements: (see pages 20)

* An equalization of group's (ethnic, sexual, etc.) status;
* Vitalismo or behaviorism will allow a new optimism about change of body and mind;
* Economic equality to end the struggle of classes is to be fostered;
* A "new person" is to be created;
* Student rights, not just of the Maestro, were to be implemented. (See Booth, 1941, page 14.) Student duties were to be conceived in such a fashion as to arrive at a new "brotherhood."

The rhetoric of this period in Mexican education, which was elaborated in a six year plan, sounds like the Cuban dialog of 30 years later. Much of the actual education was practical rather than ideological!, however. The "naturalism" and the "sex education" feared by Catholics were not likely to destroy the church - rather, if anything, to modernize it as is supposedly was becoming in the U.S. On these points Booth cites George Sanchez, Mexico's leading educational authority in some people's eyes, who was also a Catholic: (pages 71-2)

The conflict in Mexico has arisen because, unlike the American church, which is modern and in which religion is the chief concern, the Mexican Catholic church is the medieval church...which exercised not only a religious function but a political one in which economic power was essential to its existence.

Really, "formalism" is the object of educational revolt, not religion itself, according to Booth. (page 82) Perhaps the conflict in education of the 1930s was over social matters, as mediated by the political and the economic. In any case, other matters took center stage in the 1950, '60 and '70 period.

The World War II period and after saw an expansion of technical education, a slow growth in rural schools and secondary education, and an eventual booming of higher education. The middle classes had found access to higher education and to the experiences needed to assure their social mobility. James Wilkie has given us the projected and actual outlays from the 1860s to the 1960s. Wilkie observes that after the Cardenas high point in the 1930s (measured in Pesos per capita) and after Avila Camacho's reinforcement, the Aleman regime seemingly deemphasized the actual expenditures. The percentages dropped from 11.2% of the total budget to 7.1%, although the Peso level remained constant. After Ruiz Cortines' general continuance of modest levels, Lopez Mateos pushed for a new high at 21.8%, and a doubling of Pesos was involved. (See page 164.)   The ultimate meaning of these postwar statistics might be envisioned in such perceptions as Susan Eckstein's The Poverty of Revolution: The State and the Urban Poor in Mexico. (Princeton, 1977, page 173.) Eckstein, whose writings we have noted earlier in this volume, notes the strong relationship between social class and educational access and general quality. To quote her

> In general, public school allocations are distributed differently
> among the rich and poor regions of the country, rich and poor (urban
> and rural) communities, and rich and poor sections within the
> cities... School facilities were particularly inadequate in La Colona.
> There, over 2000 children could not enter first grade in 1967-8,
> about 3 or 4 times as many as could enter.

Although there were fairly immediate governmental reactions to this particular crisis, the results were insufficient. Even well-to-do areas face uneven distributions of resources as well. (See Eckstein, page 176) The issues seem to be insufficiency as well as uneven distribution and as the national level of schooling does go up, the poor continue to face disadvantages. (See page 211) The possible implication of this pattern is that political clout seems to better insure access and attainment, and this flies in the face of universalistic ideals for the system as a whole. This uneven-quality has been alluded to at the highest levels as something to be improved upon, and there has been even more candor about such matters in the last few presidential administrations.

By the 1970s the following conditions prevailed according to Clark Gill. (The Educational System of Mexico, 1974, H.E.W.)   The percentage of the total Federal budget allocated to education declined from 28.24% in 1970 to 16.74% in 1974 (page 3).   Also the state governments are seen as varying widely with respect to their financial contributions to education. (Nuevo Leon = 68.6% while Oxaca allocated only about 15%.) Generally, the Federal budget is strong in supporting elementary education (40%), but there is intense pressure to spend more on the higher levels. Private support for education is small, (page 5) and the government supports private education rather than to let the church do it. Basic problems in the 1970s had to do with:

1. Deficits in facilities;
2. The failure of students to complete primary studies (nearly 70% fail initially!);
3. The professionalization of secondary teachers (many whom lack degrees). (see page 14)
4. Tremendous over-enrollment at the national university and the National Polytechnic Institute;
5. A general lack of flexibility for students - which the new open systems (Sistemas Abiertos) may help;
6. Underemployment of graduates at various levels.

With this brief problem oriented historical review under our belts let us describe the educational structures of Mexico. We will also try to elicit the attending rationale for these structures, and finally lay out the educational policies and machinery which bring them into being. Our model of overall social development will be examined and tested to see if education conforms to it or not. We have already seen some "fit" between the expansion of technical education and the needs of the industrial order - although the latter can be variously elaborated upon.

The Structure and Rationale of Mexican Education

In this section we will spend some time on the formal structures, levels, institutions, and course of study but also more on the policy rationale governing the creation or support of these structures. We have much information on the former, but less on the latter except when the cultural missions and socialist schools were visible. In recent years the rationale may be obvious in its relationship to development, but there are still choices that have ideological veneers and varying social purposes.

There are reasonably accessible studies of the structure of Mexican education available from the Mexican government, H.E.W. in the U.S. (in 1956 and 1974 at least) and from independent sources. The 1956 H.E.W. bulletin on Education in Mexico by Marjorie C. Johnston gives the following brief outline:

> The basic structure of education in Mexico after pre-school is
> Primaria, 6 years; Secundaria, 3 years; Preparatoria, 2 years; and
> Universitaria, 3 to 7 years. But there are many other educational
> paths...(page 27).

Ms. Johnston serves that after primaria, students may start in the 5
year preparatoria, in the 6 year normal school or in some commercial or
pre-vocational study. After secondaria they can start the professional
cycles, instead of the preparatria. We note in the 1974 H.E.W. bulletin
written by Clark Gill that the three levels (elementary, secondary, and
higher) are still around. Recently, two years of preschool (years 4 to 6)
are offered before the 6 years of primary education. Next, the 3 year
basic secondary cycle has outcomes in a "general upper secondary cycle,
normal or teacher training, or specific vocational training." In 1975
some of the paths were altered. The general program and the normal
program still lead to the Bachillerato - as does some of the vocational-
technical training. Still higher education toward the Laestria or the
Doctorado augments the basic college degree or Licenciatura. The
structure must be seen in terms of its basic social purposes although
some of the latter maybe contradictory, inarticulated, and under
conflicting pressures - one might suspect.

And, so what are the purposes of elementary education - seen from
the point of view of the systems and the individual? Kindergarten,
according to Clark Gill, allows children "to develop the habits, skills,
and aptitudes necessary for children to continue their elementary studies"
(see page 5). Such are the "organic' explanations that the educational
system offers for its rationale. Gill goes on to note that:

> An effort is made to orient the children to their world and to
> encourage autonomous thinking in them according to their
> individual levels of maturity, thereby encouraging then development
> of personality and a sense of nationality.

These purposes apply to the whole of elementary education, not just
to kindergarten. The addition of the nursery schools or "guarderias," of
course, aided the working mother (and, indirectly the labor force), and
also cared for the many health and nutritional needs of the children
themselves. Besides allowing this group of women to enter the labor
force, this allows for an opportunity to make the children's behavior
patterns more receptive to later education.

How shall we view primary education and its purposes? Because of the flattened overall nature of the schooling experience most students will only experience part of these intended next six years of achievement (or 3 years if started after l0). This primary education is constitutionally mandated, as Gill observes. Most of the gains of industrialization up to the 1970s would probably have had more potential to be achieved if the bulk of the population finished this primary level. From now on, higher educational attainments are obviously necessary to achieve the goals of "modernization."

Four basic subject matter areas are covered in the primary period namely: Spanish language, natural and social sciences, and mathematics. Basic linguistic and cognitive goals are obtained for all those fortunate enough to complete the 6 years of intensive 3 year versions of this program which was established in 1969. Gill notes in 1974 that only 62% of the qualified rural students versus 83% in urban areas gained access. Besides access there is the problem of completion of the total primary program. As Gill observes in the U.S. government version (page 6): "The high percentage of pupils who fail to complete their primary studies is a continuing concern." The 1970 census showed that about 42% of the population 15 years or older had not finished this mandated program (see page 7). Still the average number of years completed, thanks to an effective 11 year plan, went from 2.2 to 2.8 years.

It would be interesting to know the following kinds of information. How "functional" for the person and the society is this level of educational obtainment? How do these levels of achievement effect other aspects of economic and social development? What is the major push to expand educational opportunities - is it just industrialization or middle class aspirations? Clearly, there is a relationship between the level of expenditures in primary education and the economic and social potential of the system. One thesis in the present volume stresses that the rationale and pressures for social development could center on the needs for "human capital" in Mexico. Social development could be sought as an end in itself, but this point assumes that another set of instrumentality's are at work and that they have considerable efficacy. There is evidence that the need for human capital is at work in the policy impetus for education as well as other areas of social enhancement. Alvaro Garcia Pena discussing "Education and Housing Present deficits and prospects..." in Latin America in the Year 2000, edited by Joseph S. Tulchin, page 327) quotes the InterAmerican Development Bank:

...human resources are the key to socioeconomic progress. This is especially true for Latin America, a region characterized by abundant physical resources but at the same time scarcity of capital and the world's highest demographic growth rates...These circumstances clearly demand that the growing population be trained, to foster social justice, best utilize available resources, and compensate for the lack of capital...educational improvements are indispensable for the success of any socioeconomic development in the region.

We offered this quote from Pena because of its emphasis on education as a substitute for the other forms of capital. Investments in primary education must in fact be equally productive to other forms of investment, but primary education may have other qualities as a pre-requisite for any economic investments - and, thus, be non-substitutable. The purposes of primary education seem manifest in any case.

Before going on to discuss the other levels of education, it is probably appropriate to put Mexico's efforts into international perspective. Harbison and Myers' excellent comparative study Education, Manpower, and Economic Growth stresses that: "The building of modern nations depends upon the development of people and the organization of human activity" (1964, page v.). These authors start by constructing a composite index for 75 countries and by noting how human resource development (mostly through education) is related to GNP levels. In terms of their composite index, Mexico is about in the middle of the 75 countries, being 39th from the bottom where the lowest score goes to Niger (1.3), and the highest is the U.S. (261.3), and Mexico has an index score of 33.0. The index is made up of such factors as teachers at the various levels, enrollment ratios, percentages enrolled in various types of higher education, and expenditure on education as a percent of total national income. More appropriately compared as a "Type III country with India, Cuba, Egypt, Greece, Italy, and Norway (plus 14 others) Mexico is the lowest scorer at this level. Yet while being at the 35th percentile with respect to the averaged range of this group's GNP, it has the lowest expenditure level (Mexico's percentage spent is only 1.4% versus a mean of 3.1 for Level III countries). Based on the total 75 countries (for the data available) only Pakistan allows less of its total national income for education, at 1.2%. Nor can Mexico claim to have an inordinately large number of children in the schooling years, at least their 26.3 percent in the 5-14 age group is only slightly above the 22% mean for Level III countries. Mexico has produced a fair number of teachers, lawyers, engineers and doctors from this base, however, and, hence, makes some points in the total index, especially as represents the higher trained part of the manpower pool. Specifically using this 1950s, early 1960s data, Mexico is fairly middling with respect to educational development at the first and second levels. For Level III countries their score of 55 falls roughly in the middle of a 35 to 89 range and a mean of 66. Mexico, however, is right on the mean for Level III countries with respect to the educational emphasis, and as of the early 1960s, a neglect of the lower two educational levels. As a "semiadvanced" country, Mexico seems unique only with respect to its efforts to effect the rural communities, not in the areas of universal enrollment. (Harbison and Myers, page 111.)

The Vocational-Technological-Professional Thrust of the 1970s

In the semiadvanced (Level III) countries, the major economic objective is rapid and massive industrial development which demands ever increasing numbers of technical personnel. Unemployment in many countries has reached dangerous proportions and is aggravated by continuing high rates of population growth. And in the field of education, there is a clamor for consolidation of compulsory primary schooling and for its extension to at least eight years. The flood of primary school leavers creates pressures for massive expansion of secondary education, and this in turn leads to a clamor for more places in universities and higher institutions. (Harbison and Myers, 1954, page 177.)

Let us see if this general pattern noted by Harbison and Myers fits the Mexican scene. Clark Gill notes the varied nature of this segment of the Mexican educational system, but he basically sees it as "supplying the manpower needs of the expanding economy" (page 9). And, the Mexican economy has been incredibly varied since the pre-Aztec period. At the lower level this recent vocational system provides an outlet for the individual who wants to leave academic schooling but with occupational possibilities. Although the above quote seems to stress that education feeds upon itself, the prerequisite is, of course, economic diversification and expansion. In the case of Mexico of the 1970s and '80s, both the more sophisticated industrial sector and new occupations like fishing (previously an under-utilized resource) would be served as well as old areas like agriculture which "lags far behind the industrial sector". Between 1970 and 1975 the number of selected types of vocational-technical institutions increased from 220 to 836 (see page 9). This tremendous increase accompanied the move toward the encapitalization of heavy industry as well as the more diversified general economy previously stimulated by import substitution. Clearly the specifically trained personnel (apart from on-the-job-training) could be in scarce supply. Sections of the newspapers with "Empleos Ofertas" could be analyzed to see what occupations were in demand. A preliminary analysis of the demands of labor in newspapers shows more interest in secretarias, solicitors, vendedores, choferes, operadores, than in technicos or even mecanicos. But, the technical recruitment pattern probably involves more direct contact between firms and employees.

The Mexican labor force continues its tripartite nature, involving agriculture and fishing as well as industry. The country has to become more self-sufficient in food supplies as well as to continue to export food for needed developmental capital. Resources besides oil could be further exploited, if the needed personnel were available. It is much more costly to use foreign technicians, as from the U.S. The demand for higher levels of technical training, and the anticipated demand as well have led to more room at the top in these educational programs. The National Poly-Technical Institute has, for example, transformed itself into a feeder program for technical specialization's at the university level as well as maintaining its role with respect to certificate training a lower levels. As Gill observes, there has been an elaboration of programs at many levels with accompanying certificates, diplomas, and titles. (As Bachillerato, Technico, Licenciatura, etc.)

Professional studies overlap these vocational-technical areas, but obviously go off into further higher specialization and socialization of the candidates. It seems from Gill's description that a total educational infrastructure is being created to match the total economic surge of the 1960s and 1970s. The ANUIES' recommendations of 1971 (The National Association of Universities and Higher Education Institutions) seems to represent the main planning activity for this expansion, and also for the proposed expansion in teacher training. The pool of skilled people is seemingly expanding to meet the basic national effort, although much of the latter seems highly capital intensive, and not needing such depth in each area as one might think. An upgrading of most occupations including teaching and other professions is being met by this recent tooling-up process. Let us discuss the structure and purposes of the highest educational levels next involving undergraduate and graduate studies and the purposes to which they have been put.

The Structure and Social Functions of Higher Education in Mexico: The Peak of the Pyramid

First as to the very pinnacle, Gill observes that "Graduate enrollment is a very small proportion of the total post-secondary enrollment and is concentrated in a few institutions" (page 15). In 1973-74 there ere only 9165 graduate students in Mexico and 2/3 of these were at the National University. Although the UNAM campus had 126,000 other post-secondary students, the number pursuing masters or doctorate level degrees is small. This set of statistics again shows where the national effort is being placed that is, squarely where the economic action is; not in higher level academics. Most of these academic specialization's have had to do with education in the past, directly in education or in specialties that are taught at the graduate level.

Undergraduate specialties are the most popular, and they are better supported financially. These program focuses include ones in "public accounting, medicine, law, civil engineering, business administration, economics, mechanical and electrical engineering and architecture" (page 15). Their main thrust (since they are not in the humanities or the social sciences as such) are to build the country's economy and the physical structures needed for its operation. As Gill notes of the new (as of 1974) Autonomous Metropolitan University which was designed in its three campuses to take the pressure off of UNAM. The latter "offers new programs in accord with national development needs" (page 16). Clearly the linkage with national development priorities has been accomplished. This happy outcome has not always been the case, as a brief historical digression concerning the National Autonomous University will reveal.

The UNAM as a Revolutionary and a Social Resource

> Conflict between Revolution and academia, between the activist and the scholar, is probably inevitable. (Michael Burke, "The University of Mexico and the Revolution, 1910-1940".)

> ...the very cornerstone of the new social order is the ideal that through education the Mexican can be and will be redeemed. "Educar es redimir" - "To educate is to redeem." (George Sanchez, <u>Mexico A Revolution by Education</u>, page 187.)

The ferment surrounding education in Mexico is obviously unmatched in any other area of social development. Michael Burke, particularly, notes of the National University that there was one kind of conflict different from the attempts to bring lower levels in line with national purposes. The National University since its modern form was attained under Justo Sierra in the 1910-1924 period was "far removed from the pressing economic and social problems" of the society (see page 254). The National University was accused of being a "school of advanced, speculative ramblings." Basically students and faculty were "insensitive to injustice." However, there seem to have been two campus groups in the early period after the Revolution. The "Universatarios" were more removed from the "Revolution," and the group labeled as the "normalistas" were followers of John Dewey's "social education."

By the early 1920s efforts were made to bring the university some what in line with the Revolution, according to Michael Burke. Under Jose Vasconcelos efforts were made to "install future leaders with a social conscience," as well as to help in the creation of a national identity. Extremely important in facilitating these matters was the brilliant Vincente Lombardo Toledano who helped reconcile "political awareness and academic freedom." One of the main problems was to reform the professional school by the inclusion of social science and social problems courses. The limited "tecnicos" needed more social purpose, which the earlier, dominant humanists had never really acquired either. The discussion over "socialist education" at the pre-college levels also affected the university, of course. The politics of the times were serious business, it did not represent mere academic egotism. Toledano's followers stressed a "radical redistribution of wealth," the latter as a way of solving society's problems - and the battle was on. The reactions were fierce, and there were moves to even greater autonomy amidst strikes and violence. Autonomy was gained, but as a consequence there was also a 75% fiscal cut! This represented a final defeat for socialism as the only university ideology. The Cardenas administration tried to support a socialist mission for the university, but this move was toward a more limited role involving teaching and research alone. Finally, only the economics department kept a strong socialist orientation, but some of the attached research institutes (as the Institute of Social Research) did focus on contemporary problems. Burke's summary says that the three decades in which the university coexisted with the Revolution led mostly to the "training of experts" (page 273) and there were only occasional bursts of social criticism.

A very sad note must be added concerning the relationship between the National University and the Mexican State. The events at Tlataloco Square in 1968 hardly helped to optimize the relationship between the two. An authoritarian state would not permit the carrying of social problems directly into the public view - an effort which had already started to create a ground swell. The conservative press of Mexico and the suppression of radical alternative media (as Por Que) had blocked the intellectual campus ferment - what ever its political hue - from a constructive interaction. The police violence which received its unleashing from the highest levels showed many what ingredients the "policy making process" can contain. Since the government had failed in the 1930s to make the university accept a socially conscious mission it is ironic in the extreme that when such a ferment spilled over and threatened to influence policy, that it reacted with such inhumanity. But, then, one must remember what was happening in the U.S. at the same moments. We will merely end this section with a quote from a teacher of mathematics at Preparatory I, the UNAM, Ernesto Olvera (as quoted from Massacre in Mexico, Viking Press, 1975, page 140):

I read a lot. I take notes. I've read Mexico: Riqueza y miseria, by Alonso Aguilar and Fernando Carmona, for instance. I learned some horrifying facts from that book; the statistics quoted in it, by the way, refer to the year 1967..For this reason alone, our fight for change is justified, for the figures in their study present a heartbreaking picture of our country. Just imagine: more than 1 million people who speak only some Indian dialect; 2 million landless peasants; more than 3 million children between the ages of 6 and 14 who receive no education of any sort; 4,600,000 laborers who tried to enter the U.S. illegally in the years 1948 to 1957; ...more than 8 million Mexicans who never have meat, fish, milk, or eggs to eat...and nearly 11 million who are illiterate. What do we need more data for? These figures are proof enough of how badly off this country is and how hard we must fight. (Slightly abbreviated)

The social role of the university is more complex, however, as it is not only a source for change, but also of social rigidity. Peter Smith in his book Labyrinths of Power (Princeton, 1979) speaks of the whole educational system and of the National University in terms of the recruitment and class patterns involved. (page 47.)

Despite these accomplishments at the primary-school level, the upper levels of the Mexican educational system (secondary, preparatory, and university) have functioned so as to preserve and even strengthen interclass barriers.

These trends are hardly typical of only Mexico, but let us look closer at what Smith says is going on. In studying the political elite of Mexico Smith observed how recent large scale admission to Universidad Nacional Autonomia de Mexico (UNAM) has been. In 1950 only 25,000 were at this old and honored university, and its adjunct preparatory school. After 1960 it has grown to over 75,000 as a result of a changed admission policy. The number who graduate has also increased. Using data from Arturo Gonzalez Cosio and Alonso Portuondo it seems that relatively few people finished their degrees in the pre-1960 days. Still UNAM's graduates, especially in law, have been over-represented in political elites. As one might expect, working-class children were not very likely (10% of UNAM's students in 1945) to go to this high powered educational institution. Smith's conclusion based on Cosio and Portuondo's data was to the effect that:

> Generally speaking UNAM did not do much to loosen up the country's class structure: on the contrary, it ratified and emphasized the system of class distinctions.

Smith gives much data that the university graduates or "Universitarios" dominate the upper offices of the society. The knowledge and skills necessary for higher office were found only among the 2.7% of the literate population in 1960 who had gone to the National University.

We, of course, are interested in more than the fact that 70% of the recent higher level political elite went to UNAM. We want to know the qualities of that education as well as its relationship to the social structure. "Life chances" in all countries are related to educational attainment and the type of education usually determines the special areas of attainment. Industrialists tend to come from technical institutes rather than Liberal Arts Universities. Hence, Smith observes the roles of the Instituto Politecnico Nacional in Mexico City and the Instituto Tecnologico de Monterrey. The affinities between education and later occupational, social and political qualities are, indeed, great. Some might observe that the lack of a humanistic education by powerful groups of industrialists may well help to explain their resistance to social policies and progressive redistribution in general. There is little direct information on this point, however.

One outcome of the excellence in higher education that is more clear is its relationship to economic growth. Alexander Peaslee writing about "Education's Role in Development" (in The Political Economy of Development, by Uphoff and Ilchman, 1972, page 334) sees Mexico as one country of 21 (out of a total sample of 37) in which "real income parallels and follows trend lines of higher education enrollment ratios." There were seven countries in this sample in which higher education enrollment ratios increased at a greater rate than did real income per capita (these included France, Sweden, the U.S., Russia, Japan, Venezuela, and Australia). Again data on Mexico indicates that they have not pushed social development much beyond the line of economic growth. Peaslee says that countries like the United States, etc., have not "overexpanded" higher education because subsequent years show a pay-off for this investment. Likewise for Japan: "This may indicate that the increasing volume of university-educated Japanese had a growing influence on the economic growth rate." Peaslee sees the overall data as showing that the best pattern of expansion from the point of economic development is to emphasize primary education first, then secondary, and only gradually shift to the tertiary level. A stress on higher education may have an incremental economic boost, but it also freezes the social structure, one might suppose. Peaslee goes on to discuss the "optimal educational mix" as to percentages at each level of the educational system. Mexico is seen as having an "instructive" history, like the Japanese, Russians, Americans, Swedes, Swiss, Danes, and Puerto Ricans (page 340). Mexico is seen by Peaslee as having a "good," as opposed to a "very good" chance in the 1970s to increase their enrollment ratios. In any case Mexico has come up to the 0.3% recommended by Peaslee for enrollment in higher education.

Educational Goals and the Policy Machinery

ARTICULO 5, VIII: Promover las condiciones sociales que lleven a la distribution equitativa de los bienes materiales y culturales, dentro de un regimen de libertad. (Ley Federal de Educacion, 1979)

On Juarez or Reforma Avenues and elsewhere one can buy from street vendors the latest Federal laws, including those in education, for from 10 to 50 pesos. These bound and unbound tracts bear the current or responsible President's name as well as that of the current Secretary of Education, in a recent instance Luis Echeverria Alvarez and Victor Bravo Ahuja. This distribution of federal laws on street corners allows the citizens of Mexico, including aspiring office holders, to zero in on the ideals of policy in various social areas. This public diffusion process is like the distribution of government pamphlets by your congressmen at country or state fairs in the U.S., but the motivation to buy such materials could be interpreted as a more avid form of citizenship in Mexico. We are now going to briefly trace the emergence of this national educational policy.

George I. Sanchez (Mexico: A Revolution by Education, 1931-1964) notes how policy and the vehicle for its implementation emerged in the 1920s. President Obregon with his Minister of Education, Jose Vasconcelos started with a missionary urge to "redeem" the indios and the campesinos. As to the policy making machinery we must turn to the historians for a description of the process. Victor Alba offers the following in The Mexicans. The Making of a Nation: (cited in

Fehrenbach, page 542)

> To an observer, the Mexican government (under Obregon) appeared
> then no different from that of the Diaz period, with its politicians,
> demagogues, ambitious generals, big landowners, small groups who
> disputed the executive power, and fraudulent elections. All this was
> too deeply imbedded in Mexico by thirty years of the Porfiriate to be
> conjured away in an instant. Nevertheless, the observer could note
> that young intellectuals filled some of the cabinet posts, there was
> great activity in the field of public education, and, above all, land
> was being distributed. Furthermore, the tone, even the physical
> appearance of those wielding power had changed; the new men were
> not the distinguished Europeanized white men of the Porfiriate, but
> men of the people, mestizos...

Rural Mexico was the first target area, and the better trained
"misioneros" would face adversity to initiate the first schools these
areas had seen. This group would then influence strategies of the next
decade. A congress of such misioneros took place in Mexico City in
1922 to pool their experiences. Education was to be seen as a prime
subject matter. Also, the rural schools, essentially to be built "from
scratch" (page 66), were to be cultural and social centers as well.
Experimentalism has always been the order of the day, according to
Sanchez (page 68), and this first experiment seemed to prosper so that
by the mid-1920s the misioneros became federal inspectors to help
supervise future progress. The well-known cultural missions than were
a subsequent attempt to institutionalize these early successes of the
misioneros. These new forms under Elena Torres aimed at bettering
teaching skills of those in-service and, also, creating popular
enthusiasm leading to the respective community's cultural, economic
and social development.

By the 1930s another phase in educational policy and policy making
machinery was attained. There was a clear need to transform Mexico's
social and economic fabric, and the "socialist" school was developed.
The Federal school system was to be an agent of the Revolution, and,
hence, accelerate the needed societal reforms (page 94). The houses of
the people of the previous epoch had successively been transformed into
"Schools of social action" and "Schools of work" now would be centers
of socialist learning and cooperation. These new forms were to be
community centered, not merely child centered. Article 3 of the
constitution was sharpened to better describe the purposes of the
socialist school, and the new form was to be seen as "revolutionary,"
"proletarian," nationalistic, "popular" or democratic and rationalistic.

Cardenas in one of his presidential messages stressed that these schools would be a "focus of sane social activity."

The most extensive treatment of the socialist period in Mexican education is by George C. Booth in his book <u>Mexico's School Made Society</u> (1941). The clear thrust of these particular policy modifications was to secularize the school, stress scientific solutions via education to Mexico's problems, and also to build a national culture. To the latter end, Booth an ardent spokesman, observed the emphasis on revolutionary art, music and dance as well as the normal course offerings. (See Chapters IV & V) The philosophy behind this emergence was a planned one different from Liberal or Fascist ones - here the cooperative efforts worked for the betterment of the society. "Igualacion" or equalization was to be one of the specific goals of such an education; this was to be urged ethnically, psychologically, and economically. The intermediate goals included the improvement of living conditions, and the school was to be adapted to assist in these efforts.

And, who were the men, and what were the forces that brought about the socialist school? The basic political history of the 1920s had seen a series of nationalistic strongmen finally devolve into the new political party, the PNR in 1929. Many of the older intellectuals like Vasconcelos had been bullied or had postured themselves into asylum, and were not available for leadership in the new decade. The Revolutionary rhetoric was still strong, but it was as a social fact not going to bring about a socialist transformation. There had been a transformation in the 1920s, however, and it consisted of two elements. The first of these was that the unholy trinity of the previous years which was now gone or under control. Thus, the "praetorian army, the latifundistas, and the clerics with 17th century minds" was destroyed. (See Fehrenbach, page 574) Secondly, "Mestizoism" was entrenched in the dominant institutions and social circles. Still Mexico had not yet emerged from the mud bottoms that had floated the Aztecs; its peasantry verged on physical death from poverty even as in the early 1930s. Also, urban life remained as bleak as scuttling cockroaches running along the dulled masonry. There had to be an economic and social transformation! Fortunately, a new generation in the early '30s had made the "schools" of the 1920s pay off. This new generation with socialist inclinations is described by T. R. Fehrenbach: (<u>Fire and Blood</u>, page 584)

> Because the younger generation had been better educated than the revolutionaries of 1917 in Vasconcelos' schools, it tended to be more susceptible to ideas and ideologies. Marxism, which before

1920 had only a foreign following in Mexico, was very much in vogue in these years; while few of the newer lawyers, doctors, and engineers were communist-oriented, most were influenced by Marxist economics, and many by Spanish Republican ideas. Thus as a group the younger men were more dogmatic and doctrinaire than their elders, and more sadist and collectivist in their outlooks. They were also more optimistic. Some carried optimism too far: They were the intellectuals who believed that with literacy the Mexican masses would become a reading public, though this had not happened anywhere in the world. The strength of this generation came from its youth, ideals, and energy; its weakness was a frequent reliance on foreign ideas...

By the early 1940s the basic pattern of education had been developed, and the country was on the verge of industrialization. The latter had been a clear policy choice as well. In the 1930s the State had grown, but populism was in the decline as mammoth state and private enterprises moved into center stage. Policy changes in the social areas were no longer as revolutionary as they were incremental in nature. The Camacho regime (1940-46) kept the level of educational expenditure up to that of the previous Cardenas commitment, but the following Aleman regime cut (per capita) popular based education harshly. As to expenditures, the Wilkies note an increase under Lopez Mateos where the funds spent per capita doubled from 1956 to the early '70s. The policy increments linked to these funding level changes involved attempts to attain one or the other of the basic value commitments. There seems to have been value commitments to both human capital and heavy physical capital investments during these years, with one becoming dominant up to the point where the other was brought in to balance the other. Yet, educational policies of the past 3 decades were certainly well established as well. According to one government source, Mexico: 1973, put out by the Banco National de Comercio Exterior, these educational policies included the: (1974, page 258)

* harmonious development of the person's faculties;
* love of country within international solidarity;
* goals of secularism, scientific progress, the reduction of ignorance, and the achievement of democracy as a way of life;
* comprehension of our problems including those having to do with resource use, political independence, economic autonomy, cultural, social, and personal integrity, etc.

These "doctrines and ideologies" are seen as being drawn from the original education oriented articles of the 1917 Constitution, namely numbers 3, 31, and 73 as elaborated upon by the "Organic Law of Public Education." The general political ideology of the Mexican Revolution is seen to have been institutionalized into policy and curriculum! Not only is economic development a goal of this emerged educational program of the recent decades, but social change remains a clear priority of what education can achieve as well. Hence, Mexico: 1973 in its section on educational policy, the one they offer to the world, states that: (page 259)

> Education also has broader social effects, such as facilitating change in social structures, assisting the end to adopt a positive attitude toward development...making social stratification more permeable, improving the form of family life...

It must be true that these values of social transformation are available for domestic consumption as well; and so one gets the impression that the revolution has been institutionalized as a set of progressive expectations. As to what groups now determine policy in Mexico, the author will only refer the reader to such sources as Gonzalez Casanova, Richard Hansen, Susan Eckstein, Martin Needler, Stanley Ross, and Jose Luis Reyna. One is only left with a few groups that one could refer to as possible sources of policy, but one suspects that people in the Ministry of Education still make the implementing decisions as opposed to the orienting decisions. There are also what may be called, for lack of a better term, consuming decisions, but we will discuss this framework later.

Closeness of Fit With Our Model

Logically in stressing human resource needs of the system as the mainspring of social development in Mexico, the specific value of education, health, and nutrition would come to the fore. Pensions, criminal justice, housing and the like might recede into second place because of the sequential and causal priority of the former three elements of social development. How does the general data presented in this chapter fit or fail to fit our model? The factors that seem to fit our chosen set of determiners with respect to social development include:

1. Allocations up to the economic growth levels, but not beyond.

2. The relative urban-rural gap, revealing that the most "productive" sectors or areas of economic action benefit the most from social development.

3. The rural catch-up of the 1970s as agriculture lagged.

4. The amount of money spent on education, especially vocational forms, during the industrialization phase (despite the setback relatively under Aleman).

5. The small number of graduate enrollments (given their "speculative ramblings"). Research figures would reflect the same constraints.

6. The low percentage of the GNP (1.4%) spent on education, given the labor redundancy.

Lack of fit with our model is seen in:

1. The Aleman educational recession, during a period of rapid industrialization.

2. The failure to produce the needed vocational-technological types of personnel in recent decades.

3. The persistence of Revolutionary purposes for education, even though glaring gaps persist.

TABLE IX
PERIODS IN MEXICO'S DEVELOPMENT AND
THE ATTENDANT EDUCATIONAL POLICIES

YEARS	PROBLEMS	POLICIES	STRUCT.
1920-1940	- National integration - cultural melding - political acceptance	- Cultural Missions after 1923 in Hidalgo - Educational modernization	Casa del Pueblo (72,161 rural villages)
1940-1960	- Achieve mass literacy - prepare for industrialization - commercial expansion	- Camacho's "Ley de Emergencia" - Expand technical training	Literacy teams
1970s	- Class integration - Coordinate higher education - Labor force - Further economic development	- Federal Act of 1973 - Preschool education	Free texts, ANUIES board, "Guarderias"
1980 & Beyond	- Avoid political de-stabilization - Complete economic development	- Clear demonstration of universality?	Appropriate structures

Significant Recent Trends: Facts Drawn From a Variety of Sources

• More than 1/4th of the total population is currently involved in the national education system. (Echeverria, cited by Gill)

• 65% of the total outlay in education comes from the Ministry of Public Education, 14.7% from state budgets, 5% from other government allocations, and only 15.3% from private sources. (Mexico: 1973)

• The higher education budget increased 5 fold from 1970 to 1975, and the number of students went from 250,000 to 450,000. (Echeverria, cited by Gill)

• "Despite the public sector's efforts in the area of education, the 1970 General Population Census registered 7.72 million persons over the age of 10 who did not know how to read and write, that is 24% of the total population of that age bracket." (Mexico: 1973)

Employment and Unemployment in Mexico

That most Mexican workers chose to remain within the existing system both as it then operated and as it was traditionally constructed, can be seen in the way those workers expressed their goals and demands...Most workers commonly expressed their goals in terms of fair treatment from the capitalists, respect from their foremen, and society at large, aid and justice from their government, and equality with other classes. (R. D. Anderson, Outcasts in their own land, 1976, page 321.)

A shanty town settler who earns the minimum legal wage (32.50 pesos or $2.60 a day in 1970) should theoretically be making 975 pesos ($28.00) a month if he works every day. Only two settlers in Cerrada del Condor, both of whom employees, were earning 1300 to 1500 pesos a month...The trouble is that most unskilled laborers cannot find work every day. (Lomnitz, 1977, page 70.)

One of the striking facts in respect of the current situation of rising unemployment and underemployment in Latin America is that whatever conflicts occur (they) seem much less intense and widespread than might be expected. What are the social mechanisms that cushion the effect of unemployment and underemployment? (Social Change and Development Policy in Latin America, United Nations, 1970, page 127.)

...while there is great social injustice in Mexico in the distribution of wealth, there is the fatalistic acceptance of the division of society between the strong and the weak, between the chingon and the chingado. (David Gordon, The Economist, 22 April 1978.)

An economist might focus upon the economically active part of the population and the ability of that group to support their households. The proportionate number of economically active persons dropped consistently from 1960 (32.4%) to 1970 (26.8%) to 1975 (25%). Of course the real numbers increased from 11.3 to 12.9, and finally to 15 million persons (the 1975 figures are projections). The main declines as to types of employment were in so called primary activities, while the main increases were in industry (18.9% to 23%) and services (14.2% to 16.6%)   Such are the gross outlines of the Mexican labor market, but what are the major concerns for the Mexican citizen seeking employment?

Historically we know that the foreign domination of the Mexican labor force - especially the rural one under the Diaz regime(1876-1911) inspired revolution. (See Zuvekas, 1979, page 127) Events subsequent to this revolution have continued rural problems of employment and underemployment as well, according to Zuvekas. Thus: (page 311)

Even in Mexico, where the principles of the 1910 revolution commit the government to serving the rural poor, and where agricultural growth has been more rapid than in most developing countries, underemployment has become a serious problem because the government's policies have in fact favored the larger farmers. Between 1950 and 1960, the number of landless rural laborers in Mexico increased from 2.3 to 3.3 million, while their average yearly days of work fell sharply from 194 to 100 and their real earnings declined fm $68.00 to $56.00. (This data was originally from James P. Grants' "Accelerating progress through social justice." International Development Review, 1972-3, 2-9)

Roger D. Hansen in discussing the "dynamics of Mexican development" has the following observations to add to the above: (page 210)

Their (rural workers) per capita rate of employment fell from 194 days per year in 1950 to 100 days in 1960 (same data as Zuvekas, above); over the same 10 year period their income dropped by 18%.

Hansen (page 210) sees "part of the difficulty in the Mexican employment picture (as) attributable to the educational profile of the Mexican work force." The latter comment takes the edge off of the terrible unemployment picture in this sector, and he further hedges by talking about the "hotly debated" nature of statistics about "disguised unemployment."

As to the Industrial labor force, Hansen an otherwise potent critic, notes their relative affluence. Thus, (page 217):

Throughout the past decade the wages paid to much of Mexico's industrial labor force have been increasing at rates well in advance of the Mexican cost of living index. While real wages may not have kept pace with the increases in productivity theory have clearly expanded the real purchasing power of workers in the industrial sector by 2 to 3 percent a year.

But, contrary to this picture, there are problems in the industrial sector with respect to unemployment and underemployment. Rawle Farley (in The Economics of Latin America, 1972, page 135) notes that only a very small part of the L.A. labor force has access to modern technology, and where it does, the levels of productivity are high. Farley sees a 40% overall level of unemployment in L.A., 15.6% in the industrial sector and 28% in agriculture. One 1977 source sees the standing army of unemployed or marginally employed in Mexico as being 8.5 million out of a total labor force of 17.5 million in a national population of 63 million. (See "Mexico in the grips of economic crises," Weekly People, 27 August 1977, page 5.) The latter Marxist source could be compared with a less radical one, namely Fortune magazine, (September, 1975, page 170). To wit:

Nearly half of Mexico's labor force is now either unemployed or underemployed, and the labor force is growing by some 600,000 a year. Surrounded by prosperity, millions of Mexicans are nevertheless on the brink of starvation.

The latter article, printed during the Echeverria regime up to 1976, observes how policy changes tried to increase farm commodity prices, raise subsidies for low income workers. and use incentives to lure industries into rural areas. Despite the new Jobs for some at Pemex plants, HYLSA (the Monterrey steel works), the Puebla Volkswagen plant, or the new heavy industries such as Las Truchas, many jobs are being lost The latter deficiencies include the loss of 1/3 of the border assembly plant jobs or maquiladores. Previously these border assembly plants made everything from shirts to television sets from components shipped in, according to this Fortune magazine source (page 177). A combination of U.S. labor pressure and rising Mexican wages has cut these jobs as well: pressure certainly this could be closing this "safety valve" very rapidly. (See on this topic, "That incredible economy," by Harold Burton Meyers.)

Fortunately, we have an excellent recent survey by the U.S. Department of Labor of the employment in Mexico. This, recent, 1979 study entitled "Profile of Labor Conditions: Mexico" notes a (1975) labor force of 16.6 million and an unemployment rate of 9 percent. The ILO is used as a source to observe that 41% of the jobs are in agriculture, forestry, and fishing activities; and 18% are in manufacturing. About 20% of women are in the labor force (as of 1975). Hard core unemployment has reached 15% in many areas and underemployment is about 4% of the labor force (page 3). This Department of Labor publication by Martha Lowenstern is an excellent source on the topic of union organization and other labor politics which we will not discuss here. This article also covers worker benefits, wages and hours, as well as conditions of employment. Let us look at what meaningful work can do for those fortunate enough to have it in Mexico.

Jobs and Security in Mexico

In Mexico the constitution of 1917 defined the major principles to be allowed in fixing minimum wages and their earliest implementation dates back to the 1931 Federal Labor Law. At present the procedure followed is that defined in the labor code as amended in 1962, which establishes (article 425, section D) the budget of the working class family containing the following items: food, clothing, housing, household expenses, transportation, attendance at cultural functions, sports, training of the worker, reading and education of the children. (From Davis and Goodman's Workers and Managers in Latin America, 1972, Heath, page 37.)

As we have observed in our chapter on the social security pattern in Mexico, it does not lack for comprehensiveness as the above quote observes. Oh, but what it were universalized or even the most typical outcome. But raises in wages for those fortunate enough to have manufacturing jobs has made for economic security. As noted above, the increases have not kept up with the increases in productivity, but at least they have been steady - and one can see the hand of policy at work. Many believe that economic redistribution in import substitution (as opposed to export substitution) economic systems leads to more concentrations of income (see Rene Villarreal in Reyna and Weinert, page 77), but some industrial workers (and their managers!) have done well in Mexico. David Gordon of the Economist staff, believes they have done too well and that the industrial sector blocks redistributive attempts (1978, page 26). We are speaking here of workers in the more productive sectors, where they have some skill in demand, partial control over the means of production, and they have a viable union. (For general discussion of these conditions, see Louis Wolf Goodman on "The Unequal Distribution of Income in Latin America.") Lowenstern, our Department of Labor source, notes the following with respect to wages. They tend to be higher in unionized industries, higher than the minimums. The latter is especially true if it is a newer industry. In the latter areas, for instance, (see page 6) when the government set guidelines of 12% in 1978, the negotiated raises ran around 14-15%. People with skills in short supply got a premium, but not where there is a redundancy of semi-skilled workers. The policy is to allow the "market" to throw the advantage to the industrialists, not to the workers. In the early 1970s real wages increased around 5% because of stable prices, but after 1973 inflation meant that bigger raises were needed - and were not typically forthcoming. Quite soon strikes showed discontent. and by 1978 some settlements of up to 40% were noted. In 1974, for instance, Bacardi the rum maker, paid out 42% in salary and fringe benefit increases, as inflation continued to skyrocket. (See Impulsa News Investment Bulletin, Mexico City, 1975, page 5.) Indeed, government responses in the form of guidelines pushed wages for workers in the most productive sectors ahead of inflation. There was no deterioration for many workers as a result of this policy - probably because of the disastrous effect of strikes upon foreign investments - a process that should not be forgotten.

There was a change from the Echeverria period where wage increases were encouraged, to the more "pragmatic" Portillo administration. In the latter case the president made a deal with the aging labor boss, Fidel Velazquez, to hold down wage increases to 10% against a background of 20-25% inflation in 1977. (Based on the Economist survey, page 19.) This general approach may not sit well with workers, as government policy evidently was trying to present a "responsible" face to its external creditors. The Quarterly Economic Review of Mexico notes (#1, 1979, page 5) that "mounting resistance even from the government's own supporters in the labor movement leadership restricts scope for maintaining rigorously strict limits on pay increases..." And, with a 1978 rate of inflation of 16 to 30% this will be hard to accept. The 16% figure is the underestimated government "price index," and the 30% is the union's estimation.

One aspect of job security which has been researched in Mexico is that of mobility via better jobs, and through the hiring of women in the first place. As to occupational mobility, Jose Luis Reyna (in Workers and Managers in L.A., 1972, page 111) concludes that:

> The evidence suggests that Mexico is undergoing a relatively
> significant degree of mobility, and indicates that...Mexican class
> structure is relatively flexible, tending to modernization in terms of
> stratification and mobility.

Reyna also concludes (page 118) that the industrial area is not the one of greatest job mobility - nor, of course, is the one of agriculture. Education has a greater impact than industrialization in creating mobility as well. Many people get their social position by ascription and there is not much downward mobility as competitive theory would predict. The "high degree of rigidity prevailing in the Mexican rural class structure is seen as leading to the crystallization of ...extremism" (page 1 18).

As to women in the labor force, there have been studies by Jopling (1974), Arizpe (1977), and Chinas (1973) and Dorothy Place, (1979). Briefly, the latter study had to do with women moving into the labor force consequent to the demographic transition. Using census data (which probably underestimates the matter), the percentage of females who are economically active ranges from 12.0% in Quintana Roo to 28.8% in the Federal District. The highest percentages of females tend to be in service areas, and the lowest in government; but about 20% are in industry. As second incomes in a household these give a needed economic boost, but we do not have a statistical breakdown in this regard.

New Jobs and the Oil Bonanza

For some analysts so inclined the critical question for Mexico's long-run "stability" is "can oil and its economic and political spin-offs change the employment picture?" Briefly, we must discuss the elements involved here, and cover some of the points of view which have emerged. To some writers this may be the most critical topic we might cover, but the oil revenues will probably not transform the pattern of social development in Mexico very directly, or even very quickly. Optimistic estimates about the creation of 600,000 new jobs partly due to oil's influence were made by the Mexican Finance Minister in early 1979 (see the Quarterly Economic Review of Mexico, 1st quarter, 1979, page 7); but this was probably too favorable a projection. Pemex gets 18% of the Federal investment budget, but other than for the construction of new plants, it may not produce many permanent jobs. As Alan Riding, the well known New York Times Mexican correspondent noted in 1979 (NYT, Sunday, 9 December 1979, page F-3):

> The thrust of the government's development strategy though, has not been toward job-creation or even job-training.

By focusing on capital intensive petro-chemical, electrical and steel industries, it is hoped that labor intensive spin-offs will emerge. Riding is uncertain whether this policy even in the long-run will affect the semi- or un-skilled, who are not among the 40% who now make the minimum wage or better for their efforts. The several year boom in the economy after the disaster of 1976 (with 40% inflation, 15% unemployment, and a business hold-out because of Echeverria's policies) may have more to do with the increases in jobs than oil itself. All in all, Riding sees a national policy aimed at real development - before the oil runs out - rather than a redistribution of oil revenues now. Also, the sale of oil could be controlled to avoid "economic indigestion."

David Gordon is one who believes that the jobs may not be in Mexico, but, instead in the U.S.! If the U.S. wants a sweetheart arrangement concerning Mexican oil, it probably will have to accept more Mexican nationals on a temporary basis. The 120 billion possible barrels of Mexican crude (versus 150 possible for Saudi Arabia) may make Uncle Sam take a different view of refried beans being stocked in its grocery stores. Much of the discussion around exporting jobs to the U.S. for oil-favors, centers on the "safety valve" hypothesis, and, truly, there are many positive values of jobs in the U.S. for the regime. Not the least of the benefits are billions of dollars remitted home to families, that raise family capital and living levels. The Mexican government itself is clear about the link between oil, its overall problems, and the "major powers," as the following quote from a New York Times special advertising section put out by the Mexican government (September 27, 1979, page 13):

> After centuries of comparative neglect from the major powers, Mexico is converting its vast petroleum potential into a spring board for development and the solution of its substantial socio-economic problems.

This same article mentions the "creation (of) hundreds of thousands of new jobs" in an article positioned over a diagram of growing oil barrels-captioned "Ixtoc. Good news for the Energy World, I'm sure!"

There are other views on the effect of oil upon jobs. David Gordon of the Economist staff notes how the new petrochemical plants, as the one called "cactus" will only have 2,000 initial jobs despite the very large investment - these plants are not meant to be labor intensive. Also, the jobs that did exist, were sold by the oil worker's unions until management got an agreement not to "expand the workplace in line with production." Hence, there will be few new jobs directly from the oil expansion, and nepotism will "keep them in the family" (page 24). It would then depend upon spin-off jobs in related sectors or in areas where prosperity has "trickled down." Liberal and radical students at the national university are especially hostile to this idea of trickling down which was originally tied to the growth plan involving import substitution where Mexico would supposedly create jobs at home by making at home what it would otherwise buy from abroad. This created

)rotected sector, and in fact led to a greater concentration of
and income.

Workers in the U.S

employers have freely admitted their willing and knowing use
:gal labor. Some have explained their motivation in terms of
anitarian sympathies for the unfortunate Mexican immigrants.
perhaps the most pervasive theme of all has been the claim that
y were simply unable to hire enough legal labor... (Kiser &
:er, 1979, page 127.)

e Kisers have edited a documentary history of Mexican workers in
lited States since World War I. After the second bracero era (from
to 1964) the situation was characterized by illegal aliens
lpelados, or those without legal documents); commuters across
ljacent border areas; and workers in the border industrialization
.ms (or Maquiladoras). The numbers of the former group in the
lr despapelados is not knowable, but surely is in the millions.
seek factory work in cities like Chicago, rather than in the
lingly repressed U.S. agricultural sectors. For these brave souls,
lrney is hazardous, degrading and subject to exploitation even
luccessful. David Gordon, writing for the Economist, believes
:e mutual solutions, but the failure of the Simpson-Mazzoli bill
this doubtful in the short run.
la-Stina Ericson, writing on the "Impact of Commuters on the
n-American Border Area" sees approximately 50,000 persons
; the Mexican border daily to work in the U.S. They aim at 9
:der cities, and are seen as having " a depressing effect on wages
trade union organizing campaigns" (In Kiser & Kiser, 1979,
8). Mostly these people are "green carders" and must work
)usly or they lose their Alien Registration Receipt cards.
20,000 with U.S. citizenship also enter on a daily basis. This
ving closer ties with Mexico, probably were born of Mexican
an-American parents but choose to live in Mexico.
)74 there were 665 participating firms in the border
ization program (up from 72 in 1967) (See page 258 in Kiser
Mexico's attitudes evidently are ambivalent because although
jobs, the program also creates foreign dependency. Attitudes
the border about these "run-away jobs" can verge on the
negative aspects as well. But 30-50,000 jobs seemingly are involved,
mostly women. With male family members remaining unemployed the
Mexican husband develops a feeling of being kept by his woman

("Mantenido") which also has adverse effects.

Basically there are many strong values in conflict concerning work and workers that pass over the border. Mexico officially wants good care of its nationals, but the conflicts make their appearance in the policy formation process.

A Summary About Jobs and a Reflection on Our Theoretical Concerns

Mexico, it seems, is short about 12 to 15 million good jobs as of 1985. A remedy for this depends for its attainment upon the level of economic activity as determined by public and private investment - and the nature of that investment. Good jobs also need healthy, well educated and skilled workers to fill them. Government policy is all important in any instance, as either human capital or investment capital is generated. We can guess that jobs only-priority now might reduce the economic base later, and we are usually cautioned in this regard. A stress on human capital would also help broaden the economic base for later development as well. Most of the good, existing jobs are in the industrial-service sector that developed from 1946 to 1970 The benefits have followed and supported these jobs as well, and only with the rise of potential for mass discontent in the 1980s have the benefits and jobs moved away from these concentrated areas. At least half of those economically active must scratch like desperate chickens in the barren fields outside the fenced areas of high productivity. But, the human tolerance for this meager level of economic activeness, grows thin.

Much of our analysis of jobs in Mexico sees them in areas where government financial policy has created them, or private businesses have followed their special logic's. Our concerns for social development and the role of social policy must see strong linkages between the economic growth strategy and whom gets what benefits in the system. A number of factors are at work that may spread access to the pay-off sector, and these include:

1. Portillo's opening of political competition so that the PRI must accommodate to these pressures for good jobs, going so far as to let the communist party surface and stir up the marginal. (See the New York Times, 10 January 1980)
2. The pressure on the U.S. to move toward a more open "Guest worker" policy. We will all watch the administration for responses here.
3. The continued policy of educating its youth in advance of the available jobs - which will exert certain pressures.

4. The continued migration to urban, productive areas by men and women seeking jobs in the productive, modern sector.

5. The pressures to put pesos into the Employment Fund, and to decentralize jobs.

The North American Free Trade Act and the Mexican Employment Picture: Circa 2000

This upcoming event involving "free trade" will do more than stir up the dust on both sides of the border. It has been described as "Mexico's fast lane to the future" (Business Week, Dec. 23, 1991). It has been pictured overall as a "romance." (New York Review of Books, Nov. 7, 1991) It is seen as banishing the Mexican Revolution (Monthly Review, Nov. 1991). It is seen as creating social, political and environmental problems (CQ Researcher, July 19, 1991). Of it President Salinas is reputed to have put it: "My people are in a hurry" (Business Week, August 12, 1991). Assembly lines supposedly will migrate from Asia to Mexico (Business Week, July 1, 1991).

Automotive News asked whether the NAFTA is a great opportunity or a dark sinkhole for jobs. The Nation asks whether it is a "fast track to unemployment" (June 3, 1991). Ralph Nader sees it as a "mistake" for Mexico (the New Republic, June 3, 1991). Is it a "Rio Grande illusion" or another "Mexican miracle?" Can it be the "ladder of upward mobility", this "Salinastroika"

A perverse consequence may be that while exporting jobs from the U.S. to Mexico - it may also be exporting pollution and other externalities. The main issue as it appears to Mexico may be the number of good jobs produced. What really will happen in this regard? For comparative purposes previous lessons could focus on the projection from the oil boom a decade ago, and on the Maquiladores over the past 15 years. One can inspect the Mexican Finance Ministry for prognostication and for subsequent results. In the oil boom example, a prediction of 600 thousand "new jobs" was bandied about, but the projections should have been suspect because of the capital intensive nature of the initial developments. As to the down-the-road impacts on the labor markets there are analyses like those of Oliveira and Garcia (1987). Data on Mexico City from 1970 to 1980 showed an increase in administrators and in "unspecified" employment, and a decline in service and agricultural workers. If the NAFTA impact is to be one of worker mobility then it probably should be in the manufacturing sector or the white collar support areas. Peter Ward (1990, page 23) sees the good, middle level jobs (which men have dominated more than women) as being in the "public space" where wages are better. One would assume that good jobs would be connected to higher productivity - although the reputed 60 to 70 cents per hour wage in auto assembly areas (currently?) would barely meet middle class life style pre-requisites. As in the U.S. good jobs in Mexico will impact the smaller number of workers in the so-called "primary labor market", not those larger number in the "secondary labor market." The Reagan policies of the 1980s in the U.S. created mostly dead-level jobs. Would Mexico's situation be different? Assembly types of jobs are such that as they improve in benefits and wages, the tendency is for capital replacement or for "going offshore" again. Where this time? Perhaps the jobs will move back to the impoverished rust belt of the U.S., the last of the third world countries because of policies there!

Perhaps employment growth based on ongoing linkage to the "global economy" has been what has increased "unspecified" types of jobs. What ever the nature of this category the likelihood is that the new jobs in Mexico and in the U.S. may not be what they are touted as being. Of 117 recent (late 1991) articles retrieved from INFOTRAC under the keyword of NAFTA very few stress jobs, much less the nature of those jobs. It is true that the hearings on NAFTA stress new jobs in the manufacturing sector, for new products for which an expanded market is (will be?) available. A multiplier, spillover, ripple effect creating ancillary employment is expected. The situation is supposed to become a "win, win" outcome!

The types of job categories not likely to expand from 1993 to the year 2000 are in the primary areas and in agriculture. The service area will see an expansion, some of which employment is in the desirable primary labor market, that is they will offer permanence, good wages, and good benefits. Manufacturing jobs will largely be in the assembly category - perhaps completely so. The Asian interest in the NAFTA is at least two fold, as Mexico initially as a competing source of cheaper labor, but also as an assembly platform for their own component parts. Strict rules of origin may be used in order to protect various national interests. If this is a step toward a boundary-free world market, it is of course very tentative.

The fluidity of capital, jobs, a know-how will make for only temporary advantages and leapfrogging types of headway for any unit so involved. Various interests will do well, others will suffer from run-away jobs, capital, and know-how! Mexico hopes that the fate of Asian countries on the Pacific rim will be theirs - that is as an elevator upward to a better way of life. The probability of this outcome depends upon the health of this global market place - which is not at all assured with continuing conflicts left unresolved by the real failure of all systems.

Crime and Attempts to Reduce It

Changing Types of Crime

...This practice of reinterpreting written law also occurs at lower levels of government. This mechanism for managing demands provides some welcome flexibility in a system generally characterized by rigidity and a lack of efficiency, but it also contributes to wide-spread corruption. (Levy & Szekely, 1983, page 52.)

"For the most part the police are conspicuously absent from the slums and lost cities, and the crime rate in these places is so high that, by 1970, Mexico had attained the rare distinction of numbering among the five countries with the highest rates of homicide in the world. (Mexico in Crisis, 1983, page 119.)

From north of the border Mexico seems a land of bribes, official corruption, prostitution, interpersonal violence, and homicide. And, gringos know a lot about these actions from their own lives back at home! As is the case, north of the border, "crime" is based upon a group of legal norms that define offenses against society. These are known as "delitos" or "ofensas." Every violation is a "delito," and there are about 2 classes of delitos. These range in seriousness from delito grave to delito leve. There are offenses against a person's body or honor. (As Homicidio en rina, where death comes about during a fight) As is the case north of the border, premeditation, treachery, and unevenness in advantage make the case more or less grave. There are special categories of crimes against persons such as parricidio, infanticidio, abandonment, lesiones (injuries), difamacion, and kidnapping. Besides crime against persons there are, of course, property crimes such as theft (robo), embezzlement (abuso de confianza), fraud (very badly defined), and bribery (mordida). Unlike gringo America there are some differences as to sex offenses, so called. Rental of one's body is not a crime, but soliciting may be. Both wives and prostitutes can push prosecution of violation, or rape. Consenting acts that do not create scandal are not punished. White slavery (Lenocinio) is punished, but persists because of the mordidas! The persuasiveness of the latter was brought home to this writer because of the availability of motel space after midnight, when we inadvertently drove toward Mexico City from the border on a busy holiday weekend!

Generally violations of public morality could receive a range of punishments. Obviously, the use of drugs (or estupefacietes) is very serious and is covered by Federal law. For Mexican nationals (not gringo turistas) it is possible to maybe allow a minor, first-time offender to be treated with leniency. A "mule" who is transporting large quantities of drugs is treated very differently than an addict or a person carrying minute quantities.

Our major source up to this point has been Alberto Maysgoitia (see A Guide to Mexican Law) who has presented an outline synthesis of the Mexican legal system. But what can we say about changes in the criminal law and justice system, especially as broad policy may be involved.

The immediate post-revolutionary decades seen a variety of responses to visible crime. Constituted authority tried to maintain public order and identification with national goals. Normally punishment came either swiftly or not at all. One president to-be, made a name for himself by not accepting a free automobile. Thus, Cardenas paid for his auto out of his salary, and set a well-known example! Local vigilante justice may have prevailed, or perhaps the lack of justice led to feud. Mexico's reputation for "barbarousness", whether deserved or not, came out of the near anarchic post-revolutionary decades. The John Huston type films that gringo audiences seen showed greed, violence and death against a revolutionary scenario. Gringo audiences seldom seen the idealism, humanism and soul searching as in the Bunuel film "The Lost Ones" (Los Olvidados). The latter tried to bring understanding to the actions of people and youth caught up in these perilous times.

As recently as 1964, Norman Hayner described crime and delinquency in Mexico in the following manner: Juvenile delinquency is largely an urban phenomena. Only two cases were reported in Oaxaxa for the whole year ending August 31, 1945 (see page 170). There is a movement of this delinquency in Mexico City that is related to other urban phenomena. In the latter, it seems to reflect the Chicago-urban ecological insights. Thus, the deteriorating housing of the horseshoe shaped area of Mexico City which contains the "Vecindades" has the highest rates of delinquency. Taking he statistics at face value, Hayner also sees most delinquents as being without homes.

According to Hayner (page 174) prostitution also followed the general urban pattern especially that having to do with deterioration. The officially ignored "zones of tolerance" had been obliterated by the late 1940s, however. Mordida kept the latter institution alive, although it probably changed in form. Thievery is very common and often involves collusion. Clearly the link between most prostitution and theft is to poverty.

In trying to generalize, Hayner sees Mexico as having proportionately more offenses of personal violence than north of the border (see page 179). The latter are also linked to the "passionate, often inebriate nature of working class crime." Nor is this category linked only to urban environments; only the means of destruction differ. In rural areas, according to Hayner, machetes and knives are substituted for more expensive guns! As of the late 1950s, homicides seem to be increasing in rural Oaxaca, but decreasing in Mexico City. Perhaps there are clear trends relating violence to some pattern of folk-urban experience. Theft seems to be largely an urban problem, and probably is not all related to poverty.

Some changes are noted by Hayner's data and implied by his comparisons. Urbanization and industrialization create a different environment for families and individuals. The social glue in the State of Oaxaca is certainly more adhering than in the Federal district. Much of these differences are reflected in an anthropological film study by Laura Nader who studied the control processes in Oaxaca and in urban United States of America. This film called "Little Injustices" revealed a serious attempt to use the law and other local institutions to preserve social peace. Mexico City's atmosphere at some points in time flat-out encouraged theft, bribery and prostitution, although Hayner believes that the incidence of petty bribery, extortion and syndicated crime are **not** on the decline. The recent (mid-1980s) attempt at "moral renovation" reflected the special cases of corruption involving Mexico City's mayor, police chief, and the top executives of such mammoth concerns as PEMEX. While petty bribery was almost customary in some sectors, and kickbacks and payoffs festoon the middle levels, monstrous collusion reaches to the top levels of government and business. Yet moral "renovation" also has a foothold, and the author's experience has many more incidents of completely honest dealings. It is rewarding when an airport security policeman refuses a gratuity for a favor that is done. It is refreshing when a lost tourist card is replaced without any unusual payments. It is soothing when one shops all day and sees no short changing!

Much of our discussion of crime so far has stressed what is called blue collar crime north of the border. There is also white collar crime and crime in the suites as opposed to the streets. Hayner is well aware of the higher levels of crime (see page 210) in Mexico. Using Edwin Sutherland's definition of white collar crime as being committed during the course of one's occupational activities, Hayner comes up with a series of examples - by no means uniquely Mexican in nature! The big mordida takers tended to live in the fashionable colonias of

Cheputlepec, Roma, del Valle, Tacubaya, Cuauhtemoc, etc. The castle-like housing of a former bribe-taking mayor of Mexico City reveals the pattern for these activities. Besides low salaries for public employees and previous traditions supporting it, Hayner suggests that bribes work like an incentive system to speed up the services involved.

Crime as Unrest and as Facilitation

According to Durkheim, crime is also functional. It is a necessary prerequisite for social change. In order for the collective sentiment to be flexible enough to permit positive deviation, it must also permit negative deviation. If no deviation is permitted society becomes stagnant. (Reid, 1982, page 113)

When a revolutionary group robs a downtown Mexico City bank in order to fund its activities and to draw out an over-reaction from the authorities, then we have a good example of crime representing social unrest. When the amount of street crime goes up in the form of robberies, muggings or petty thievery than we may be viewing responses to the difficulties of survival in current Mexico. When the upper classes make illegal money transfers then we have a similar connection of crime to societal stimulation, although the magnitudes, motives and impacts certainly differ. When public officials plunder their own treasures or rapaciously demand kickbacks until they can retire with the plunder, then society seems to have lost control. One would like to ask the Emile Durkheim referred to above quotation just how much crime is needed for society to avoid stagnation! Perhaps a more helpful way to view crime would be through facilitation theory. William Bonger, and more recently, Frank Tannenbaum argued that "criminals are as much a part of the community as are scholars, inventors, scientists, and businessmen" (Sue Titus Reid, page 139). For any of their behaviors to exist, society must provide a facilitating environment. Given the continuous crisis which Mexico seems to be in, people will resort to behaviors that are facilitated by the positions, intersections or occupations that they occupy. Low police and public official salaries facilitate bribe taking. Deviance by short-cut taking citizens or tourists facilitates bribe giving. If a PEMEX official or Union chief sells a scarce job, the situation obviously has facilitated this opportunity in an economic sense. Facilitation theory as economic theory is somewhat less deterministic, as long as the opportunity is there. As computers and credit cards replace paper documents and cash in Mexico as they have to a greater extent in the United States of America, then computer crimes and credit

DIAGRAM II
SEXENIOS & POLICIES (Model From Skidmore & Smith)

LEFT	CENTER	RIGHT	YEAR
CARDENAS - Land Distribution - Nationalization - Economic & Social Expenditures Over Administrative - Concilatory to Labor			**1930**
	A. CAMACHO - More Dificit Spending - Revolution Died in 1940? - IMSS in 1943 - Emergency Law		**1940**
		ALEMAN - Revamped Social System - Education Collapsed? - Minmum Wage Dropped!	**1950**
	RUIZ CORTINES - "Unproductive Investments" Ignored - Decrease In Poverty Index An Alemanista?		
L. MATEOS - "Balanced Revolution" - Actual Spending UP - Minimum Wage UP - INPI, ISSTE			**1960**
		DIAZ ORDAZ - Continued Balancing - Borrowed Past Ideology - Actual Administration Expense Up - Peacefull Until 1968	
L. ECHEVERRIA - 170 Pieces of Legislation - Educational Reform; ANUIES, CONASUPO - Human Settlement			**1970**
	PORTILLO - Conurbation Commission - SAM Announced - Plan Global Desarrollo, New Master Plan - Peso Devaluation		
		DE LA MADRID - Attacked "Financial Populism" - SEDUE, SPP, etc. - SAM Axed - INFONAVIT Then Eartquake - Outdid IMF On Austerity	**1980**
	C SALINAS - "Salinastroika" - Continue Privatization and "Modernization" **PROSANOL?**		**1990**

card frauds will replace older versions. Facilitation theory is, to repeat, an economic theory of crime, and when one reacts from economic desperation at the bottom of the social order, the impact can be to steal back the wealth, amenities and services of an exploitive society. One of the reasons for the great fear of "blue collar" crimes is the nearly conscious recognition that crime from below is a thrust for change. Criminologist Richard Quinney sees much of lower class crime as a form of "primitive social agitation" which may or may not lead to social transformation. Quinney (in Class, State and Crime, 1980) also sees such crime as "reactionary" because it typically victimizes other lower class people - not the holders of wealth and power. When the latter does occur, then martial law is installed!

Crimes of a political nature such as diversion of government funds to help support the dominant party, selling influence, unethical manipulation of public resources and industries, and so forth depend on the facilitating opportunities. Roger D. Hansen's book on The Politics of Mexican Development has three pages of examples of high level political crimes (1971, pages 124-27), and he basically deals with the ruling PRI party as "La Cosa Nostra." Hansen also cites Jesus Silva Herzog who claims that "Politics is the easiest and most profitable profession in Mexico" (page 125). The author remembers a 1930 description of politicians in his own home state as being "The best that money could buy!" Mexico has no monopoly on such behaviors.

Middle level crimes also have their particular patterns of facilitation, and there are in Mexico as elsewhere people eager to buy their way into the "action". While the popular press may focus on mayhem, violence, sexual crimes (as depicted in the tabloid ALARMA), the large newspapers and less sensational magazines mix stories about crime and immorality with their other fare. When Edwin Sutherland wrote his book on white collar crime he noted several categories, to wit: restraint of trade, rebates (kickbacks), patent and copyright violations, false advertising, unfair labor practices, financial manipulations, and war crimes. Based on this mid-century list from the United States of America we would have to amend it to fit the Mexican pattern of facilitation. As to restraint of trade, this was seldom deterred north of the border. Cases were not prosecuted until 70 years after legislation was passed. In Mexico when PEMEX decided that gas stations would go to private hands, they often went to a few "revolutionary politicians" who then had an "absolute monopoly" (see Hansen, 1971, page 12). Concerning kickbacks, these may be the largest source of wealth going to the middle levels, but data are minimal, of course. Miguel De La Madrid's demands for "moral renovation" are aimed at middle and upper levels where the payoffs may approach universality where decisions involve the relative advantages to be doled out. As to patent and copyright infringements, it is known by the author that many products bear false brand names - but these mostly show up in marginal market areas. As the Mexican consumer market grows this category of crimes may find a more common pattern of facilitation. There is a world-wide pattern, given various tariff practices, to manufacture products without benefit of franchise. The import substitution policies for the general economy may well facilitate these practices. False or misleading advertisements are another of Sutherland's categories of middle level crime. Again Mexico's market facilitates this activity as it expands and correspondingly develops consumer resistance and skepticism. Mexico has a fine consumer organization and magazine which hits hard at sleazy practices (see Revista de Consumador). There are also other groups offering counter advertisements to try to reverse the effects of legal, but pernicious advertising, as the anti-smoking ad put out by IMSS on "Mortal brand" of cigarettes. Probably more pernicious, but also legal, are such practices as over the counter pharmaceuticals which, although banned in other countries, are sold freely and do not list the side effects or counter-indications. The Revista de Consumador ran an article on such practices in 1983.

As to unfair labor practices, the category would have to be revised somewhat, but Mexico could write its own chapter on the practices involved. Yet despite the corruption, cooptation, attempts to stifle dissent, and use of goon violence, there are autonomous, powerful, membership-centered labor groups in Mexico that have to be given their due. The totally different political structure means that the specific categories of crime would vary according to their pattern of facilitation.

While "war crimes" have less relevance to the Mexican experience, financial manipulation might be the ultimate middle and upper level area for big crime. North of the border we have become aware of the massiveness of crimes such as the California Equity case which transferred over 300 million dollars illegally. The scope or magnitude of some such crimes defies the imagination, although in Medieval England they knew that harsher punishments would befall the person who stole the goose from off the commons than for the person who stole the commons itself. The recent overvaluing of the peso, which was supported by debt saddling foreign loans allowed the upper classes of Mexicans to trade pesos for dollars and essentially rob the country blind. These "sacadolares" or "dollar looters" actually made off to Swiss, Panamanian, Texas, and Floridian banks with an amount probably as great as the total foreign debt which Mexico now faces. Although the transaction was legal, if not very patriotic, it basically was the theft of the commons. (See Judith Hellman's excellent description of the facilitation involved here, 1983, page 222.) The government's response was to nationalize the banks to stop this financial hemorrhaging, but not before the well-to-do had absconded. Let us now look at the policy area as Mexico has attempted to deal with crimes at various levels.

Criminal Justice and Policy

> In this century Mexico has moved away from the notion of imprisonment as punishment or revenge against the delinquent toward a more humanitarian concept of the treatment of prisoners. The idea is to help the human being who committed an act against society to cure himself, and if the person is detained in jail it is so that society will not be hurt again. (Alberto Mayagoitia, 1981, page 50.)

Although Mexico has a constitution and set of criminal law concerns similar to the United States of America, they do not share much of what is called the Common Law tradition. Trials by jury are rare, for instance. Basically as Mayagoitia points out the Mexican legal system stems from the old Roman Law and more recently from Spanish and Napoleonic codes. Mostly statutory laws are the same throughout the country, and tend to follow the lead of the Federal district, although some states have arrived at unique precedents. The revolutionary constitution of 1917 has set many of the basic rights, including guarantees in criminal proceedings. Article 13 sets down equality before the law. Article 14 claims due process and guarantees non-retroactivity. Article 18 deals with detention prior to and during trials. Articles 20 and 21 have to do with the proceedings and the possible punishments, and number 22 deals with cruel punishments. In fact no use of the states death penalty has been made since the late 1940s, and most have abolished it. Lastly Article 23 has to do with double jeopardy. Such is the constitutional basis for policy.

Much of Mexico's approach is seen as being "preventative." They have "preventative policies" and "preventative prisons." The infamous "preventative" Lecumberri prison is also known as the "black palace" (See T.R. Fehrenbach, 1973, page 637). Fear of such incarceration is meant to be preventative! The administration of this institution is political rather than through a professional cadre. The preventative policy evidently came about because of the lack of career professionalism on the part of previous police forces. Hayner notes that prior to the 1960s, "Career policeman did not exist in Mexico" (page 186). Then each new recruit had to undergo a 4-month training internship. He was an "internado" who had to live in special quarters. There were other types of police than the latter, but only a small number of these exist - as the "secret service" which deals with selected federal problems.

Another way in which Mexico's approach is preventative is the attempt to change the life styles of the lower classes. No more heavy drinking and fighting! The injuries and homicides amongst the unemployed and the weekend boozers are to be ended by a "revolution in recreation," according to Hayner (page 218). Baseball, soccer, football, basketball, etc. were to create "dignidad" and new group status's. The Sport Promotion Administration had 14,000 teams in 1961 in the Federal district. Today one can go to these "Sports cities" or to any park, such as off of the Reforma in Chapultepec and see these weekend activities. Thus, the disproportionate number of violent crimes would be prevented. Hayner notes the nation-wide slogan by recreational leaders of "mas deportes, menos vicios" (more sports, fewer vices).

Needless to say, such weekend activities probably produced a labor force on Monday that was less bent out of shape - except for athletic injuries. In any case, a clear national policy was aimed at lower level "crimes." Legislation was aimed at middle and upper level crimes but the "bite," probably made most unenforceable. Imprisonment was also to be "preventative" for all classes of people. Overcrowded prisons, with few services and relatively long sentences were used to deter. Except for the well known conjugal visit opportunities to help maintain families or sexual identities, (prostitutes are allowed too) there was little good to be said for these institutions. It was also true that some remunerative jobs were available where skills could be learned and applied. Much of the knowledge of Mexican prisons came in the late 1970s when there was concern over American prisoners in Mexican jails. Thomas G. Sanders and Kenneth Frankel, writing an American university Field Service Report (September, 1977) basically confirm the harshness of prison life, and also the unfairness of the processes leading to imprisonment. Torture, forced confessions, inmate violence, bad sanitation, minimal food, lack of medical care, and forced work are standard features of the system according to these writers. Good features evidently include leniency (3 days counted for every 2 served peaceably) some extracurricular activities such as basketball or soccer and, evidently, conjugal visits. Supposedly there is a range of prison conditions in Mexico from the more progressive Santa Marta in Mexico City to the black palace of Lecumberri, with others in between. Evidently no national survey of prisons exists and a "policy" of using fear of the worst prisons as a deterrence is in force. In Federal prisons in the late 1970s evidently half of the prisoners, were there for marijuana offenses - for which such deterrence or "prevention" is supposedly necessary. Other offenders described by Sanders and Frankel were serving sentences for murder, rape, assault and also property offenses of robbery and embezzlement. Mostly these were "blue collar" offenders and one wonders where other offenders may be found. Perhaps Mexico has its "country club" varieties for middle and upper level offenders, as in Estados Unitos del Notre.

Based on the amount of money spent on prisons and paying police, judges, defenders, and so forth, the outcome could be not different than described here. The "use" of non-political prisoners to harass political ones (as the students in the late 1960s and early 1970s) shows that prisons have clear control functions - not necessarily geared to concepts of universalistic justice.

Crime Control and U.S. Involvement

We have not stressed the international picture with respect to any social policy area. We did note the importance of the border and the role of the U.S. with respect to border industries, migrating workers, tourism, and various reactions to Mexican polices north of the border. The recent U.S. attempts to "interdict" the drug flow have probably had little positive impact on the trade. Much of this activity has a variety of other purposes, which we will not be privy to. Exchanges of favors to release middle class, U.S. drug offenders has directed some attention to joint matters, as has the assassination of U.S. agents. The very recent attempts to extradite a "cult" murderer show a spirit of cooperation. Flight into Mexico is no longer safe haven, but borders all over the world are permeable to all sorts of low and high level crimes - in both directions! In order to trace some motives for social policy we have to trace the growth of police activity aimed at political unrest. The relative proportion of "traffic cops," "Federales," and internal political police probably has led to an increase in the latter. Well dressed FBI type agents with automatic weapons and silver badges inside their billfolds have obvious functions in the current context.

Mexico, like most "modern" nations, has great redundancy in order to control "crime as unrest." One does not need to go to South Africa, Chile, Ireland, or a dozen-dozen other illegitimate states. Perhaps it takes a combination of vicious leadership and a failure of the usual, sub-critical control activities for the "police solution" to be the final solution. The American writer, James Baldwin, wrote about the countering "Fire Next Time", but those activities usually are also self-limiting and insufficient to modify systems. Much more powerful in the long run is the dispensing of rewards in a more "legitimate" fashion, not an ad hoc one for limited purposes. Crime as unrest is something most systems can not easily acknowledge either, and as of this writing Gringos are trying to come to grips with the "riots" and "looting" after the Los Angeles police-court catastrophe.

Mexican Cities as a Test of Our Concerns With the Pattern of Social Development

> We are, however, of the belief that the Monterrey pattern is not atypical in Latin America and that adaptation of migrants is fairly successful. Man is a far more adaptable animal than he is sometimes given credit for. ("The social and economic context of migration to Monterrey, Mexico." Browning and Feindt in Rabinovitz and Trueblood, 1971).

> Formerly they were often the work of squatters, or Paracaidistas, who occupied vacant land and built homes for themselves. Many of the houses have gradually improved and now seem substantial in construction, and adequate in many respects as living units except for the frequent absence of basic urban services. More recently the number of squatters has declined as mushrooming land values have driven owners to assert and maintain title to and control of their property. (Oliver Oldman, et al, Financing Urban Development in Mexico City, Harvard, 1967, p. 25)

Our two introductory quotations, the former drawing on Wayne Cornelius' optimism about the upward trend of urban life, and the latter stressing at least the diminishing of shanties, could offer a hypothesis about the levels of social development in Mexico's cities and the direction of the forces at work. In proceeding let us:

1. Review the history of urban settlement in Mexico;
2. Discuss the urban condition today;
3. Look at the main policy-planning inputs affecting urban social life; and
4. Cover the main non-policy forces affecting the quality of urban life.

A History of Urban Settlement in Mexico

Archaeological evidence shows pre-classic centers at La Venta, San Lorenzo in the Gulf Coast area, Tlatiloco and Cuicuilco in Central Mexico and La Victoria in the Mayan Area. These "town and temple" settings precede the more extensive urbanization at Teotihuacan, Tikal, Tula, Monte Alban and, finally Tenochtitlan.

We do not intend an archaeological summary of urban life here except to say that there were solid reasons for this urban growth before the Spaniards decided to replan Mexico City in the 1530s. These reasons or factors, some of which are still operative included:

* the need for social focal points to integrate the dispersed and heterogeneous peoples.
* the similar needs for market centers to handle and exchange the "surpluses" of the separate ecological niches which collectively made for a more prosperous life.
* the need to handle problems in other areas of culture because of the lack of the "compression effect" found in old world, river valley, hydraulic civilizations.

Indeed, the centripetal movements toward the cities obviated the disparateness of the cultural ecology of Mexico. The super scale of cultural activities at such places as Monte Alban and at the pyramid city of Teotihuacan showed the desire for cohesion and its products. These elite centers were self-serving and egoistic, but they were also products of their own hinterlands and were open ended in many ways. Historians and archaeologists have variously debated what was happening and here is one version:

> Whether or not an 'urban revolution' occurred is debatable, but there is no question that concentrated population in so many sites had an incalculable impact on culture. Teotihuacan and Dzibilchaltun had urban populations of at least one hundred thousand, and very likely greater. The arts always thrive with greatest vigor in an urban milieu, and intellectual growth is enhanced as well. At the same time, the stratification of society is inevitable. So, too, is a central administration to maintain order, promote public works, provide justice, set regulations to perform, in short, on a more simplified scale, and functions familiar to city administrators of our own times. And although the details of how these early people of Mexico accomplished all this still evade us, there are signs of considerable efficiency. (Michael C. Meyer and William L. Sherman, The Course of Mexican History, page 17)

The most efficient of these urban centers probably were always in the valley of Mexico - which may have had its own kind of "compression effect" (after Robert Adams) because of the geography of the 3,148 square mile valley. After Teotihuacan, there was the empire of Anahuac, the capital at Tenochtitlan, and finally in 1531 the Spanish Mexico City redesigned to fit their needs. Gordon Schendel's <u>Medicine in Mexico</u> waxes eloquent about the Aztec urban achievements especially the dual aqueducts that allowed continuous bathing!

Perhaps the achievements of New World cities including those of Mexico could be listed.

* they allowed social identification for diverse peoples.
* they stabilized regional life even though there was also competition between centers and between regions, and resultant rural dependency.
* they provided orderly production and marketing and a fairly rich economic life for masses of people.
* their engineering skills, from lake drainage, aqueducts, and the Chinampas, were passed on as part of the technical heritage.

Negative aspects included the post-classic tendencies toward militarism and plunder. The social hierarchies, although not as pronounced in the uneven terrain of Mexico, probably were a form of overburden - leading occasionally to total collapse. Even the more benign rulers, such as the Toltec of Tula, probably could not make this life a secure one. Still public services in pre-Hispanic Mexico City were considerable and Diego B. Lopez Rosado had documented these in <u>Los Servicos Publicos de La Ciudad de Mexico,</u> (editorial Porrua, S.S. Mexico, 1976).

A special note on the cultural tone of pre-Hispanic cities must be offered before we move to the colonial experience. Probably the pomp, grandeur, gore and orgiastic quality of these classic cities is overblown by the <u>National Geographic</u>-type portrayals and the heart removal episodes on the high alters. The day to day building of vast urban scapes took the same mundane planning and incremental plodding as are found elsewhere, although Teotihuacan and Tenochtitlan probably differed in many ways!

According to Francisco Jose Alvarez y Lezama in the <u>Encyclopedia of Urban Planning</u> (1974, p. 688) "Most of the urban designs of Mexican cities had been controlled by the Law of Indies." Meyer and Sherman in their history text describe life in late colonial Mexico City in the following fashion: (paraphrased)

Visitors to Mexico City who recorded their impressions usually commented on the fine buildings and broad, straight avenues. In the 17th century, travelers asserted that everything one could desire was available... Foreigners remarked on the excellence of the city's construction, with its plazas, fountains, and sidewalks... Color was everywhere...

Such was what Prescott had called the "Venice of the Western World" which had been completely rebuilt after Cortez - for the usual reasons of destroying the cultural and political hegemony of the past. Mexico City, according to Robert Fried in Great Cities of the World, (1972, p. 649) was the largest city in the New World until New York superseded it temporarily in the 19th century. Fried clearly states, however, that the grandeur of Mexico City was based on the exploitation which "reduced the mass of the Mexican population to conditions of squalor and serfdom that generated and fueled the armed revolution of 1910-17" (apart from the rural sources of discontent?) We will return to Fried later in order to discuss "policy making for the (federal) district," but let us continue about the colonial period.

The Mexico City plan of the Spanish started with the central plaza or Zocalo which was rimmed with the central government offices and leading church structures. The plan of 1524 had a square mile of land for the conquerors and what was outside of this was left for the scrambling poor. Neither Fried nor Alvarez y Lezama would accuse Mexico City of being well planned in this colonial period, however. As we have noted, the rules from the Laws of the Indies supposedly dominated developments for several centuries. According to Alvarez y Lezama it was not until the mid-19th century that the characteristic boulevards (as the magnificent Paseo de la Reforma) appeared. These were based on the Parisian models of Georges Eugen Haussmann. Gradually the modern form emerged and this included the following:

* more open spaces, parks and gardens
* some diagonal streets were utilized to unite the city and its
flowing geography
* public works and important buildings (as railroad centers, theaters,
etc.).
* occasional grid designs--these were used in the Queretaro and
Puebla plans.
* the monumental, world-class, religious and secular art products of
the Federal district appeared.

Diego Lopez Rodada's volume on public services in Mexico City shows this 19th century expansion. The latter included increments in potable water, communication and transportation, public buildings, mercados, and even cemeteries.   Let us discuss other urban developments in Mexico before we examine urban planning and policy. The modern cities of Monterrey, Guadalajara, Juarez, and Queretaro each have their own pre-Hispanic, colonial and modern antecedents, and we will briefly discuss them as we have for Mexico City.

Another Mexican City: Guadalajara

John Walton notes the historical experiences of Guadalajara in a manner relevant to our tasks. The pre-colonial periods are mentioned only in terms of a local, "hostile population" which was trying to protect its water and land. The followers of Cortez founded at various sites the city of Ayuntamiento as the administrative center for what now covers parts of seven states. This nearly independent region spawned the crown center (Audencia) of Guadalajara in 1575 - which Walton claims (p.31) was economically dependent upon Mexico City and Spain. "Classical colonial" development followed, and the rural Encomiedna system delivered its agricultural "surplus" abroad. The classical pattern included, rich folks at the center, then the small middle class, and, finally the poor at the outskirts. Conflict in the hinterland may have boosted the city's population, as well. Even independence, probably, did not remove this pattern of regional economic dependence. In fact, the persisting historic pattern has continued problems of housing, land use, unequal access, spatial segregation of classes and sewer and water problems, according to Wayne Cornelius, (Latin American Urban Research, volume 6, 1978, p. 15) into the modern period.

By 1800, according to Walton, Guadalajara had 334 city blocks in a rough rectangular form. Besides its center there were "barrios" with distinct cultural and class characteristics. As Alejandro Portes describes for Latin American urban patterns, the small upper class is near the plaza, and the poor exist without benefit of amenities or planning at the edges (see p. 19). Walton notes that early 19th century growth was rapid and was partly caused by rural conflict. Latin American cities are like the "strategic hamlets" of Vietnam fame! Still the rural dependency continued, and even within the city "basic services...were slow in coming in poor neighborhoods" (see p. 33). Further aspects of development in 19th century and early 20 century urbanization in Guadalajara included "land speculation and soaring prices." The Revolution subsequently did little to break up the class-ecological segregation that the previous speculative patterns had laid down. Even though there was much revolutionary fervor in the state of Jalisco, the basic social-spatial pattern persisted. A strong state governor, J. Gonzalez Gallo, did much to change the physical appearance of

Guadalajara in the l950s, but the dominant commercial pattern persists - and continues to segregate the poor. Modest industrialization has not changed the basic social structure of the city but has augmented congestion, pollution, slum living, land speculation, urban sprawl, and general poverty. We will discuss the contemporary planning below, but will close this discussion of Guadalajara by observing that there seems much continuity from Empire and colony through the Revolution to the strongly class segregated patterns of today in this example. Labor and unrest regulating functions are apparent as well.

Queretaro: A Smaller Version of the Same Processes

Andrew Whiteford's study of the social classes in Queretaro gives us a limited picture of that town's development. Whiteford's data from the 1950s and before compares the social classes in this Mexican city and in Popayan, Colombia. Both were colonial cities, and had been administrative and commercial centers in the Spanish Empire. Fernando de Tapia founded Queretaro in 1531 and it was meant (as typical) to be the seat of political and religious rule for a vast area. As Whiteford notes, Queretaro was an important historical center and became a capital of a poor, but central state.

The nature of this city is such that it dominated a mountainous region with some mining, and some agricultural wealth. Queretaro was a city that attracted some commercial and more industrial development, however. The early reasons for its being were largely centered on the administrative roles, where the region's hacendados dominated from town centers. In the early 1800s Queretaro's water power and local cotton supply led to the first substantial textile operations in the New World. Mostly this involved making cotton sacks for the region's silver. The combination of exploitive patterns and limited access to resources would make Queretaro the center of considerable conflict and violence in the seventy years after 1850. Many of the wealthy moved to the safety of nearby Mexico City, according to Whiteford (see p. 15). Some of these events led to a departure from tradition and the old class patterns, and in the 1950s the town was connected by first-class roads to the outside - which enhanced its industrial potential.

While there are variations in our case studies the following seems true:

* the urbanization was originally planned as a form of colonial domination. (See A. Portes)

* their early development strongly fixed the relationships between social class ownership and situation in the city. Labor became more manageable in this relationship.

* neither capitalism, industrialization, modernization or Revolution has greatly changed the pattern.

* much of the "modernization" stressed commercial interests and has enhanced social segregation.

* planning has not changed matters, such as have been implemented.

As to these last points let us look at Monterrey, Mexico to see if it adds or detracts from these generalizations.

Monterrey, Mexico as a Test of the Effects of "Modernization" in Some Sectors

What is now the third largest city in Mexico, Monterrey at 2 million plus, follows Guadalajara which has about 25% more. But, Monterrey as the "Pittsburgh of Mexico" has a strong attraction for migrants from all over the country. What of its history?

In the 1570s Luis de Carvajal was "given a commission to pacify the Northeast" of Mexico (Meyer and Sherman, 1978, p. 162). Not finding suitable mineral wealth the area became a source of Indian slaves to those mining elsewhere. Under colonial rule this was not a formula for tremendous growth, however. It would only be when the industrial revolution hits Mexico in the early years of the 20th century that Monterrey would expand. Under a "progressive" governor, Bernardo Reyes, American, German, British and French investors started steel production in such companies as Compania Fundidora de Fierro/y/Acero de Monterrey. But there were also significant developments in beer, cement, glass, textiles, brick and soap in this town as well during the Diaz period.

What can we say of the pattern of Mexican urbanization based on this last brief case study?

* colonial reasons for existence affect contemporary patterns.

* Industrialization as <u>one</u> of the recent causes of rapid influx can alter earlier patterns socially and physically - but mostly by increased concentration and segregation.

* Monterrey is a blue collar town that is slowly being transformed by economic development.

* the change from only 186,000 people in 1940 to over 2 million in 1980 has transformed this city. (as revitalization of its El Centro)

* transportation and proximity to the U.S. of A. are additional factors whose history must be appreciated.

Let us now turn to a growing border town to see if we can add other historic generalizations to our knowledge of urbanization in Mexico.

Urbanization in Ciudad Juarez

As a border boom town there has clearly been a reciprocal, if not symbiotic relationship across the international border. El Paso's "urbanization" is a dual creature of the processes in Juarez. Oscar Martinez clearly has shown in his volume on "Border Boom Town" how this interaction has taken place. Perhaps it betokens the larger reciprocity between Mexico and the United States at various junctures, which we increasingly can acknowledge.

Martinez is doubtlessly correct about the role of U.S. policy in creating a need for various products (tourist "needs") and services (vice?) south of the border. Mexico's own needs to link Juarez with the rest of the country and to stimulate the border's growth (as with "free zones") has also affected these border urbanization processes.

Descriptively Juarez is a flat, sprawling city set along the concrete basin of the international river. Its El Centro is aging, but shows some commercial vitality (not as much as Nuevo Laredo or Reynosa, perhaps, given the former's greater size). Recent years have seen commercial and public development to the south, away from the international bridge. Some fine shopping complexes, cultural centers, and meeting areas are set in amongst the more dingy concrete and adobe settings.

The growth of Juarez does not reflect the typical circumstances of Mexican urbanization because of the immediacy of cross border processes. Clearly, national economic and political policies are central to its fate, as the need to integrate and make viable its hinterland that also determines its macro circumstances. Given Martinez's fine history of Juarez and Ugalde's depiction of the willingness to accept poverty and high unemployment as a policy, we will not go much further in this brief case study. The "dual factory" border industrialization will have a variety of effects on many border towns having these maquiladores. Of greater short-term effects are those associated with international migration and the relative peso-dollar evaluations.

The Urban Condition in Contemporary Mexico

In Mexico City, 1952 figures indicate that 11% of the city's population live in Jacoles (Squatters Shacks), 14% in colonies proletarias (low density, relatively substantial squatters' huts without urban services), and 34% in Tugurios (traditional slums). (Harley Browning, "The Demography of the City" in The Urban Explosion in Latin America, 1967, p. 102)

Mexico City is one of the most polluted cities in the world. It is estimated that 4,600 tons of carbon monoxide, nitrogen oxide, hydrocarbons, and other contaminants are emitted daily. These combine with large quantities of dust blown in from the ex-lakebed of Texcoco, forming a mixture which one could call "smost" (smoke dust). (Alan Riding, New York Times, 1982)

Excellent sources exist on the general conditions in urban Mexico and these are listed below, along with some of their major conclusions. One of the better brief summaries is by Luis Unikel ("Urbanism and Urbanization in Mexico: Situation and Prospects", in Hardoy, 1975, p. 393). Although this article is heavy on the general nature or urbanization, its overall generalizations for Mexico should be noted here. Unikel claims the following major Mexican trends:

* a decreasing rate of urbanization.

* more concentration in cities over 50,000 - but not in Mexico City.

* the "urban structure" will include three very large cities (Mexico City, Guadalajara, and Monterrey).

* more regional cities achieving regional dominance - but with continuing overall presence for Mexico City (see p. 405).

Unikel is, thus, noting the spread of urbanization's throughout the nation. In this rapid process, however, evaluation must be critically applied or Mexico's urban problems will worsen. There must not just be money but appropriate concepts. Increasingly however, planners suggestions are being ignored! "Planning" in the sense of a public focus has not had a big role in Mexico as we will note below. Let us however in this section review various aspects of the urban condition in Mexico as:

* Physical and spatial conditions.

* Housing and quality of accommodations.

* Public access to facilities.

* The nature and effects of in-migration.

Physical-Spatial Conditions

In Francisco Bullrich's New Directions in Latin American Architecture the cultural quality of Mexico City is described in the following way:

> In Mexico City the colonial past is a powerful background and although it is often rejected at the level of social consciousness, it continues to control the extended historical conflict, the attitudes, the spiritual reality, the town and the landscape. On the other hand, Buenos Aires nearly lacks colonial architecture, and most of the city center looks very much like Paris and London.

The present writer as a former participant in local city planning, has had much the same impression of processes in Mexico City. Even with its breathtaking towers of modernity, a side glance or turn leads to another century. Probably there are solid economic, architectural, cultural, and environmental reasons for this survival.

Schteingart and Garza have most directly described the city's basic spatial structure. There were actually few changes from Tenochtitlan during the colonial period. The dispossessing of the Catholic Church did make a real estate market possible in the center of the city, and this also spread the upper classes to the western fringe (see p. 68 in Garza and Schteingart). Diaz further developed the infrastructure, including the development of areas for working-class housing in the North and East. Incidentally, the latter areas have only recently been served by Mexico City's great metro system. After the militant phase of the 1917 Revolution, the bourgeoisie started their rise to power via urban rents and propertied self enhancement. National policies under Camacho and Aleman led to an urban in-migration which filled the

cracks and surrounded the city as well - especially in the northern areas
where the industries were the big attraction. The next spatial phase was
that of housing governmental and business bureaucracies downtown,
with the poor filling in the decayed segments (or vecindades).

Garza and Schteingart also observe that the growth of Mexico City
occurred additionally with the incorporation of communally held lands
(p. 73) and that although the outcome could have been progressive, it
instead served to "obstruct orderly urban development and encouraged
land speculation.

Much of the focus on spatial areas in Latin America (and Mexican)
cities has been on the periphery, but this could miss the larger action
and the relative stability of internal developments. It seems true of
these developments, however, that they are underlined. Unikel (in
Hardoy, 1975, p. 415) says of Mexico that:

> The majority of sectoral development plans - as in Mexico - do not
> define zones or cities that should grow more rapidly than others, or
> which economic sectors have priority in investment allocated to
> each region. This circumstance aggravated by disconnected plans,
> can cause such serious problems as the formulation and undertaking
> of investment programs and projects whose objectives are
> incompatible with development (in the short or long term) of the
> nation, a region or a city.

Such incompatibilities surely affect the spatial environments and the
physical living circumstances. Unikel goes on to urge that "national
planning should include the spatial factor (geographic distribution or
spread of investment) on an urban as well as a regional scale" (p. 419).
Much of Mexico City's pattern is based on the filling of this particular
"hydrographic basin" and the tying of the parts together with the
surrounding regions has left a pattern just short of chaos. Unikel cites
Hardoy on what should be done:

> In this respect, Hardoy has suggested the promotion of new spatial
> systems of cities that break with colonial and neo-colonial models
> and exploit the advantages of gradual national and Latin American
> integration.

We can continue this section on physical and spatial matters with a
quote from Oscar Lewis on the settlement patterns in the Vecinidades.
It is probably true that upper and middle class Mexicans manage spatial
matters through housing and community manipulation, and the poor are
more completely vulnerable to oppressive physical arrangements.

A type of housing settlement like the Vecinidad, which brings
people into daily face-to-face contact, in which people do most of
their work in a common patio, share a common toilet and a
common washstand, encourage intensive interaction, not all of
which is necessarily friendly. It makes little difference whether this
housing and settlement pattern is in the city or the country...In all
cases it produces intense interaction, problems of privacy, quarrels
amongst children and amongst their parents. (Lewis, 19, p.)

Competition for space, high densities, juxtaposition of varied uses,
absence of zoning, and the poverty of planning, thus, all affect the
spatial outcomes. The original Spanish "great pattern" spreading
around and out from plazas and plazotetas was modified by the later
importation of European motives and models. The competition for land
along major boulevards led to strips of affluence through the urban core.
Elite and, then, middle class dispersal then led to sub-urbanization and
sprawl. Many spatial features follow world patterns, others are unique
to the culture and environments found in Mexico.
    Let us conclude this section on spatial aspects of Mexican cities
(particularly Mexico City) by looking at Jane Cowan Brown's
examination of Patterns of Intra-Urban Settlement in Mexico City.
The latter is an application of the "Turner Theory" (not to be confused
with the frontier Turner thesis) of low income settlement in Mexico.
This theory, in short, says that:

New migrants settle upon arrival in the city, not in marginal
settlements at the urban fringe, but in center city slums or in
centrally located 'bridgehead' settlements which serve as reception
centers for new migrants.

The move then, subsequently, is to final peripheral areas. Briefly
this study concluded that: (p. 165)

Our findings for Mexico City show that Turner's functional
priorities of location, security of tenure, and amenity appear to be
valid for the Mexican case, and that intra-urban settlement pattern
which Turner suggests appears to have been characteristic to Mexico
City until about 1950.

Jane Cowan Brown believes (p. 165) that this pattern may have
been accurate only during this earlier historical epoch, and that there are
also three areas of low-income settlement in Mexico City (not a central
and peripheral one as Turner believes). Supposedly Mexico City is in

the "late transitional" period, where in-migration is becoming less important, but this is by no means certain.

Housing and the Quality of Accommodations

Urban poverty shows up clearly in housing, which seems to have improved slowly in recent years. Although housing is scarce throughout Mexico, the shortage is felt particularly in the Federal District. (From Oldman, Aaron, Bird and Kass' Financing Urban Development in Mexico City, 1967, p. 24)

By 1970 the UAMC had a housing deficit of 577,000 units, which represented 44.6% of the total dwellings in existence at the time. This included 242,000 units needed for "families without housing," 148,000 units in need of renovation due to deterioration and 187,000 units needed to eliminate "overcrowding." (Garza and Schteingart, 1976.)

The above authors note that there are three basic categories of sub-standard housing:

* Vecinidades which are tenements in the older North and East parts of town, which are slums known as Zones de Tugurios. They have communal toilets and generally inadequate services, for instance.

* Jacales or cardboard, tin shacks which are the "worst type of housing in the Federal District" which are regarded by all as "temporary".

* Colonias Protelarias which include over 300 residential areas around the city which has sprung up in the past 35 years. Previously the squatters or "paracaidistas" have new built "casas proletarias" and (except for shortages of services) are now somewhat established.

This Mexico City and Federal District pattern is not found in all other large urban areas, but Walton's study of Guadalajara observes the following:

With respect to urban housing, Guadalajara again compares favorably with other Mexican cities yet still reflects a condition of absolute deprivation among the poor. For example, it is estimated that only 22% of the housing stock is adequately constructed - the lowest proportion in the country.

Walton (using Ibanez and Vazquez, 1970) also notes that this town has the lowest proportions without drainage or sewerage and some of the greatest overcrowding. Most of the bad housing is found in the two Eastern sections of town, Libertad and Reforma. It is strange that the terms "liberty" and "reform" should lend themselves to such misery! The Northwest section, Hidalgo, has the best housing. Most of the "uncontrolled" growth is in the Northeastern, Libertad area. The glorious planning has not kept this city from the road to deterioration in, at least, the physical impact area of its in-migrants. Whether the residents are as happy as Cornelius and Browning and Feindt (as regards migration to Monterrey) say they are, must be considered against the physical assaults which these environs are capable of.

In Cornelius' list of "Principal Problems of Nine Latin American Metropolitan Areas" both Guadalajara and Mexico City are listed as having "Land use/housing" problems right on the top. A footnote to this last phrase notes that several problems are "analytically impossible to disentangle," and these included "land speculation, uncontrolled urban settlement, housing deficit, and deterioration of housing stock."

Oscar Martinez's study of Ciudad Juarez has numerous photos of the various colonias around this great, border, boom town. Despite a range of nice housing and new commercial and cultural centers (as the Pronaf Shopping and the nearby Cultural Center) the physical base of housing and commercial is old. The gleaming concrete of bridges and river bedding as viewed from the El Paso side can be deceiving. The basic wealth for solid residential areas is just not present. Middle class housing, including suburban and high rise types, are present, but they are gems set in aging adobe.

Without discussing the slum conditions in all of the cities, let us note that the urban housing issue is centered in the basic processes of political economy - just as it is in other countries. All of Cornelius' nine Latin American countries examined for problems place Land Use/Housing in the top three categories. Basic inequalities in wealth are matched by such inequalities in housing and associated amenities. On the other hand, excellent quality housing is readily available in any reading of Excelsior's advertising pages. As noted in our section on incomes, the top 10% have some of the most beautiful housing in the world.

Let us additionally deal with another factor that affects the housing pattern in Mexico. Oldman, et al. citing as IMSS study ("El problema de la vivienda en Mexico," 1965) notes that rent controls cover many of the high density areas of Mexico City. The latter is true of 710,000 in the "Horseshoe shaped downtown area known as old Mexico" (p. 137). Critics say that such efforts "freeze land use patterns," "hasten deterioration," and hinder labor mobility. Probably the cause of the poor housing is structured in poverty - not rent control. As to why rent control is not ended Oldman et al, observes (p. 145) "political feasibility in Mexico probably requires compensation for some or all tenants who suffer from modification of rent control." To put it in terms of the main thesis of our book, rent control is part of the effort to avoid urban revolt as are a hundred other measures. These authors (p. 146) note that "political feasibility and economic targets appear to conflict." The authors finally note that rent control does affect a million residents, but it does "prevent changes in land use patterns and it is also an inefficient form of income redistribution." The loyalty of urban workers clearly is involved in this aspect of social policy. It does make for a stable work force as well - perhaps too stable for some entrepreneurs!

Urban Planning in Mexico

The Encyclopedia of Urban Planning (by Whittick, 1974, p. 684) notes the following pattern with respect to city planning in Mexico. "At the national level there is no legislation referring to urbanism, and there are still several persons with political power who believe it should not exist. The same could be said about regional and local levels."

Yet, some efforts at urban planning exist, and the state of Nuevo Leon has tried to mitigate the effects of its heavy industrialization. Engineering considerations have been of more concern that have social elements, such as in the social effects of architecture. But there have been laws on construction, water supply and sewage in all cities according to Francisco Jose Alvarez y Lezama (pp. 684 695). Between 1958 and 1969, at least four other states or regions also tried to get more desirable outcomes from urban developments. The latter efforts were in the states of Veracuz, San Luis Potosi, Jalisco, and Colima

As to professional practice it is estimated that only about 50 people have the needed training in urban planning in the whole country. Many of those who are involved merely improvise. The striking boulevards of Mexico City (as the Paseo de la Reforma) come from the partial emulation of Georges Eugene Haussmann's works a century ago. The diagonal avenues, public parks, and gardens show French and English influences, we are told.

According to Alvarez y Lezama, much of the early "planning" came from a burst of capital building in the 19th century, and their basic geometry either oriented toward the palaces, theaters, public buildings,

TABLE X
ASPECTS OF AREA PLANNING THAT MAY PERSIST FOR THE NEXT TWO DECADES

(Formal response of any planning unit - DDF, nearby states, Federal government, deligacions, etc.)

YEAR	LAW OR REGULATION	IMPLICATIONS FOR MEXICO CITY
1958	Ley To Fraccionamientos: Comprehensive regulations on creation of colonos.	- Showed lack of sanctions against violations in Satellite City and the Pedregal
1976	Human Settlements Law: State can intervene on a consistent basis - with a hierarchy of decision making	- Seems to be a basic document, consequences remain to be seen.
1977	Regularization of Land: Allows and implements full titles for people in colonos.	- Seems aimed at Mexico City, although there will be examples in all urban centers.
1978	Conurbation Commission: Regional development planning (see Ward, page 118).	- As part of the Echeverria & Portillo large scale planning effort, it was aimed at Mexico City.
1980	Conservation Buffer Areas: Open areas are a planning and an ecological necessity.	
1982	New (DDF) Master Plan: Zoning for MZMC (?), stressed population limititation.	- Supports consolidation of centers (ESES VIALES?).
1982	PRUPE: Zones of conservation.	

and monuments or flowed around them. Railroad patterns, basic avenues, water and sanitation courses also helped form the core patterns. Much of the rest grew like topsy, we presume. Buildings, either public as the wonderful museums or private as the massive hotels, merely took up preferred ground in an otherwise agglomerated form. As in the U.S., the circular traffic rings seemed to rope in the central city - or provide a "noose" (as James O. Wheeler notes of U.S. cities). Recent attempts to handle traffic congestion have led to slashes through the core, and were probably more unsettling than the metro-construction.

The author is familiar with changes over the last 15 years in Monterrey. These plans were assisted by Harvard planner Kurt Munn, then later Guillermo Cortes Melo and others revitalized the central area of this industrial community in North Mexico. Much of this development recaptured the city center and the main lines of approach. The elite of Monterrey had similar kinds of motives for revitalization as Yankee planners have noted of the U.S. with its decaying cores but potential value when renewed. Also there is a possible "gentrification" as an affluent, talented elite may reclaim some areas of the cities.

Blake Fleetwood writing about "The New Elite and an Urban Renaissance" in the New York Times magazine (Jan. 14, 1979, p. 16) notes the affluent young retaking desirable parts of the cities from the poor. Evidently a smaller scale process is going on in Mexico City. Alvarez y Lezama notes that since 1955 several neighborhoods called Unidades Habitacionales have appeared, "some well planned but generally very expensive." It seems that clear areas of land on the outskirts are also used for these bright new communities, as Lomas Verdes northeast of Mexico City (p.690).

Planning as such is largely limited to private decisions in the freed-up central areas and in newly developed peripheral areas. It is usually without benefit of master plans, and much of it may well enhance such future problems as traffic congestion and pollution. A planning law of 1953 for the Federal District was superseded by the Urban Development Law. The former dealt mostly with physical aspects and the latter went slightly beyond the deal with administrative procedures. Garza and Schteingart note that: "neither the new law nor its predecessor is informed by a comprehensive vision of the city's growth process..." (p. 77). The word "plano" is often used very loosely.

Still we would be amiss if we did not mention one of the more striking plans which has been put forward for the decongestion of Mexico City. Ervin Escalante in his volume on New Towns: Antiquity to the Present notes the plan for "Ciudad Paralela" which is to accommodate three million people between Cuernavaca and Yautepec in the state of Morelos. Professor Escalante's plan is to use tunnels to link this parallel city to Mexico City, and uniquely use the downward thrust of Mexico City's sewage to generate electricity and fertility in the lower down state of Morelos. To move beyond incrementalism, such startling innovation may be needed.

Most of the forces which affect Mexico City are beyond planning in a public sense, including the very destructive 1985 earthquake. Let us conclude this chapter with a brief review of these other elements.

Beyond the Policy Sphere

Analysts of American poverty policy such as Fox and Cloward do not see the poverty as existing beyond policy, but as being the result of it. The Black movement to northern cities was a direct result of prior agricultural policies, for instance. The absence of a policy could also be construed as a plan or a policy, although we should specify whom is laying this sort of negative policy down. As to our problem here, is there a realm beyond social and economic development policy concerning the nature of Mexican urban life? Is there life beyond legislation or the concerted efforts of public and private sector executives? Does the absence of formal planning mean that there are forces at work that could be brought into the policy or at least accounted for?

Probably a limited view of policy should be adopted when it comes to matters of positive responsibility, and a broader view when it comes to matters of explanation of general forces at work. The lack of funding and general enforcing of Mexico's great constitution is a clear "cause" of the failure of many Mexicans to achieve social development. It is not the only "cause", however, as private decisions of citizens have an autonomous range of efficacy that clearly determines macro outcomes as the peso flight of recent years. Let us note a set of forces that can greatly improve the quality of urban life. The first will be factors seemingly more in the social-economic policy sphere and the second list being those in the citizen's domain.

This decision paradigm stresses that there is a considerable sphere beyond formal policy, but obviously linked to it in "causal" ways. Situations where there are no offered "incentives," or programs, and where there is no push from circumstances determined by public (or corporative) entities are indeed beyond existing policy. Let us briefly examine what sorts of evidence bears on this private side of the ledger with respect to the urban scene in Mexico. We might hope to get an indirect reflection on our thesis by finding out what the government and dominant groups are not willing to do.

First, as to the physical situation, the government has never provided comprehensive settlement plans other than for the unrealized and, perhaps, fanciful varieties such as those offered by Escalante. Housing needs are offered to key working groups, but for other poor migrants it is only the "central niches" (after the Brown-Turner thesis) or the peripheral shanty-towns that offer havens. Surely 4-6 million people live beyond the active, positive policy space in most senses in Mexico City. Obviously with the value of land going up, with congestion and the middle class demand for space, the active policy sphere will further block shanty-town developments.

What about the distributions of urban amenities? As in rural areas these are linked to certain regions or patterns of development. There are, of course, civic amenities which are more or less universally available, as parks, boulevards, public recreation, roads and free non-commercial productions. These latter amenities do augment the lives of many, and we have discussed them elsewhere. They are indeed the aesthetic payoff and contribute to better, if not best, levels of living.

Individual Choices That Affect Urban Areas

The cooperative study of migration into Mexico City by Munoz, Oliveira and Stern notes the zones of origins of these peoples (pp. 117-123). Some come from nearby areas, but many more come from distances of 300-500 kilometers. The tierra caliente is a main point of origin although other urban areas seem to produce some considerable migrants. The north-east produces minimal in-migration to Mexico City, and this may instead go towards Monterrey or to the U.S.

Another individual choice that affects urban conditions is one involving a decision to join a relevant voluntary organization. Butterworth and Chance (in Latin American Urbanization, 1981, p. 142) have studied the founding of a voluntary association in Mexico City by a group of migrants from the Mixtec region of Oaxaca. This group, the CPMO (Coalition of Mixtec Oaxacan Communities) is not aimed at the condition of migrants in Mexico City. This paradoxical quality may be based in the elite formation that guides it, but here is what Butterworth and Chance observe:

> At no time at these meeting are needs of migrant families or individuals in the city discussed. The Coalition is entirely dedicated to the amelioration of conditions in the Mixteca.

Obviously based on Oscar Lewis' observations in Mexico City, those by Martha Lomnitz, and those by such writers as Wayne

Cornelius show active involvement of individuals and their collective groups trying to affect their level of living. The choice of local leadership is an important matter in the barrios of Mexico City, and the variability of leaders reflects the character of the urban neighborhood (See Cornelius, p. 161). As to demand making, Cornelius shows a considerable list of achievements for five colonias, (see p. 188) as, for instance, provisional electric service, school construction, piped water, public phones, child care centers, bus service, etc. The first successes of such community action are to get inspection tours by appropriate officials. Events that tragically demonstrate conditions (as a fire set by an original owner to flush out squatters) can also demonstrate their plight and help to achieve their goals (see p. 191 in Cornelius). Overall, Cornelius sees much fear and uninformed behavior by these migrants, however, and this "greatly reduces the willingness and capacity of the migrant poor to challenge the political system as it presently operates" (p. 229). The present writer's conclusion is that there are individual choices within limits that affect the quality of urban life as the squatters or "parachutists" move toward established status in the city. Job policies may have more to do with this achievement than does the mere effort to establish permanent housing in the colonias. For the middle class, which we have not discussed here, there are some common ingredients, but the natives of this city, seemingly lack the fear to approach their leadership and are more aggressive.

Non-Individual Factors Affecting the Urban Quality of Life

Probably the best way to visualize non-policy, supra-individual forces at work would be to look at case studies of the major Mexican cities. Oscar Martinez's study of Juarez details many such forces that affect the quality of urban life. These include such factors as the access to the U.S. for workers, U.S. policies that made tourism attractive (as prohibition and anti-prostitution pressures), the boom times caused by World War II, and such natural phenomenon as water shortages. The table on the next page shows the kinds of non-policy and policy factors which affect the prosperity and other qualities of five major Mexican cities. For Juarez there are, of course, many policies to promote its vitality and to avoid such historic problems as depopulation, (and over population!), economic stagnation, economic dependency, and pernicious vice. The use of "zona libres" and currency devaluation to attract the American dollar were effective policies at various points in recent history. Tariff schedules, according to Oscar Martinez, have aided Juarez as well. Naturally the border development and industrialization programs have had their effects in many fortunate and unfortunate ways (more women are hired in the factories than are men). Luis Unikel says that joint planning with El Paso, Texas is possible (p.420 in Hardoy, 1975). Ugalde, et al, stresses that the main policy (or non-policy) that affects the barrio called Juarez is the toleration of high unemployment.

The Housing-Land Situation: Big Costs for Some

The state was often viewed as a liberal entity that was interested in developing a form of welfare society engaged in national planning and spreading the benefits of economic growth to most groups...such a conception underlay much of the writing on housing...To understand specific state responses, therefore, a more holistic, class based, political-economic approach is required. (Housing, the State and the Poor, Alan Gilbert and Peter Ward, 1985, page 3)

We have taken the general view of all social policy areas that the provision of social benefits serves other functions. Can we correlate the provision of land, housing, and services with these background elements? Alan Gilbert and Peter Ward ask where the crucial decisions are made, whether by housing administrators or at higher levels by budget makers. Is the model one of technocrats backed by authoritarian rule? Probably, but to what ends? Scarce land and building materials are big ticket items where big decisions have to be made. What does the provision of such materials reveal about the process, motives and the role of the state?

We are most concerned with the land, credit, or materials provided or stimulated by the state and its agencies. Knowing that many build on their own resources and that we are focusing on the remainder, we do not wish to offer examples of a dual system. The latter supposedly consists of a formal market with private provision and an informal market involving a "petty commodity" basis for construction. Both types of housing rely upon the same political-economy. What has been the history of this activity?

The 1970s seen a self taxing 5% on wages for some workers. INFONAVIT did increase the housing stock (Ward, 1990, page 55). For the less lucky there was the older land acquisition process with do-it-your-self instructions: Scrounge! When agencies were set up during the "interventionist" periods their budgets were skimpy and there was a debilitating inter-agency strife and competition. (Ward, 1990, page 64) The whole policy explosion of the Echeverria period came after a spectacular, but painful period of growth. The first 3 years of the sexenio were especially ones of policy initiatives before other factors set in. It is true according to the details which Ward offers that in terms of land provision the programs established were supposed to be self-financing in the long haul, had budgets covering only administrative costs, and were characterized by competitive strife. (1986, page 64) The alphabet soup of other agencies active in the nation, Federal District, and large states (like Mexico) may have had different names up to the late 1980s, but behaved in the same fashion. As to motives involved in the process of bringing the landless into ownership, Ward says (page 66) that regularization with land ownership was "an end in itself." While this is possible, what he seems to be referring to is that "It became the key ingredient around which state-community mediation was channeled." This outcome is hardly an end in itself. The 1970-76 period did seem to end the crisis of the "unserviced and unrecognized settlements" that had been reached by 1970. (page 67) After 1977 "invasions were no longer tolerated" (page 68) and the "process of streamlining and technocratization has continued since 1982." (page 71) The "free for all" was over, and the key political mediation process was established.

As to the affordability of land, Ward (page 77) has a subchapter on this topic. Land sells (when available) for $2.91 to $4.98 per square meter versus $8.2 in Bogota - supposedly then a bargain in Mexico. The average size of lots in Mexico City is 234 sq. meters. It is relatively then more obtainable as long as the mediation process is adhered to. Not all have access to this process it seems. Non-owners in the colonias populares remain a political problem for the powers that be Ward assumes. Provision of capital or credit for building held the same sort of prospects for the individual and the political system. The typical owner of land in urban areas moved from scrounging to petty consumer purchases of building materials. Only in rare instances was housing pre-built for populations. The 1985 earthquake was one such instance of building finished housing.

In his 1990 book Ward discusses the rehousing of "the low income residents most affected by the earthquake in the downtown area of Mexico City (page 194). A World Bank loan was obtained and the government wrote off its portion of the enabling "loan." 28,000 previous households were rehoused and half as many homes were rehabilitated in ways that created new inequalities. "Many groups were in effect bought off." (page 195) For our purposes the process fits the parameters of the Piven-Cloward model about as well as any. The pressure to rehouse was great starting right away after the earthquake. This writer was on the scene shortly after the earthquake, and noted the demonstrations. The damnificados (refugees) were not to be ignored, and more broadly represented those previously left out of the system's benefits. The housing-land deficit up into the 1990s continued to be officially over 2.5 million units which evidently the "market place" will have to resolve - or some focused political response.

A recent (The News, March 15, 1992, page 8) opinion article about the housing situation sites a contractor in the cement business who sees the housing deficit of 6 million units, with INFONAVIT producing only 10,000 a year. Mexico City mayor Manuel Camacho Solis says that the problem can not be solved by the market alone, a new "corporative system" is needed. Much of the problem is supposedly hidden because of the informal nature of the housing market, and much of the lack of market responsiveness is supposedly because of the frozen rents. "Corruption and inefficiency" are often blamed for previous programmatic failure, but a better argument about "frozen policy" can be made. Another whipping boy for the housing deficit is the government's "populist policies." When the economic pie is small, perhaps only this is the only kind of policy format we will obtain.

Cities: Costs and Conflicts

He (Castells) identified the provision of the "means of collective consumption"...(cf. the means of production) as the locus around which conflict would evolve, increasingly with the state cast in the position of protagonist responsible for providing the means of consumption. In effect this politicizes the issue and brings to forefront state intervention and response to social conflicts that arise.

Harvey's (1985) work, in contrast, emphasizes the logic of capital accumulation processes by different income groups, and identifies contradictions arising in the process of capital accumulation, and in particular to over-accumulation crises. (Ward, 1990, page 4)

So what is happening in urban and organized rural settings? What is the locus of the conflict, and how does it help us to understand the motives for certain patterns of social development?

Urban hegemony of Mexico City (and other urban centers) since Mechica times represented a universal process existing elsewhere and through time into the future. It may not be otherwise. Policies to augment urban fortunes can hardly be offset with half-hearted policies of "decongestion." Cities exist by and for the extraction of wealth wither from the earth or the labor process in their respective hinterlands, and the actions in Mexico are no different. There are phases in this process,

TABLE XI
POLICY & NON-POLICY FACTORS
AFFECTING MEXICO'S MAJOR CITIES

CITY	SOURCE(S)	NON-POLICY FORCES	SOME MAJOR POLICIES AFFECTING IT
Mexico City	Cornelius, Oldman, et. al Robert Fried Garza & Schteingart Margaret Hooks	In migration massive Resource shortages Income inequality, locational advantages 1985 earthquake	DDF policies and resources Property tax reform Decision to decentralize intervention in land market Rent control, expropriation: El Centro
Ciudad Juarez	Oscar Martinez Antonio Ugalde et. al. Nestor Valencia	Ups and downs due to U.S. Economy, U.S. policy changes, water shortages, failure to link needs with El Paso	Maquiladore Program, Pronaf Program, Articulos Gancho and free zones, Peso devaluation, border industrialization and development programs
Monterrey	Browning & Feindt Balan & Balan Luis Unikel	Wide spread migration Income inequality, elite autonomy, local advantages	Support for heavy industry in National scheme
Guadalajara	John Walton Luis Unikel Cornelius F. & L.O. Dutson	Industrial dominance, High attraction, Absentee ownership, striking, Class-ecology relationships	Industrial park scheme, Gov. sponsored housing projects, New public Transportation
Cuernacaca	Nord	Decentralization from Urban dis-economies, Attractive environment	New highway linkages, reformed property taxes

and the costs and conflicts vary accordingly. Broader interests and games than those from within the metro areas are involved, and this has often been the case.

Since the Law of the Indies, the dispersal of native lands to the conquistadors, and the systematic exploitation of the hinterlands via the encomiendas the primacy of city life has been assured in Mexico. After independence the Porfiriato pushed the plundering until revolution slowed down the process. The antidote of Cardenas was to change the emphasis, thus allowing for some rural peace. The push to industrialization and Import-Substitution-Development propelled the urban areas further ahead as unbalanced islands of prosperity. Money lavished upon urban infrastructure, money paid for urban wages and amenities catapulted these areas leagues ahead of their hinterlands. Monterrey with its heavy industry grew without a substantial, consuming middle class and with a different relationship to it's more barren hinter-ecology than for Mexico City or for Guadalajara. Ward's chapter "The paradox of dominance, yet dependence" (1990, page 1) deals with the processes by which Mexico City became what it is. Different products lead to different outcomes and so deliberate policies one way or another may be of less importance in determining the "global" relationships. Ward stresses how state action helps to "reproduce inequality", and it remains to be seen how policy can undue these structured inequalities. The 55% of the Mexican population living in urban areas does well in the aggregate. Benefits do fall into middle and upper-middle spheres, however, or to those groups whose loyalty is needed at the moment. Increased spending on behalf of various constituencies who can throw sand into the machinery is common. The net result of these productivity payoff processes give 20% of the population almost 40% of the GDP today. Half of the services developed are utilized in the ZMCM as well.

The costs of living this way have been apparent to many, and have consistently raised policy issues of decentralization and dispersal of resources. The impact of the attendant policy dialog however, is such that people seek their fates by private solutions. This is what many see as most desirable in any case, because of the political externalities associated with state solutions. For some the economy and economic well-being are at their best with the state leaving productive channels open (after dog handling labor into obedience) and then keeping the avenues of the consumption centers clear of non-consumers and complainers! The urban areas and the organized rural areas then become the policy focus in what is touted as a win-win situation, but really is a win-lose, lose one. Yet commerce for all the folks - each in their own shopping niche - is one great liberal goal, and the cities are the major locus today as seen by the lavishing of resources in these areas.

Commitments made to the producing-consuming factions in Mexico City and elsewhere will propel this dynamic into the 21st century. Suburban flight of the consuming classes and the subsidized offering of amenities and services will caste the urban priorities into metal - with little left over for other constituencies. The NAFTA may offset the primacy effect, but only recreate the dynamic elsewhere.

CHAPTER VI

MEXICO'S LEVEL OF SOCIAL DEVELOPMENT AS SEEN BY OTHER STUDENTS

The new national bourgeoisie had developed the economy and kept social peace, but they had not solved a great number of Mexico's problems, nor had they abandoned developmental attitudes characteristic of the late nineteenth century. (Michaels and Bernstein, 1976, p. 705.)

The evident worsening of the income distribution (IBRD, 1975; M. Singer, 1969) through the 1950-1970 period provided the second line of attack. This was seen as due to the growing imbalance of the economy as industry and urban services expanded more rapidly than agriculture (leading also to massive internal migration) on the one hand, and to the concentration of national income in profits, on the other. In this way, the two lines of the critique were combined to a single assault on the orthodox view of the Mexican growth process. (E.V.K. FitzGerald, "The State and Capital Accumulation in Mexico," The Journal of Latin American Studies, November, 1978, p. 267.)

We need to broaden our perception of Mexico's achievements or lack of them. The above quotations from Michaels and Bernstein and from FitzGerald attempt to depict the general process and its mixed results. Statistical data exist that would help us to document progress in separate areas, if we are to trust these data and agree on what it is that they indicate. We are basically trying to measure what the editor of the Statistical Abstract for Latin America, James Wilkie called "social modernization." Many attempts by such writers as Wilkie, Cumberland, Gonzalez Casanova, Ayala, etc. have left us with "poverty indexes," Gini coefficients, demographic contrasts, and levels of achievement. Many non-social statistics could be used, as Martin Needler's data on defense expenditures; May and McLelland's material on the amount of land used for domestic and export food production; level of income tax as a percentage of G.N.P.; and various Federal expenditures by areas. We can use both social and non-social variables in attempting to describe the parameters which account for Mexico's pattern of social development. We know that the pattern is one of great unevenness, and we can, if we wish, use such words as "Dualism's" or "marginality." Wilkie sees social change as being outdistanced by economic change by 3 to 1. Even the spirit of supposed "communism" under the 1930's Cardenas regime did not bring a great transformation; and Wilkie doubts whether such great social changes ever occurred. The latter author believes (p. 269, 1970) that "social improvements have come in times of (an) expanding economy," and even here the cost of administration has reduced the social impact. For our part we have stressed that social enhancement has had the conscious (or reactive) purposes of producing/controlling a viable work force and, additionally, to dampen politically focused unrest. Perhaps Wilkie's assertions do not conflict with our perceptions about the motives for improvements.

Let us proceed here by doing the following:

1. Outline the economic linkage to social improvement as seen by a sample of economists.
2. Compare more strictly political parameters to the course of social development.
3. Defining the social policy pattern that is unique to Mexico by a set of contrasting qualities.
4. Offer a bottom line for the above.

A Sample of Economist's Views of the Linkage to Social Development

One excellent digest of what some economists have offered about social enhancement is given by the English social scientist, J.E. Goldthorpe. This writer briefly covers the works of Arthur Lewis, a Nobel Laureate; W.W. Rostow, who has received fewer prizes; and also A.O. Hirschman, Celso Furtado, Gunnar Myrdal, Seers and Streeten, and Polly Hill Humphreys. We will have to deduce some of their positions concerning the economic-social development linkage in some instances, but in other cases these writers are quite explicit.

Concerned as Goldthorpe is with the disparity between rich and poor nations, he naturally relates the views of these economists toward forms of "backwardness." Basically, Goldthorpe asks: Why are some so poor?

The answers are supposed to inspire "How to do it" types of solutions where the typical one might stress "psychological modernization." Although the latter solution is not one we might stress, let us look at the range of proposals. As one example, Arthur Lewis, writing for the United Nations in 1951, advocated adequate incentives in poor countries, where:

> The public sector must perform all the tasks which in developed
> countries had come to be thought of as its traditional
> sphere...providing a good sound infrastructure of roads and other
> communications, education, public health and other public and
> social services.

Social policy is linked closely with infrastructure in Lewis' approach, evidently.   There is much legitimacy here for social development to be the responsibility of the state, as the social basics are also built into the total system.

Let's look at a very different model, one from the political right. According to Goldthorpe, W.W. Rostow sees the whole process of development as a series of stages that finally leads to the mature capitalist form. The mature stage, then, is the place where "the welfare state, redistribution, social security, and leisure" come in! It is not to be a completely benign form of "Monopoly" game, but it is one where the social benefits merely have to wait for the game to be fully played. Rostow is setting the time table for such "uneconomical" activities, and Milton Friedman has probably better stated this particular position. If this is Rostow's last word on the subject of social enhancement, then it seems to ignore the prior role of policies, both economic and social in bringing about the later, advanced stages. Recent assessments of this approach show dismal results.

Goldthorpe goes on to cover the topic of "balanced versus unbalanced" economic development and the related ideas of "sector," "big push," and "enclave" economies in the writings of Rosenstein-Rodan, Ragnar Nurske, Myrdal, and A.O. Hirschman.   The implications of an unbalanced model is that the social development pattern is likely to be linked to economic development on a regional basis - which is precisely one of the problems in Mexico even with some attempts to geographically spread industrialization.   The subsequent tensions of unbalanced states may spur "spread effects," but the immediate social and economic lag seems unbearable. Myrdal and Hirschman favor unbalanced growth versus no growth at all, however.

Concerning sectional notions of growth, Celso Furtado is a neoclassical economist who writes about Latin America and emphasizes "capitalist wedges" in traditional societies. The result of such patterns can be a variety of forms of underdevelopment in which labor and capital can not be adequately used (See p. 153 in Goldthorpe). Under these circumstances, an adequate social policy seems unlikely, but sector or dual development is possible. Now let us look at a more complete set of concepts for dealing with regional disparities as these are found in the writings of Gunnar Myrdal. Goldthorpe deals with Myrdal in terms of his main concepts which are also a way of analyzing regional imbalances. Some of these concepts include "backwash effects," "cumulative effects," and "spread effects." These processes have their impact upon such conditions as preparation for production, levels of living, attitudes toward life and work, and general governmental policies. Also, very important for Myrdal is the general nature of political and social institutions. The latter have much to do with the determination of social policies as well. Based on such an analysis we could see the previous colonial institutions as starting the development process not only with ports and roads, but with such amenities as sanitation and education. These social developments would be in the form of human capital to match the economic infrastructure. Although there is much pessimism in Myrdal's analysis, especially for Asia, his institutional line of thought reveals ways of reversing "vicious circles." The latter is achieved precisely by moving some of the aspects of social development to the fore, and, hopefully, reversing the negative processes. Let us go beyond this small group of analysts reviewed by Goldthorpe to writers who work more closely to the Mexican situation.

With An Eye to Mexico: Essays of Greater Relevance

Dudley Seers and Polly Hill Humphreys are two among many economists who are in favor of a more "realistic" economics of development, by that they mean one which pays closer attention to the particular forms economies take when studied comparatively. We will take their advice and look at other economists who are "realistic" about Mexico, first Louis J. Ducoff, a U.S. government analyst, who in 1970 wrote of "The Rural-Urban Gap in Development: Mexico's Experience." He notes that in 1967 while GNP was at an all time peak level, a "contradictory dualism" which posited extreme deprivation existed along side the heights of economic development. Using a family income survey made by the Bank of Mexico he seen rural families as having incomes only 43% of that of urban families. (1970, in Zimmerman and Duwors, p. 110.) There was also a greater income concentration in

Mexico than in the United States. To quote Ducoff: "The top 5 percent of family units got 17% of the total income in the U.S. compared with 29% for Mexico in 1963." Trend data moreover, (he cites an ECLA study covering the period from 1950 to 1963) indicates that this gap is widening between the lowest income sharers and the upper groups. (Sec p. 113.) Ducoff does qualify these economic assertions by noting the following:

> The income trends among the various sectors of the population do not of course reflect the wider benefits derived from public policies in Mexico for increasing social investments such as the greater coverage of the social security system, greater educational facilities, improvement in health and housing services, etc., which have continued to expand.

Ducoff goes on to observe that these benefits have had less impact on rural families. The economic reasons for these regional imbalances have to do with the "extreme concentration of industrial development in only a few states or localities." Whereas, the Federal District had 40% of such activities, 27 of the Mexican states only accounted for about 1/5th of the total. Such is an unbalanced, sector economy, and it reflects the importance of the political geography in the social development in Mexico. Social development clearly follows the planned economic development in this country, but this is not what is being advocated, because it is unprogressive socially and economically. Myrdal's models of upward movement away from the vicious circles could start with social enhancement. Ducoffs observation that the gap evidently widens with increased economic development is matched by rough correlation's supplied by Gayle D. Ness (See The Sociology of Economic Development, 1970, p. 8). Ness correlates a number of social measures with GNP levels and while the number of physicians goes up, as does literacy, school attendance, female life expectancy; so do measures of inequality - as measured with Gini coefficients.

A volume with specific knowledge of our question about the competition of economic and social goals is Wilford's Monetary Policy and the Open Economy: Mexico's Experience. This book has a chapter on Mexico's developmental policies from 1954 to 1974, and while the book is concerned mostly with monetary and fiscal policies, it does note when social expenditures occur, and when they occur optimally from the point of certain other policies. We are, of course, trying to clarify the relationships between economic plans or exigencies and the implementation of social development. Basically, Wilford sees four time periods during this 20 year span as differing significantly in the government's ability and/or willingness to spend for social development or to make public investments - the latter two, not being synonymous. Wilford's first designated time period was the 2 years of devaluation, 1954-55, which were not ones of great expenditure of any type in the public sector. From 1956 through 1960, prices were stabilized and much of the government's spending was as a result of borrowing - as opposed to taxation. This "stability" continued through 1968 when economic development goals (as via import substitution industrialization) were being served. Profits were not significantly taxed, although the middle class was now feeling the "bite." We would predict a conservativizing impact of this fiscal policy, just as in the U.S. where social development has become stalled. This new import substitution policy (protectionism) also weakened the agricultural sector, according to Wilford. (See p. 109.) A "disruptive" change occurred from 1969 to 1971 along with world inflationary movements. These last events led the government to "decrease the growth rate in public expenditures." Finally, Wilford observes a further period of "economic disruption" from 1971 to 1974, when especially after 1973, "political and economic pressure led to expansion of government expenditures and to growth in domestic credit." (See p. 110.) The growth in public expenditures (including aspects of social enhancement) and in domestic credit tend to be encouraged at the same time, it seems. With the 1970 recession and these additional pressures of a political nature, "monetary and fiscal policy became less consistent with development policy," according to Wilford. The relationship of macro economic experiences to social development in the 1975-85 period seems to be consistent with these earlier patterns.

In these latter assertions we have some support for the idea that departures toward greater social enhancement can follow the Fox-Cloward thesis as well as the macro economic exigencies. Wilford observes that with the disruption of the 1970-76 period "income redistribution acquired increasing policy importance, and Mexico began to face a crisis in the agricultural sector." (See p. 129.) This latter shift probably meant less vampirism from agriculture to pay for industrial expansion. Oil revenues could have substituted for this blood letting from the agricultural sector - but this seemingly didn't occur. All in all, these material from Wilford seems to reveal that social development is highly dependent upon overall fiscal considerations, but the political unrest of the 1970's had an evident effect as well. Most important, the Wilford materials indicate that social development did not grow autonomously, but rather it seems to be the results of conscious policy that meshes with other policies.

Another source which discusses the relationship between economic development and social enhancement is Luis Serron's <u>Scarcity,</u> <u>Exploitation and Poverty</u> (1980, University of Oklahoma). While not predicting a viable income for all, even with a declining birth rate and economic redistribution, (See p. 235) Serron may be quoted about the effects of the economic growth pattern on social enhancement (p. 122).

> Economists who are familiar with trends toward capital concentration in Mexico emphasize different facets of the impact of such concentration on Mexican life. (Carmona 1970: 89; Ganzalez Salazar 1971: 547; Tello 1971: 637-38). They point to: (1) a necessary correlation between, on the one hand, capital concentration and, on the other, exploitation of labor, forced savings, and the division of the labor force into an employed and an unemployed sector, with the unemployed sector exerting a depressing effect on the employed sector, (2) dependence abroad coupled with imbalances within and between the various sectors of Mexico's economy, concentration of income and incapacity of the industrial sector to provide employment for the growing population, plus high rates of exploitation of labor.

The "necessary" nature of this relationship evidently accounts for the trend toward greater disparities in the future as well. Serron's views are echoed by many other observers as well. Judith Hellman notes the "human costs" in the following quote: (1978, p. 82)

> The development strategy chosen by those in power in Mexico has led to a high rate of economic growth accompanied by social neglect and economic inequality.

Can any other view of the situation be reasonably held?

Whether the forces at work in the shaping and timing of such policies is now to be seen as the results of the hard economic facts of Mexican life (including class struggle) or as the result of certain political images will be discussed in the next section. Did, in other words, the Indian-oriented populism of Cardenas, the economic die-casting of the Alemanists; the limited compromising of the group that favored a "balanced revolution" or the later, minor alterations under Echeverria need to be manifest in <u>those</u> particular fashions? Are other factors causing these macro policy changes than merely those of the fiscal evolution of the country and its national and international vicissitudes?

More Strictly Political Models of Development

In an age when the left-hyphenates "political-economy," it is hard to talk of the primacy of one academic abstraction over another. We would note that, as far as political models are concerned, there is many a slip between political intent and economic and social outcomes. We could define politics here as the competition of rival ideologies or as the relative clout of factions, but we, more importantly, are going to ask what have been the "political" as opposed to the more strictly economic considerations perceived or actually operating in Mexican development? We are, of course, referring to public discussions, not those to which we may never become privy to. That we are often dealing with ideologies or paradigms-in-the-mind with respect to development should be apparent when we look at the writings of many of the observers of the development situation. As an example, we will quote Dudley Seers view of the political-economic aspect, in this case the ideological view of investment, which we are ultimately concerned with in this chapter.

> There is a well-known, indeed classical, argument that inequality is necessary to generate savings and incentives and thus to promote economic growth - which as we have seen, can be taken as an indication of some types of developmental potential. I find that the argument that the need for savings justifies inequality unconvincing in the third world today. (See p. 9 in Wilber, 1973.)

The larger context of Seers' remarks is to note the exaggeration of economic incentives - especially when they aren't forthcoming. Seers is saying that the western economic axiom about the route to development, is in reality, a political ideology, and these are the kind of convenient fantasies that are offered by many western developmentalists. We might ask what have been the academic-political ideologies about Mexican economic development, and whether they offer us economic truths or more politically relative ideologies. The gist for our discussion can come from the nature of public actions in these areas, or the scribblings of the politicians and pundits. We have a later chapter on the language of social reform that will pursue this further.

It seems much easier to make comments about the role of the "economic" or the "political" by looking at the amounts of the Federal Budgets allocated and spent in each area as James Wilkie has done. Whatever former President Lazaro Cardenas' motivations were with respect to national autonomy, the preservation of national resources and oil, and so on, it was possible to trace the actual fiscal outlay for the social budget. Wilkie can say that "Lopez Mateos' ideology of balanced revolution did not get under way until 1961 when social outlay actually approached Cardenas' record." (1970, p. 159.) Even with these fiscal statistics, which were not easily gathered (see p. 289), it is still difficult to judge the role of economic imperatives or of political visions. There are alternative paths to "development," or we would be stuck only with "growthmanship." As a matter of record, however, Wilkie notes that little was spent on the social emphasis during the violent years; only slowly picking up in the peaceful years until the relatively dramatic rise with Cardenas. Subsequently there was plateauing or regression under Camacho, Alaman, and Cortines, then "truly dramatic rises during Lopez Mateos' term." (See p. 161.) To answer our question about what are the actual motive forces, we would have to break down the data more than Wilkie has. Much writing about Cardenas stresses political visionary activity, but the clear needs of nation building around the presidency had to be served as well.

A recent Ph.D. thesis by Keith Haynes on one of the shapers of the political pattern stressed the role of Alberto J. Pani on Mexico's "corporatist" system. The latter was meant to regulate interclass social relationships, and avoid the blow-up which flat-out entrepreneurial autonomy would bring about. The fullest, early applications of this "moderate" approach came under Cardenas, and persists today. The management pattern established by P.R.I. tracks close to the Cloward-Piven theory which we are pursuing. The Pani-type approach allows for the development of a management strategy as the base for the push to economic development which accelerates in the 1940's. Pani was an adviser to seven Mexican presidents, and his influence was great.

The shift to the particular type of industrial growthmanship since Cardenas took one political view of the economic to heart and, hence, transformed the revolution. "Import substitution industrialization" which was to be pursued was more than an economic strategy as well, as it clearly stresses nationalistic autarky, not to mention the creation of an extremely affluent island within the nation. The shifts from the socio-political consolidation under Cardenas, first to the hell-bent-for-development Alemanists, then to the "balancing" of this thrust, followed crudely a line tracing economic exigencies, emerging class interests, and the fading Revolutionary rhetoric. The shifts did not allow sharing by those on the margins, and the "dualism" was heightened. (More on "dualism" and "marginality" later.) Social policies, in any case, also followed this economic qua-political or political-qua-economic mural of national enhancement. Our discussion should not allow political ideologies to float in space, as we can imagine how they may serve class interests, and these ideologies seem to exist in a manner that appears to be almost sui-generis viewed from the outside. And, their final reification in the Federal and institutional budgets, leaves the "why" questions unanswered. The Ducoff and Wilford studies tell us more of the "what and when" than of the "why," but they do note what the emerging development in Mexico did and did not stress. Consider the following comment which notes the varied outcomes of this developmental process. Adam Starchild, writing in Americas (July, 1979, p. 27) observes that:

> The developmentist philosophy of the past three decades, which dictated the production of consumer goods at the expense of capital goods, is in the process of being scuttled.

The current stress on huge developments in steel, petrochemicals, ammonia, and other basic products shows the intent, shared in much of the emerging 3rd world, of laying the foundation for solid economic growth. A problem solving bird in the hand is being substituted for several birds in the developmental bushes, we are being told. To cite a New York Times analysis of what is currently happening ("Mexicans decide to use oil wealth to develop industry," Minneapolis Tribune, March 22, 1979, p. 6A):

> Although a newly approved National Industrial Developmental plan recognizes unemployment as "the most important obstacle to be overcome," the government has discarded the idea of stimulating socially-valuable but inefficient labor-intensive industries.

According to this New York Times report from Mexico City, the result would be a diminishing of dependence upon oil revenue from 35% of the foreign exchange total to about 14%. There is more than a little nationalism in this plan, and it is also a way of avoiding the problem of "drown(ing) in our oil reserves," the latter presenting many battles over distribution and redistribution! By running the country at a 2 billion dollar deficit, rather than a 3 billion dollar surplus, they avoid an internal scramble, one might assume. Under this "philosophy" as Starchild called it, social progress for the current "marginals" is going to take much longer, although there are supposed to be economic windfalls for almost everybody. Yet, the infra-structure and its appendices may still not be able to tolerate these huge masses of underfed, under-educated, and unhealthy people, not to mention their discontents.

We might ask why should changes in development plans take place at the time they do. The recent collapse of oil revenues; the weight of foreign loans; or the increased threat of open dissent (or its destabilizing suppression) probably have much to do with timing. Clearly, the ideological view can be that now is the time for people (some of them?) to "bite the bullet," and to move the economy one way or another. Starchild notes that there are "compensatory benefits" that help tide the various constituencies over until more lush times return. Housewives, for instance, could get low-cost natural gas, as long as the steel mills and the pipeline to the north do not absorb it. There is clearly a model in the Mexican planner's mind about what the risks, tradeoffs, opportunities, and alternatives are. The synthesis that emerges constitutes a dominant political ideology - it surely can not be an economist's axiom alone. To justify economic growth by slowing consumer goods (especially to the lower orders) is clearly a political ideology - not the synthesis of economic concerns alone. It would be equally feasible to finance the needed capital holdings from a variety of sources, and class clout, no doubt. will-out! Foreign borrowing is an additional option for planners. Many people identify with the idea that all personal consumption should be curtailed for these purposes of capital formation, not just that of the poor. But, alas, current ideologies and interests may not be so inclined.

Many of the politically acceptable metaphors see the process of capital formation as not only tapping the "marginal" poor, but also the laboring classes. Observe the following quotation from Raul Prebisch, who has much influenced Mexican development planning - as his ideas about protectionism and import substitution:

> Continuing growth of surplus as a result of steady increases in productivity is essential for regular development of the system based on the consumer society. This process is brought to a halt when the distribution struggle intensifies as labor siphons off not only those productivity increments but also the surplus accumulated earlier. In other words, when the surplus is threatened, the distribution struggle jeopardizes not only capital formation but the consumer society as well. (*Americas,* January, 1979, page 3.)

Prebisch, whose article is entitled "Development and Social Justice" notes how this is "especially hard fought if the lower strata participate in the struggle." This Argentine economist who would have us engage in a "grand strategy of development and social justice" of the kind McNamara is said to have initiated at the World Bank. Prebisch asks us to renounce "simplistic formulas" for development, and calls (like McNamara) for "a faster pace of development" and an "enlightened policy of international cooperation." The implication of the latter is that the answer lies in a larger pie, but that the world in the meantime is essentially a zero-sum-game-situation where any erosions of profit (or legitimate consumption?) are a total detriment. The sacrificing appears to be a bit lopsided, but there is also a political offering being made here. If the haves will be more "cooperative," then the have-nots will hold still until a larger pie is prepared and baked. Interestingly, Prebisch also sees the consumer society as being "incompatible with (the) eradication of poverty." This might be considered, overall, a middle-of-the-road position from the main spokesperson for the Economic Committee on Latin America. The position hedges, it seems, on subsequent income redistribution, and the imagery has as much political as economic appeal. In so far as the grand strategy" involves "international cooperation" it may also be an unrealistic scenario. The less than cooperative U.S. responses concerning the more or less reasonable $2.60 PMCF of natural gas proposal, shows that international cooperation will not include giving an economic edge to a Latin American country.

We must finally ask if political ideology has any efficacy in generating social modernization. In our third chapter of this volume we discussed the values espoused by "liberalism," "socialism," "indigenismo," and even of the "Revolution" itself. Open ideologies of capitalism have little legitimacy, we are told, but ideologies of the left have several handicaps as well. Supposedly the latter, when expressed by the government, have a tendency to cause a panic - witness the supposed reaction to Lopez Mateos when he declared that he was "going to govern to the extreme left within the constitution." (See Roger Hansen, 1971, p. 169.) Although Mateos was apparently trying to cope with and to compete with the far left, it was said to have caused a flight of capital out of the country. Other problems with the ideology of the left as an open banner for social progress are that efforts to achieve "communalism" and "socialism" in the 1930's did not lead to great achievements or at least ones that count today - although they apparently gave much legitimacy to the Mexican presidency. Hansen's book on the Politics of Mexican Development notes the breakdown politically of population (originally from Robert Scott) into three groups. This breakdown reveals why no ideological thrust develops towards the system, if it is correct. The first of these three groups is one consisting of 25% of the population which is seen as being "parochial," and one which expects little from government - it represents passivity and resignation. The largest group consisting of 65% are said to be "good subjects" and they are politically quiescent and characterized by total distrust, hence, they are easy to control. Only the remaining 10% are sophisticated and these "participants" are takers!

The latter consist of government and business leaders and they manipulate ideologies to their own ends, which also creates the immobilizing distrust of the "good subjects." With this total scenario it would seem that only cynical uses of ideology are feasible. Elites need only to co-opt the ambitious - so far.

In summarizing the role for the political as we have approached it, we might of course see it as an epiphenomenal one, that is, of secondary importance in influencing social development. Yet. there are political metaphors which may keep the "good subjects" from revolting. It may also be the case that the economic gains of the 7th, 8th, and 9th deciles of income receivers has something to do with their acceptance of the "status: Turtle's pace."

It is difficult to add up all of the political and economic views presented here so far. The author tends to agree with David Felix who notes how policy itself creates and maintains a "dualism" in Mexico. Although there is no real separation or "marginalization" because the poor do exist in the one economy, they are obviously not it's beneficiaries. According to Felix:

> Behind the increased income concentration and widening dualism of
> the 1940-1975 boom were public policy shifts from social
> reformism to growthmanship, as well as polarizing dynamics of the
> marketplace. (P. 113)

The results of this "growthmanship," given the nature of this system, led to a <u>shifting upward of the social budget to meet the demands of the upper and middle classes</u>. Felix notes (p. 113):

> With public investment contributing nearly half of total fixed
> investment in postwar Mexico, the burden of adjustment has fallen
> on educational and other social expenditures. Educational outlays
> per capita in constant prices rose in proportion directed toward
> secondary and higher education. The post-Revolutionary focus on
> rural education as an equalizing force, particularly strong under
> Cardenas, as deflected by his successors toward meeting the demands
> of the middle and upper classes. In 1970, only 26 percent of the
> rural primary schools went beyond the first four grades, and only 9
> percent of all rural pupils completed the four grades. On the other
> hand, the rising share going to higher education has serviced the
> wealthiest 15% of Mexican families.

We have chosen this rather banal (and somewhat incorrect notion) of a "dualism" to describe how the economic pie gets cut for social development. It seems that a political decision has been made to elevate part of the social structure at the expense of another. Mexico's social expenditures seem to have enhanced the "dualism" on behalf of economic growthmanship.

Let us turn now to a description of the pattern of social policy and development in Mexico as others have seen it.

Defining Mexico's Social Policy

There must be a universalistic set of criteria by which to describe the pattern of social development. After examining such a set of criteria we will cover the views or research of a number of other analysts of the Mexican social development scene.

Social policies can vary in many ways. Social policy can vary with respect to the philosophical view of the social ends to be achieved; for instance, are they to be ameliorative or more redistributive? Mexico's revolutionary rhetoric seems clearly to be typified by the latter, but its practice barely meets the former. Secondly, social policies can see the "mode of operation" as being individually oriented or group oriented. Clearly Mexico's social policies are <u>group oriented</u> or manipulated, if that is your preference. Does the policy mode stress the participation of the client? We would have to say that there is <u>little direct participation</u> of the client in the designing or execution of Mexican social policy, although there supposedly is in the background pattern of political participation. The ultimate mode of operation of social policy could be universal or selective, and again we find universalistic ideologies, but <u>very selective</u> application - as with membership in the social security programs. The main locus of decision making can be in the client group, the professionals who deliver the service, with the members of the ministries, or beyond in some elite. While teacher and student were to have formed the "Casa del pueblos" of the 1920's, a group of professionals and bureaucrats emerged in the educational realms of the 1930's. Social security has become very formalistic, although its membership may sense belonging in a broader organization. Probably the strongest efforts at client participation in decision making have come from the National University at some points in its conflict-ridden history. (See Donald Mabry, 1982, Chapter 10.) One can ask generally how the mode of operation responds to clients who do not respond properly. What is the response to perceived "deviance?" Without much systematic evidence one would assume that a failure to qualify for the service or the benefit would be the result. There seem to be <u>fairly severe penalties</u> for telling untruths to social benefit workers, as for instance those listed under "sanciones" in the "Nueve Ley del

Seguro Social." (1971 Edition, p. 234.) These penalties can be pecuniary or follow what ever disposition results from the application of articles 210 and 224 of del Codigo Penal para el Districto Federal.

Three other elements that can be looked at in our analysis of Mexican social policy are the nature of political inputs, the contribution of the social sciences, and the relationship of the policy to the general process of social change. As to the nature of the political inputs, these can represent translations of political ideology, and they can be democratically initiated. These inputs can be intrusive into the actual operations or merely concerns for goals and funding. And, they can be interest group oriented - as opposed to a broader conception of public interest. We, and many other observers, have attempted to understand the political inputs in Mexico! Clearly, the Revolutionary ideology as embodied in the 1917 constitution is manifest, and creates even today a "strain" toward change. The reader will have to consult such analysts as Gonzalez Casanova for an estimate of what the prospects for "democracy" in the policy process are. As to how intrusive the political process is, one could ask members of the National University on the one hand or IMSS on the other, and perhaps get different answers. With Revolutionary rhetoric going full blast, and gaps between promises and delivery occurring, one might expect considerable feedback into the political process as a result of this. At various points in the late 1950's, late '60's and early '70's the feedback heated up.

As to the contribution of the social sciences in the policy process, the following observations are offered. First, there is a question that can be asked concerning the "hand maiden" role of the social sciences - do research results initiate policy or merely legitimate existing policy? Corollary questions that could be asked have to do with whether social scientists sit on policy boards, whether they can criticize the process at some point, and how the evaluation process is carried out. Clearly many social scientists are in such Ministries as Education, Indigenous Affairs, and labor and Welfare. As in the U.S., however, there are as many lawyers as researchers, and one gets the impression that there is even little drive to legitimate policies after the fact. Social scientists seem to be utilized in the processes having to do with the elaboration of the policy, more in the cost-efficiency areas than in the initiating or evaluation activities. Internal criticism was more typical in the early decades when powerful political leaders of the stature of Toledano or Vasconcelos had not been housebroken by the "institutionalization" process. Evaluation of policies seems external to the process, but fortunately there has been sufficient talent and opportunities to publish for this to occur. The effect on appropriate audiences by writers for

Siglo XXl or The Instituto de Investigaciones Sociales, UNAM or El Colegio de Mexico or the Fondo Culturales is probably minimal. This small body of university social scientists does have a significant impact on their colleagues in policy making bodies, however. Roderick A. Camp's research on the political technocrats in the Mexican government shows an increase in graduate education, but 56% received their basic degrees in Law. It was true that 13% had arts and letters degrees, but only part of these groups were social scientists. Probably economists were the largest social science group amongst these "technicos." (Latin American Research Review, Volume XX, Number 1,1985, p. 101).

Finally, we should look at the relationships between historic forms of social policy and the general direction of social change. We could postulate a move from laissez faire approaches to ameliorative approaches, to curative approaches or preventative ones, and finally to more positive forms. Mexico moved from a laissez faire period, we are lead to believe, after the governance of Porfirio Diaz. The public health measures of the 1920's were ameliorative and preventative, and did their job. Individual medicine was two decades away, and people were left with self or traditional cures. Mexico may present a greater range of types of approaches than does the U.S., and their social security system -however limited in memberships - does present an alternative, positive model for its participants. Policies in the employment area, corrections or criminal justice, housing, or care of dependent groups have not moved significantly along any continuum that we can perceive - except, perhaps, a demonstration project notion. As to the ultimate relationship to social change these policies seem to stress the modernization of the client, and in fact see the latter as "deviant" if personal "modernization" does not accompany the process. Urbanization is linked to many of the benefits, and this must complicate the planning process. Mexico's goals have always considered the various constituent groups in final calculations, and youth have been central in the minds of planners. Yet, youth also die of starvation or fail to become educated because they are not let into the benefits system. Family planning has become a reality, although some outside observers still accuse the system of being fixated at the laissez faire level. (See Serron, p. 202.)

There is a quality of Mexican social policy which stresses comprehensiveness almost as a way to make up for the lack of achievement with respect to more universal participation. The urge to encompass human needs is visible in these social policy formulations. The belief that individual housing should have an integral relationship to the community's larger purposes fits with the social ethos of many great community planners. One must suspect that Mexican social policy makers have always been aware of the evolutionary processes by which society successively transforms itself. Mexico may well have a genius in this regard, even though it can be seen in other lights.

Several Efforts to Evaluate Mexico's Social Policy Achievements

The histories of both Mexico and Brazil reveal the essential interdependence of economic and social development. (Clark Reynolds, "Mexico and Brazil, Models for Leadership in Latin America," p. 453.)

Clark Reynolds is one to seek "lines between social and economic change." We can inspect his model to see how compatible it is with our model of social development in Mexico. Reynolds assumes that there must be a balance of concern for the economic and the social or there will be a general reduction in policy space in the public sector. The delicate link between social needs and their realization (which is public policy) could be missing or substituted for by something less nurturing. Policy space, on the other hand, is increased (see p. 454) by developing human as well as physical capital. Hence: "The better educated its society, the broader the social dimensions of policy space." As to the general dimensions of policy space, the following may be considered: Class conflict reduces the dimensions of policy space - because of the needed costs of substituted repression. Policies that favor growth over distribution will ultimately create more demands for public sector improvements, Reynolds believes. (P. 454.) Mexico has (as does Brazil) a "growth first, social progress later strategy." More typical of Mexico is its concentration on internal matters, until relatively recently.

But, what of Reynold's views concerning the specific relationships between economics and social policy? Reynolds sees growth in either as allowing growth in the other. (See p. 462.) Balance between the two may be called for, but in actual circumstances one of four other strategies may come about. These more typical strategies would include: First, Growth with Coercion. Social policy is relegated to the future, as under Diaz Ordaz, and from mid-1950 to the end of the 70's there was little improvement in distribution. Secondly, Growth with Cooptation, where "highly visible social projects...create an atmosphere of change." The demand for labor, supposedly, will eventually create real change with this approach. The opposition is bought off or destroyed; the old carrot and stick approach we discussed elsewhere.

TABLE XII
CROSS NATIONAL COMPARISONS

COUNTRY	HIGH/LOW	VARIABLE	MEAN	S.D.	MAX VALUE	MIN VALUE
Mexico	(54.49)	Schutz Coeff.	80.85	11.90	99.35	57.78
Australia	(99.35)	"	-	-	-	-
Guatemala	(57.78)	"	-	-	-	-
Mexico	(193)	Soc. Wel. Ind.	193.32	34.36	259	112
New Zealand	(259)	"	-	-	-	-
Congo-Leop.	(112)	"	-	-	-	-
Mexico	(65)	Soc. Ins. Exp.	75.22	39.20	135	0
Belgium	(135)	"	-	-	-	-
South Korea	(0)	"	-	-	-	-

This approach involves vague promises without specific social policy elaboration, and supposedly produces instability (see p. 464). Thirdly, there can also be an <u>expansion in the public policy space where economic reform will favor a broader group</u> (now only 35% of the GNP is in wages and 65% is in capital - whereas in the U.S. over 60% is in wages). If there was a reversal of these percentages then great changes in social participation would occur. This third strategy would only work in a growing economy, and so much diversification is unlikely so that a fourth alternative becomes likely - or, at least, considered by many. Since conservatives raised the fear of capital flight when Echeverria tried the third approach in the 1970's (many, actually getting on planes with bags of money) it is likely that some will consider a more drastic approach, namely <u>revolution</u> or very radical reform. This fourth type, according to Reynolds, will only lead back to the first type, namely growth with coercion. While these types seem to fit Mexico's history at various points, they do not give us much choice as he defines them. Because coercion, and cooptation seem so dismal, and innovation so likely to meet defeat, we only have revolution - which is like landing on the "go directly to jail" space in a Monopoly game. Let us look at another comparative view of Mexico's social policy and development.

Robert Jackman has followed a long line of comparative researchers in giving ranks to the performances of a sample of countries, including Mexico in this case. This ranking of performance data is useful in the setting of expectations about what Mexico could or should be able to do We do find right off that the relationships between aggregate wealth and distribution of benefits is not very positively correlated! Jackman's measure of performance is social equality and he approaches it in basically three ways (p. 11). First, Social Insurance program experience (which is an attempt to gauge political efforts at redistribution); Secondly, the Schutz coefficient of income equality; and, lastly, a "social Welfare Index." The latter two are attempts to quantify how material goods have actually been distributed

As to Jackman's three measures, social security systems are seen as establishing minimum standards by transfers across the life cycle as well as with vertical class contributions. The second measure, the Schutz coefficient is one of policy impact or of "actual equality." (See p. 15.) The latter reflects "command over economic goods," and is similar to the Gini Index in what it measures. The third measure is oriented toward the actual distribution of material goods (p. 21) such as have to do with health, nutrition, protein consumption and live births. Jackman notes that these variables "unmistakably tap conditions of social-welfare."

Let us look at some data to put these measures into action. Jackman observes the obvious in telling us that aggregate levels and distributive measures are quite different in what they reveal. We can accept that, but let us get something to sink our teeth into! Essentially, Mexico is used as Jackman's case study to argue that income inequality is related to amenity inequality, such as to health and nutritional variables. But, even such data (which Jackman takes from the works of Hoivik on Amenity inequality) under-estimates actual inequality. (P. 23.) We will offer Jackman's data on Mexico by comparison to the high and low examples also given. Here in very abbreviated form is where Mexico stands: (pp. 210-215)

Based on selected data from Jackman's study we find Mexico to be near the bottom on the Schutz Coefficient. Like the Gini Index, which correlates at +.95 with the Schutz measure, Mexico's wealth distribution reveals little policy impact. As to the social welfare index, Mexico is right on the mean. The significance of this measure is that it seemingly contradicts the Hoivik data presented in this same volume. The three measures are, indeed, not measures of the same dimension (hence, strongly correlated), but the "Social Welfare Index" seems to misrepresent some aspects of the picture. It would seem that the non-communist world is a very sad place if Mexico is at the mean with respect to the distribution of material benefits.

As to the Social Insurance Experience measure, Mexico is slightly below average, and this may reflect the poor distribution of its programs as of 1960 (or, indeed, 1975). This six category index is one of government efforts for five programs over 27 years - or 135 years of experience. Mexico had most of its programs after 1943 and 1960 - and they covered no more than 1/3 of the population. Their index level could certainly be improved upon, but more than likely Mexico's middling score reveals the sorry state of things in general in the countries measured. The issue may be as Jackman observes, how does one measure bottom level poverty, without under-estimating its extent.

One study by Kreps and Kuykendall ("Growth Without Equity: The Case of Mexican Income Distribution, 1958-68") attempts to gauge what life is really like at the bottom of Mexican society. Rather than using an absolute poverty line approach like Gary Fields (1977), these writers proceeded with per family income based on an internal cutoff measure of $300 pesos (U.S. $ 24). This avoids an "external" and supposedly more arbitrary measure of social development. We mention this study here because it is a way of measuring the effects, and hence, the real parameters of social policy - rather than with empty words or numbers. It goes without saying that: "The proof is in the pudding," which seems to be the reason for our whole volume. In other words, rather than looking at the numerous social policies written into laws - the Library of Congress has a special section of such documents we can instead see what the policies deliver to their constituencies. Kreps and Kuykendall conclude that: "Choosing a poverty level that encompasses the poorest 5 to 10% of the population, the position of these poorest apparently has deteriorated both relatively and even absolutely between 1958 and 1968." This would imply again that the policy, if there is one with respect to income redistribution as the constitution implies, has failed. (See p. 18.) If the 40% level is chosen then, these authors find that the poor have gained "more" than the non-poor. This latter measure is the one advocated by Robert McNamara at the World Bank, and it seems one that is more likely to meet some success - depending upon what "more" means. There are broader ways of measuring the success of social policies, and let us look at another comparative study that included Mexico.

While our present volume is an attempt to gauge the reasons for, the extent of, and the general characteristics regarding Mexico's social progress on the basis of a broad review, others have made quicker assessments. Lloyd G. Reynolds in his volume <u>Image and Reality in Economic Development</u> (1977, p. 257) focuses on the social, economic, and political characteristics of 15 countries. While we are mostly interested in the social characteristics, we will mention some of the other qualities to put the latter into perspective. Much of this data used by Lloyd Reynolds was taken from a larger sample of 74 countries made by Adelman and Morris. Mexico as one of these 15 non-socialist, non-oil or mineral (as of 1970!) economies, with over 2% growth rate, received good "grades" ("A," "B," "C" and "D" were the score indicators) from Reynolds. "A" was, of course, a good or excellent score, and Mexico received the following letter grades: (p. 259)

1. Size of subsistence sector	B
2. Extent of Dualism (Traditional-Modem)	B
3. Extent of Urbanism	B
4. Size of Indigenous Middle Class	A
5. Extent of Social Mobility	A
6. Extent of Literacy	B
7. Extent of Mass Media	A

The average grade for Mexico, on a three point scale, was 2.6, in fact this was the second best score in a group of 15 which included such countries as Brazil, Columbia, Iran, Kenya, South Korea, Nigeria, Pakistan, the Philippines, Turkey, and the winning Venezuela at a score of 2.7. This sample is not one of the biggest winners in the race for development one would have to admit, but they have resources and promise.   By Reynolds data compilations Mexico ranked first in political indicators (as sense of unity, degree of party competition, administrative efficiency, and political stability) in the sample, being faulted with a "C" grade for "too much centralization."   As to economic indicators, Mexico (at 2.6) outdistanced all but Venezuela (at 2.9) where rate of GNP growth, gross investment rate, abundance of natural resources, effectiveness of financial institutions are amongst the submeasures.   How are we to view these good marks - an overall tie at 2.6 with Venezuela versus the average of 1.6.   Latin American countries, Reynolds observes, do better than African or Asian (except Taiwan) in general.   Does the nature of the comparison make Mexico look good?   Is Mexico really a social and political giant as well as an economic "miracle?"   We have previously discussed Mexico's unevenness - which these kinds of measures by Reynolds fail to pick upon (except for extent of dualism - which this material seems to deny). These materials supposedly reflect levels of attainment, and the possible outcomes of social and economic policy.   We at best have a comparative perspective on Mexico's achievements, but even when these particular indicators are utilized, we are not sure what knowledge we are acquiring about actual experiences of people.   The chosen indicators and their subjective scoring (as a "C" for too much centralization) raise the issue of value judgments - which we do not want to duck.   Let us summarize what we have learned about policy dimensions and achievements in Mexico from these sources, and, then, discuss what could be described as a more universalistic approach to the utilization of social policy in such settings.

What Typifies Social Policy in Mexico: A Summary and Some Lessons

Men can not live without creating, influencing, and utilizing social policy. (W. Cohen)

By now we are aware that the Mexican Revolution and its subsequent rekindling have led the nation to an evolving commitment to broad based social development.   At times social development has competed poorly with economic growth, and the social spin-offs from the latter have been slow in coming.   But, what can we generalize about the style of social policy and development in Mexico in terms of its inception, elaboration, and possible self-renewal?   What typifies the locus of decision making concerning social policy?   What are its boundaries in terms of what is included or not?   What are the arguments made politically for changes in social policy? How is social policy fitted to the total planning process? What are the ultimate counters used to evaluate success or failure? Are more limited "programs" stressed rather than broad-goaled social policies? (A social worker could execute the former, but only a planner with a mandate could accomplish the latter.) To what extent are ad hoc responses made instead of more systematic, universalistic, value based types of responses? What kind of reactions typically come after policy implementation has obviously failed? These are the kinds of questions that more universalistic approaches are taking, as Tropman, et. al's Strategic Perspectives on Social Policy. (Pergamon, 1978.)

We have tried to answer some of these questions here but basically argue that good programs have been extended mostly as supports for other national priorities - that is, national consolidation and economic growth. In this chapter we have typified Mexico's social policy as group oriented; quite selective even though the ideologies are universalistic; comprehensive in scope where applied; strongly punitive for lack of compliance; dominated by external priorities; acculturationally oriented; and occasionally preventative. We agree with Clark Reynolds that coercion and cooptation have been more the norm in determining the scope and shape of social benefits than has a basic broadening of the base of participation. This is not to say that there has not been innovation, dedication, and massive commitment to the achievement of truly transformational goals. We would reject for reasons of failing to represent distributional aspects the type of studies done by Lloyd Reynolds, but these comparisons can be instructive starting points. Jackman's analysis shows the need for multiple measures, and for what we would call radically descriptive approaches.

For a government or an apologist of that government's policy to analyze the social development results of a country only by stressing the positive accomplishments would not be "radically descriptive." Nor would a discussion of a country's good intentions. We must find measures and indicators that go to the heart or root of the matter, and, perhaps, the Wilkie index of poverty shared one quality with what we have in mind. The latter tried to encompass the experience of being poor in Mexico. Ultimately the question of poverty comes down to the F. Scott FitzGerald-Hemingway issue: You are a poor or rich depending upon how much money you have! But concepts like "life chances," which Ralf Dahrendorf has recently reviewed, have something to do with root experiences. Nor are we talking merely of government expenditures, or such factors as numbers of doctors available or hospital beds. Yet overall, such measures have their place in a truly descriptive grid of qualitative and quantitative measures. These measures would handle the problems of distribution, and not merely deal with mythical averages. Economic measures additionally can compliment social measures, and would mutually validate one another, hopefully. Multiple measures of the same social phenomena may be called for, but the costly process of statistic gathering often means that multiple measures have come from the same sources and share the same problems. Such a summary volume as the present one is over-reliant upon official or interest-seeking sources, as well.

The Bottom Line Concerning Economics, Politics and Social Policy

If we are to believe such writers on the macro-institutions as Nora Hamilton who has studied "The Limits of State Autonomy," then we must perceive a "limited number of options" in the Mexican policy process. (See p. vii, 1982.) This limitation stems from the role of foreign capital and domestic "grupos" in the private economic sector. We must have a workable model for the larger process that specifies what groups in fact are so inclined, and what options they face. Hamilton's book has a Library of Congress card that classifies it to include social as well as economic policy. The latter is more evident and only a few references to Ejidos, rural education, socialist education, city services, income distributions, the price index, public works financing, and the seventh day wage are made. The basic thrust of the volume is upon the economic policy decisions that are made during the various early administrations (1930-1940's). The rise of the progressive "new alliance" under Cardenas is seen, however, as a series of economic moves (agrarian reform, wage increases etc.) that brought social peace and more "progressively" prepared the base for capitalist expansion. Basically the "socialism" of the period was confused with the "mixed economy." (Hamilton, p. 140.) The main non-capitalist experiments were "eclectic" and failed. The state would be autonomous, however, and control both capital and labor - the limits of state autonomy toward the former meant the doom of Mexican progressivism, however.

What does this thesis offer us concerning the policy process in Mexico? As to the notion of state autonomy being limited, we have no quarrel with this idea because any model (both conflict and systems approaches) must account for given outcomes; as the kinds of needs met and unmet. "Met" needs, however, begrudgingly approached, have reasons for being just as unmet, non-redistributive "needs" do, however alienating their lack of "satiation." To repeat our model using a U.S. of A. example, the social security acts of the mid 30's and the War on Poverty acts of the 1960's have a scenario in which it can be said that certain "motives" (interests or trade offs - not unmet needs) can be said to have been decisive. As with any other "act" or "decision," the sequence of forces leading up to their expression have not only been sufficient, but have a nature that may be fairly well characterized. The social development policies of Mexico can <u>not</u> be best seen as an expression of national values, their constitution, the dominance of progressive or conservative forces (alone), or the outcome are gained on the basis of the collectivity of contributions, and that they may be "overdetermined" as well.

Mexico's social policy "achievements" must be seen as a result of options picked up or as a result of their likely consequences. Either a state with relative autonomy or capitalist dominated forms - (making up the triad which Peter Evans (1979) refers to) must maximize their social investments. The triad of groups (limited state, internal and external capitalists) can not squander their investments given the exigencies of the labor market and the possible level of popular political expression. The exploitation of the existing autonomy of the Mexican state could have meant a move to more progressive outcomes as groups flexed Revolutionary legitimacy. This outcome, however, is not to be, given the surge to capitalist development and the parallel absorption of the peasant and working classes into authoritarian structures (Hamilton, 1982, p. 268). The need to pacify or "countervail" the subordinate classes probably represents the bottom line concerning overall social expenditure. The specific direction and magnitude of actual social expenditures remains to be explained. Nora Hamilton is herself unsure how social policies emerge, and of what nature. Although the "progressive alliance" had its impact (versus rural Chile or Peru?), the social development programs are seen as both cause and consequence. Thus, "peasant and worker mobilization was both cause and justification of the radicalization of the government program." (P. 274.). It was followed by a temporary "abdication of its (the State's) social control function" (p. 277); and then a subsequent need to control the subordinate group's economic and political demands lest "the state would be undermined." In political terms the right won; and the conservative alliance was victorious. After this point, mostly forces from outside the state would change the direction of minimal social expenditures. Given this political history, we have only a small range of phenomenon to "explain." Perhaps we should spend our efforts on something beyond what merely seem to be "techniques of domination!"

According to Hamilton, several contradictions establish the "limits of reformism and the fallacy of efforts to 'humanize' capitalism." (P. 265.) The perspective of our present volume does not lead us to deny these outcomes; indeed it specifically stresses the very limited nature of reformism, and the narrow pretext for its expression. Neither do we see these limited expressions as taking on a life of their own or of raising demolished expectations. These policy expressions probably have more "perverse" consequences. Our current position is more like that of Alvin Gouldner and his view of the "welfare function" in modern capitalist society.

In Alvin Gouldner's The Coming Crisis in Western Sociology (1970), there is a discussion of the "shift toward the welfare state" and the relationship of this shift to academic sociology. Gouldner notes that stability demands are met by certain mechanisms that reduce or head off social disorder. The latter disorders are manifestly more important to the system when they occur in or near the labor markets or the political arenas. Disorders in other sectors (culture, social values, popular expression, life styles, family arenas or social interaction) probably allow tension reduction, but produce no potential vector of force against the existing system. Even the conflict avoiding sociologist Talcott Parson and the other early functionalists finally accepted the possibility of avoiding key conflicts via the welfare function - albeit on a selective basis. Basic change is avoided by such internal amelioration and only external (and improbable) sources of change need then be avoided. With our stress on the system's manipulation of social inputs, we are, indeed dwelling on techniques of domination. The sources of macro change at this point, are indeed obscure - but not unfathomable.

CHAPTER VII

THE AUSTERITY TURN OF THE EARLY 1980'S & 90'S AS A TEST OF OUR MODEL

> At a time when the average Mexican believed that his country had been plundered by its political elite (Where did all the oil money go?), and when the virtually bankrupt public sector lacked the resources needed to rebuild support through massive populist-style social welfare and public works programs, an anti-corruption campaign made good political sense. (Cornelius, 1985, page 99.)

Let us trace what happened to social policy and social benefits during the "austerity crisis" which started in the summer of 1981. Previously we noted a variety of views about what was actually happening with the quality of life in Mexico, as DuCoff's observation that while income distribution worsened, wider public benefits improved conditions for many. Did these circumstances reverse themselves after 1981? The devaluation of the peso, surging inflation, a decline in employment opportunities, zero economic growth, major business failures, capital flight were part of the economic back drop against which social life would improve or decline. Judith Hellman describes this economic disaster and how Mexico had to come to terms with the International Monetary Fund and the Bank of International Settlements. Lopez Portillo reacted with strong measures including bank nationalization, but one must remember that Portillo had already reduced the "populist gestures" to the poor which previous president Echeverria had engaged in. (Hellman, page 227.) Hellman notes that pressure from a well organized labor sector helped to preserve assistance in very desperate areas, but some cuts were made before the summer of 1981. Portillo's regime no longer had the resources to achieve cooperation of powerful organized sectors. The I.M.F. formula was to include new taxes, financial "reforms," decontrol of "non-essential" items, and a general belt tightening. One million Mexicans would loose their jobs; there would be increases in the cost of government services; and wage raises (as of January 1,1983) would be held to only 25% despite the inflation running over 100%. Hellman observes of the latter that "The state's capacity to impose this level of austerity on the working class is striking in view of the severe decline in the standard of living which had already been felt in 1982." (Page 231)

As to this latter observation Wayne Cornelius (1985, page 97) cites the view of economist Abel Beltran del Rio who argued in 1983 that "Mexico complied excessively with the terms of its agreement with the I.M.F." The latter quote has more to do with the contraction of the money supply, than it does specifically to the support for social programs. As part of the "draconian cuts in public investment" De La Madrid "exceeded its I.M.F. targets for both reducing the public sector deficit and limiting new public sector external indebtedness..." (Page 93.) In real terms total public spending was down 13% and on public works it was cut by 50%.

Who Bit the Bullet?

If one were to have followed these events in Mexico in the New York Times articles by Alan Riding and Richard Meislin this is the picture of the austerity under Portillo and De La Madrid which emerged. Riding (NYT, Sept. 7, 1982) notes that Portillo appointed a left of center, "Nationalist" economist by the name of Carlos Tello Macias to direct Mexico's central bank. This was to coincide with the nationalization of the banks. Riding notes the business community's hostility to the bank seizure (Sept. 2) a week or so later Riding writes about the "Taming of Mexico's passion for more" (Sept. 12, page 26). To quote Riding:

> Even during the good times, inflation eroded the real wages of many
> workers and peasants and, for them, the outlook is for hardship and
> even hunger. Just last month the price of corn tortillas and bread
> doubled overnight. The middle classes are also feeling the squeeze
> of unemployment and inflation. Having enjoyed a consumer boom
> over the past 4 years, they are now seething at the prospect of a
> lower standard of living. (Section B - page 1, 26 NYT, September
> 12,1982.)

One would almost assume that the biting of the bullet is a generally shared activity, but Riding observes that the middle class mostly lost such amenities as foreign travel and would probably not go hungry! Strangely one group who have been hurt were U.S. citizens with

TABLE XIII
SOCIO-ECONOMIC EFFECTS OF THE MEXICAN AUSTERITY PROGRAMS
(By Aggregate* Groups in Mexican Society)

GROUP	GENERAL EFFECTS	SPECIFIC POLICIES	NET CHANGES
Government Workers	Projects cut or delayed	Public sector good and services up in cost, public spending down 13-50%	Slowed improvements in salary and benefits
Middle Class (Workers)	Annual inflation rate over 100%, gains from 1978-81 period wiped out (Cornelius), reduced consumption	Taxes raised on consumption (10-15%), imports down, CONASUPO stores for the affluent	Small says Riding (1984, p. 152), less home building
Lower Class (Employed Non-Union)	Open unemployment doubles from 1982-83 (Not as much expected?)	Government subsidies reduced, official minimum wage down 23%	Substantial losses, critical subsidies maintained
Lower Class (Marginally Employed)	More underemployment? (45 to 50%), "Informal Economy" absorbs more	COPLAMAR underfunded then dismantled	More strain on family "safety net"
Peasant (Workers)	Stagnation persists	S.A.M. dismantled	More strain on family "safety net"
Peasant (Marginally Employed)	International aid greater than internal?	COPLAMAR never reached, except for some clinics	Remain "super-marginalized"
Students	Lower classes froze out reversing trend, cutbacks and closures	Tuition increases, "punitive cuts" in subsidies	Dual class system reinforced as to access to higher education
Union Members	Inflation losses not restored by wage increases	Wage increases held to 40% vs. 81% inflation	Significant but not catastrophic losses

* By aggregate we mean those with a single or multiple common, identifiable membership or experience (as union members or students).

money in Mexican banks and investments. According to Riding these "peso prisoners" (October 26, 1982) owned at least half of the 12 billion dollars in Mexico's nationalized banks. But the effects of the economic moves had more diverse effects. The steep peso devaluation, according to Thomas Hayes (NYT, Sept. 15), supposedly has increased work available in the border industrialization program. These Maquiladores would not be harmed by such economic measures. Portillo himself got strong support from the left during his last months in office and according to Riding (Oct. 1,1982) Portillo received over 12 million dollars in small donations to help pay the debt off and also reimburse the former bank owners! When Portillo went to give a speech at the United Nations on Oct. 1, 1982 (NYT, Oct. 2, 1982) he noted that "our efforts to grow in order to conquer hunger, disease and ignorance have not caused the international crisis." Portillo further noted how capital flight in search of "high interest rates, tax havens and supposed political and exchange stability" decapitalizes whole countries. The larger picture presented by Portillo is that the whole country was victimized! Perhaps this imagery, which is seemingly correct, took the edge off for the individuals in pain.

The incoming president at this point (De La Madrid) spent several months early in 1982 touring the country. Supposedly, according to Alan Riding (NYT, May 25,1982), the president to be received a good education about the country's social problems and began to talk about them in terms of specifics rather than "empty phrases." The following quote from De La Madrid supposedly shows that he has come to see the "country through the eyes of poor."

> When people say that they have no drinking water, that is times
> they must share water with animals, when you realize the indices of
> infantile malnutrition and sickness in depressed zones, obviously
> you have an emotional reaction. I have reiterated that the greatest
> challenge facing Mexico lies in the inequalities between groups,
> classes and regions of the country.

Unfortunately, this quote is followed by another agenda setting issue. "People are demanding the control of inflation as a priority." The latter issue may not be consistent with transfers of money to solve health, potable water or income maintenance problems. Two days later, De La Madrid also reiterated the "moral renovation" issue (see NYT, May 28,1982). Non-monetary policies as well as inflation control may both steer priorities away from basic social problems of the lower classes.

At this time De La Madrid was into the 3rd year of his Sexenio. Wayne Cornelius characterizes the first years as ones of "short term crisis management" (1985, page 83). The language of the current process stresses such notions as "Renovation," "competitiveness abroad," "decentralization," "structural changes," and so forth. Cornelius believes that De La Madrid "has had considerably less policy space." After a brief summary and an inspection of our table on how groups have fared from 1981 to 1985, we will conclude this chapter by discussing efforts to keep the lid on - given the incredible austerity crunch.

Table XIII on the next page shows 8 groups and what general things were happening to them. Also policies that seemed to impact them most are noted, as well as net changes (very speculative!). Obviously each of these groups were impacted by most of the austerity measures, but some groups were specifically targeted (gasoline users, telephone users, students in Universities, etc..) for changes. Some observers of the impact make statements that say the burden, as usual, was unevenly shared. Alan Riding (1984, page 152) observes that "The burden of 80% inflation, however, was carried mainly by the poor majority, whose wages rose by only 45%." Continuing, Riding claims that: "The middle classes were forced to reduce their consumption and foreign travels, although crowded restaurants, tourist resorts and shopping centers over the year-end vacations of 1983 and 1984 suggested little change in the expectations."

Unions asked for wage and price control, but this was not granted or attempted by De La Madrid. On the other hand the possibility of general strikes meant that labor would get some of its due. Labor had benefited just as the white collar middle class and government employees had during the oil boom years. Expectations of continuing improvements were tempered by the several economic experiences of 1981-85, of course.

In summarizing our ramblings about who bit the bullet it seems to have been the middle and lower sectors of Mexican society. Obviously some businessmen faced retrenchment, but the upper middle classes only slowed general consumption and recreation. De La Madrid did keep the subsidies on such essential food supplies as corn and cooking oil, but the main experience was of further deterioration in nutrition and life circumstances for the majority. It is doubtful whether the "Family safety net" or the "informal economy" took care of all the problems which austerity induced.

Attempts to Keep the Lid On

Because of widespread opposition to an I.M.F. agreement from labor and political parties, the letter of intent sought to reassure the public that the austerity program would be guided "by a criteria of social equity and protection of lesser income groups"to protect the standardof living of the working class. (Riding, 1982.)

Discussing the "Social Crisis" in Mexico, Alan Riding observes of the government's general response to social needs that: "Because resources are limited, they are invariably assigned where political pressures - rather than objective needs - are greatest." (1984, page 233.) Such may be the universal nature of the welfare game! Political forces in Mexico are not always very apparent especially to the outsider so we could assume that the above statement is tautological in that those who are recipients are by definition those with the most political clout. Although we are not going to describe the political process in Mexico, we can probably agree that, the recent victories of C. Cardenas show that the opposition can be organized!

The faction of most danger to the P.R.I. regime is probably the very well to do segment on the right that has maintained ties with the top military and various foreign powers. So then if welfare is retrenched, and there is no "provocative" response from an organized left, then what is the nature of possible political unrest? Probably P.R.I. and its allies had feared a spontaneous revolt of the kind that 1968 generated although some may now fear the ballot box! Any regime that must have a base of reasonably solid support against such an event, or a regime must be able to deflect public anger. Cornelius notes that:

While De La Madrid has not garnered broad public affection and support for his policies, he has won respect for his firmness and political decisiveness. By September, 1984, there was less public anger directed toward the De La Madrid administration than toward its predecessor, and much less of an air of crisis. Indeed the crisis had become almost routinized. Much of the public appeared resigned to a long, painful recovery process. As De La Madrid himself put it in a meeting with labor leaders, 'Mexico is coming out of its problems. Not all at once, nor with the speed that everyone would like. But with firmness.' (Mexican Studies, 1985.)

It seems that the previous Lopez Portillo's regime became the lightening rod for the discontent in general, and the austerity in particular. As Cornelius notes, events during mid-1984 could have sparked open conflict, there being fire bombings and the assassination of an important political journalist. We seem to be talking about state craft on a broad scale, rather than the functions of social policy in particular. Let us review the main initiatives in social policy since the Cardenas regime, and the parallel political conditions. Our model suggests the primacy of certain motives or "functions," but it may be as economist D. Sykes Wilford implies - you need to have a lot of money coming in, before you can distribute any! Social development has this one necessary prerequisite.

The 1920 to 1940 period stressed nationalistic education and some public health. Nation building and the creation of a viable workforce were apparent motivations. With the move toward industrialization in the 1940s, there had to be some token gestures toward the needs of workers, even though I.M.S.S. would not be extended for many years. The balancing period of the late 1950s and early 1960s was the most clear congruence with our model, as the lid was partly blown off. The CONSUPO program tried to dampen some unmet basic needs. Echeverria from 1970 to 1976 promoted countless pieces of social legislation aimed at rural and urban workers, and it was clear that the effort was the result of pressures from the bottom - especially by workers. As needs were met, the political right, we are told, reduced Echeverria's initiative if not his will by 1974. Programs like S.A.M., COPLAMAR, INFONAVIT, etc. were aimed at specific groups - many of which had the capacity to either "raise hell" or drag their feet in the labor market. The gradual expansion of social benefits does loosely fit our model although those of writers like Carmelo-Mesa-Lago who earlier had stressed sheer political clout fit less well, perhaps. Nevertheless, many see key workers as an elite in Mexico because of their disproportionate sharing in the social benefits. Yet the middle and upper classes have done the best at the total hog trough of benefits amenities and transfers. The so-called redistribution by social benefits aimed at workers amounts more to manipulation, than to a full measure of equity. The oil boom benefits probably did "trickle down" to some extent and if D. Sykes Wilford's book had been written in the mid-1980s it would probably have shown how social largesse and public expenditure expanded in the 1978-81 period. (See Monetary Policy and the Open Economy: Mexico's Experience: 1977, especially Chapter 6.)

What of the 1981-1989 period; surely the pressures are upon the regime - even if "routinized" as Cornelius suggests? Operating with "limited autonomy" (as Nora Hamilton suggests) and a reduced "policy space" (as Cornelius suggests, 1985, page 85) the Mexican state still has options and trade-offs. If the economic cupboard is near empty, it can still stress some acceptable concepts of equity, forbearance, sacrifice ("ask not what...."), or patriotism. We have already noted the efforts at deflection to other issues, and could also note the non-monetary substitutions which the regime could offer - as with recognition of otherwise "illegitimate" political status's. By definition, these and other tactics worked from the point of the regime.

In analyzing "the crisis of the Eighties," Judith Hellman notes the pattern at work in the even more explosive 1970s. (1983 - Chapter 8.) While the left tries to demystify the "Revolution," there still are guerrilla actions, bank robberies, kidnapping, wildcat strikes, and demands for more democracy. The worker demands for a "democratic tendency" or autonomy was outside of what Echeverria had allowed, or hoped for, in his "apertura democratica." Factions within labor actually went beyond the cap-in-hand request for cooptation. They were demanding a fundamental restructuring of Mexico's political economy. Union's had done this relatively apart from the academic parties on the left as well. Not only oil, steel, chemical, electric, telephone, and railroad workers were involved in this ground swell. Teachers, the largest union in the country formed the "Revolutionary Movement of Teachers"! Many of these reactions were in response to <u>cuts in existing social benefits</u>, and that is what finally may spell the end of previous patterns of domination and their success at holding the lid on. Even rural areas are moving to "clearly articulated ideological positions" from the previous "clientelistic/personalistic independent peasant movements" that were so easily demolished with carrot or stick in the past. (See Hellman, page 250.) The costs of keeping the lid on have evidently gone up, but Hellman stresses the need for a positive alternative before the system can be transformed.

As to our general model as a guide to understanding the implemented social policies of the early 1980s, let say the following.

1. Pressures have been met with much flexibility by the regime in distribution of social largesse.
2. When programs are cut, it seems that this creates a relatively spontaneous basis for popular militancy. *
3. Adjustments within the existing benefits pie will merely shift the direction of pressures.
4. Final outcomes are not predictable on what we have offered by way of analysis here. The next elections may end the PRI pattern of control, in favor of what we can not predict either.

* The background to the U.S. "riots" of the spring of 1992 included a cut from 19% of targeted federal programs to a mere 6% of the same fund sources. No one would want to predict when the

arrangement would go this bad, and more elements are involved than this might imply. More likely as a response are the consolidation of groups in the presidential or state elections. Cynics believe that the National Solidarity efforts were an attempt to keep the voting box lid on, but more of this later.

POLICY
TALK

Salinas con Colosio

Presidential word play

In this age of "modernization," what could be more appropriate than a computer analysis of President Salinas's state-of-the-nation address? While many analysts were preoccupied with what Salinas *meant*, the Mexican Institute of Public Opinion, a political research group, decided to find out what Salinas *said* – word-by-word. The institute ran Salinas's *informe* through a computer for word counts and then compared it with the first state-of-the-nation reports of all presidents from Miguel Alemán to the present. The first discovery: Salinas's was the shortest first informe in modern Mexican history (two hours, 15 minutes). Highlights:

The most popular words were low-risk warm-ups: "Mexico," (21 times) and "Mexican" (16 times). Only Gustavo Díaz Ordaz outdid Salinas on a safe bet like "Mexico" (25 times).

The true winner – surprise! – was "modernization," which came out of the dust and took over the address. Salinas managed to use his catchword – which was uttered once in De la Madrid's first informe and never by anyone else – 14 times.

Along with modernization, there was a lot of "respect" (11 times) and "justice" (10 times). Neither of those words had been popular with previous presidents, who referred to justice an average of three times and to respect an average of twice during their first informes.

Mexico's crisis is officially over – at least in presidential informes. De la Madrid had referred to it eight times in his first state-of-the-nation speech; Salinas mentioned it but once.

Another word inching toward extinction in the Salinas era is "government," used just three times by Salinas compared to five by De la Madrid and 18 by Adolfo López Mateos, understandable considering Salinas's shrinking government. "Development" wasn't mentioned at all by Salinas, though used an average of five times by previous presidents.

The word "democracy," popular with opposition leaders, has never had star billing in presidential addresses. Four of the last eight presidents skipped over it altogether. Luis Echeverría, however, used it most: five times. Salinas used it four times, compared to De la Madrid's three.

– Cindy Anders

INFORME

CHAPTER VIII

THE LANGUAGE OF SOCIAL TRANSFORMATION IN MEXICO: ACADEMIC AND POLITICAL VERSIONS

....there are plenty of hard words there... (Lewis Carroll)

The language of social intervention, reform, and modernization in the Western world has varied much historically in its denotative and moral qualities. In Mexico's 75 years since the revolution there has also been a range of expression. Aside from the language eulogizing the "Revolution" itself, there are common words that are threaded through the speeches, slogans and media offerings. In Mexico planning ("el plan") allows an authoritative moral quality. Development (desarrollo) probably has increased in usage as the bureaucracy grew and the needs for legitimation did likewise. Serious policy decision making made "politica" a buzz word in the proper context. Additionally the concepts of power (poder), change (cambio), mobilization (movilizacion), legitimation (legitimadad), and movement (movimiento) are thrown onto the screen. The political-social lexography would also include certain frequencies of use for "strength," "Nation," the "people"(used more selectively today?), "workers," and, occasionally, "struggle."

In this chapter, let us look at the language used to describe the Mexican efforts to improve people's lives. We will use some historical references from a variety of sources, with emphasis being upon the political sector as this is aimed at the national public. There have been many efforts to do content analyses of the language of politics, as the early studies of political propaganda by Harold Lasswell and his associates with their world attention survey. Some analysts, like writer William Safire, have merely tried to catalog usage in the form of common use dictionaries. One of our goals will be to try to understand how social transformation has been depicted in the mainstream of

Mexican life and politics. Some of our examples are drawn from key national documents, others from presidential pronouncements, and others from academic observers of the process - who may not be all that supportive of what is/was happening. We assume that if we do our job reasonably well that we will shed light on the motive aspects of social development. We may also be able to perceive changes of significant sorts.

In fact we can perceive ideological change in the Mexican Revolution, just as Wayne Olson has shown in his recent article on "Crisis and Social Change in Mexico's Political Economy." (Latin American Perspectives, Summer, 1985.) The following quote from Olson notes changes in the language of legitimation:

> The particular issue that the Mexican state has emphasized as the basis of its legitimacy has changed with its role in the political economy. Thus, during the Cardenas administration and the transition to import-substitution accumulation, land redistribution and anti-imperialism were the basis of the state's legitimacy. During the "miracle" the state's role in promoting national economic development was emphasized. After the onset of the crisis, Echeverria attempted to demonstrate that the alliance existed and to ensure the credibility of the ideology through social justice programs (i.e., land and income redistribution). (1985, page 22.)

Currently, according to Olson, the move to export-substitution accumulation necessitates other changes in the political-economy and in the parallel verbal-legitimation efforts. As part of the current economic effort, tariffs will be reduced, state enterprises sold, ejidatarios made more capitalistic, and price subsidies dropped. Significantly, although there may be more efforts at democratization, this may not offset the reversals because of the moves away from income redistribution. If we accept this portrait of the country's political-economic thrust, what language will be used to legitimate the social effects of the actions and policies? Let us look at a sample of academic observers of the policy process first, and, then, establish a chronology of terms describing the implementation of the "Revolution."

Academic Language Used to Describe Mexico's Transformation

The Mexican political system has been defined as corporative, populist, authoritarian, and patrimonial - Corporative centralism. The Mexico which emerged from fragmentation of power and from the regional struggles that followed the Revolution, is often credited with the implementation of policies of economic development under conditions of political stability. In order to achieve such aims, a corporative regime characteristically employs "cooptation of leaders; vertical or sectorial policy compartmentalization; permanent institutionalization of access; juridization or legalization of group conflicts through labor and administrative courts; state technocratic planning and resource allocation; a political culture stressing formalism, consensus and continuous bargaining." (Lomnitz citing Schmitter, 1974.)

The above set of ingredients also includes physical repression and "anticipation of intimidation!" With such a list, we may not have to go any further. However, there is a larger context to the policy process, its language of legitimation and its motive forces. We agree with writers such as Hodges and Gandy that a full analysis would also include the rule of Mexico's ruling class, and not merely a focus upon the executive policy process. The Lomnitz quote above would help us to anticipate key parts of the process and the motive forces at work. Our purpose remains to elicit the key motivations for the elaboration of social development at various points in Mexico's recent history. We do realize that the question of <u>whose</u> motivations (interests?) have hegemony is central to our concern - motives do not float bodiless in space!

The following academic case studies are not in any historical sequence, and only constitute a sample of the known universe of such studies. Some of these authors have been discussed at other points in this volume, but here we will focus upon their insights into the motives behind the policy process and the language used to legitimate certain actions, decisions, and rationales. Our first source by Grindle is entitled "Public Policy and Political Change in Mexico," and it is a good place to start because of its comprehensiveness, relevance, and general critical nature. According to Grindle, the six year term of presidents has its effects on the deployment and implementation of the policy process. Both constraints on innovation as well as the greater opportunity for responsiveness (to whom?) are noted as consequences of the Sexenio. To quote from Grindle:

Each new administration is concerned with making its own impression on public programs quickly, and newly recruited officials take over duties with little commitment to pre-existing plans. As a result old policies which have failed are reintroduced in the guise of new solutions; old mistakes are repeated by inexperienced cadres, and many programs which prove to be promising in one administration are shelved in the next. (Page 167.)

The basic motive proclaimed by Grindle is "Plazismo," or "the propensity to invest in highly visible, but developmentally questionable projects such as remodeling public parks and thoroughfares." (P. 170.) One can certainly question whether bureaucratic careerism, timing, and self-enhancement via "plazismo are the major motivations for social policy developments. One might agree that the "eternal return' to previous regime's policies does help account for the lack of linear progress. The supposed outcome wherein we find the "bureaucracy's inability to design comprehensive plans for social and economic development" (page 175) needs more supporting evidence as an explanation of Mexico's uneven development. Must we blame selfish, bureaucratic careerism? As the author herself notes, many CONASUPO administrators were committed to the goals of redistribution, even if this did not involve a radical redistribution. (Page 179.) Grindle's analysis moves us toward the position of Max Weber and Roberto Michals that we are all going down the tubes in the 20th century because of the motives of bureaucratic incumbents. Too much is left out in such types of analysis. Surely government personnel have important motives which they probably both present and obscure with the language they portray policy alternatives with. Besides staying in office, remaining near the seats of power (and the "bite"), many government workers do not want the opponents of the Revolution to take over completely. There are also other functional perquisites for the game to go on at all. As the Mexican system has been constituted, it must maintain stability by being "inclusionary."

Our next source for the analysis of the language of social reform in Mexico is Susan Purcell's The Mexican Profit Sharing Decision (1975). In discussing the "authoritarian decision making process" she observes how the system incorporates its critics, and hence, demobilizes them. More to our point she notes that: (page 139)

Controversial legislation is also justified in terms of the "revolutionary" ideology, which guarantees that its legitimacy is unassailable. The use of the prevailing ideology in this way has been called "the mobilization of bias." In Mexico, the mobilization of bias against the interests of private groups is a frequent tactic of the government. It also serves to reinforce the integration of the authoritarian coalition by emphasizing the nation rather than its component parts.

The language of the Revolution is used to gain consensus for the totality. This is not a surprising idea for us at this point. She further notes that during the crisis years of growthmanship in the early 1960s the national profit sharing commission, the president (Mateos), and several key groups came to an open position of unity over this policy of potential redistribution. (Page 122.) Although the projected benefits were meager and favored business interests, labor acquiesced. In the battle that finally laid the format for the profit sharing plan, verbal definitions of the program with one slant or another filled the air - not always offering light on the issues. Was profit sharing really "redistributive" as business claimed it was? Was an alternative proposal of a month's bonus really not "profit sharing" as some of the more liberal claimed? Were the non-sharing directors really just "high-level assistants," and hence very eligible to receive profit-sharing - and thus receive a disproportionate share?

Apart from showing the verbal-ideological battles over a key issue Purcell notes an interesting time related aspect of the decision making process.

> A decision made in response to a violent outbreak follows a similar pattern. A substantial period of time will be allowed to elapse between the outbreak and the decision so that the latter will not be interpreted as a response to the former. The labor unrest of the late 1950s, for example, was not followed by new legislation benefiting the labor movement immediately, but approximately four years later. (Purcell, 1975, page 137.)

Thus, the "patrimonial image of the president is reinforced" by this delay, even though the amount of time may vary in other instances. Legislation coming from the president or attributed credit-wise to the president constitutes the initial language of social improvement. Evidently in the family planning decisions noted a decade earlier the same type of calculated timing delay existed as well. Because we say that an attempt to offset disorder is an important "motive," this deliberate pattern of delay makes our task for proof somewhat more difficult because of the lack of immediate response. On the other hand, if the assumption of purposeful delay to avoid encouraging other demands is correct, then it shows the concern to be precisely in the area we have been eluding to.

There is no shortage of attempts to describe the basic nature of the Mexican policy making system. We have discussed Clark Reynold's views of the economy of Mexico elsewhere in this volume. (See *The Mexican Economy*, 1970.) Reynolds, in another source, analyzes the "tactics of stabilization," such as with devaluation. He observes, however, that such economic policies may have contrary results in actual "destabilization." Over all, he sees an historical move from "stabilizing development" on to "shared development" - and this seems to involve fairly optimistic language in itself! To document this transformation he notes that:

> The poverty index falls more rapidly for the 1950s than the 1940s, although the growth of per capita product took the opposite trend. It follows from these tentative measures that rapid economic growth might well have been a necessary condition for major reductions in poverty, although the data before 1925 indicate that rising per capita product was by no means a sufficient condition for rapid improvement in social welfare. (1970, page 47.)

Various linkages between economic growth and social improvement are postulated in this formulation by Reynolds. The inevitability of a positive correlation between growth and distribution is nicely questioned by Reynolds, but we have already assumed that economic growth is not a sufficient condition for social modernization to occur. For our purposes here, we could search the political rhetoric for arguments that everybody has a stake in growthmanship - which is obviously not always the case! The notion of "shared development" itself seems to imply that a positive relationship between growth and equity exists (existed?) in Mexico.

Many writers, as Menno Vellinga (<u>Economic Development and the Dynamics of Class: Industrialization Power, and Control in Monterrey, Mexico</u>, 1979), show discrepancies between the rhetoric and the delivered reality. Vellinga observes how the "normative model" serves to maintain "the legitimacy of the system which is threatened by political practice." (Page 53.) With this modality, the ancient authority and administrative pattern of the Diaz regime reoccur as the "eternal return." Judith Hellman observes (<u>Mexico in Crisis</u>, 2nd Edition, 1983, page 17) that some of the great legislative breakthroughs for the Mexican working class came without great fanfare as when the dominant political figure was the crusty and conservative General Venustiano Carranza. These breakthroughs came about "due to the political and strategic needs of a conservative on his march to national power." Zapata had already denounced Carranza for his lack of concern, but words have a minimal effect on history.

Let us make sense of this sample of academic views of the language and practice of social reform. Besides the observation about cynically offered policy carrots and the opportunism associated with them, what

else can we say about the process? Clearly Mexico's progressivity in
social policies came out of intense political competition, where each
utterance, posturing or delivery was spawned out of an ongoing
conflict. The need for powerful allies, must be seen as partial
motivation for the strong rhetoric of reform. It is clear that much
conscious, willful intent is involved in the process. The offering of
policies from Cardenas on, is much effected by the timing of the
Sexenio, as well as from the fear of what a caving-in to pressure might
do to the process. It is probably true that "Plazismo" type motives
survive along with revolutionary ones. The Mexican state needs
"legitimacy" in order to get the kind of "policy space" for any kind of
move, including toward social reform. If Wayne Olson's position is
correct about the needs to legitimate the political economy of export
substitution, then we should be able to observe that trend as well in the
political rhetoric. Let us briefly summarize the latter.

Political Versions

Table XIV presents a brief chronology of the language of social
reform since 1910. Based on these examples, and some depiction's of
the periods and regimes, let us see if our academic observers have
adequately described the action. It is probably true that political rhetoric
has always been "hot" in post revolutionary Mexico, although the first
decade, the Cardenas administration, and the sexenios of Mateos and
Echeverria may have run somewhat warmer. The first decade involved
cannon-like exchanges of rhetoric, plans, slogans and songs - not all of
them being full of meaning. Competition from the radical Toledano
faction in the late 1930s pushed the rhetoric, at least somewhat to the
left. The "balancing of the revolution" under Lopez Mateos may have
involved a move as "far to the left within the constitution" as possible,
or it may have been a series of propaganda victories matched by a very
few deeds, such as the extension of social security. Echeverria in the
early 1970s is seen as moving the political rhetoric to the left, and of
matching some (opportunistic?) deeds to the words. Since 1976, the
ideology has cooled although occasional tough actions (like Portillo's
nationalization of the banks) call for tough words. Many must feel like
Luis Cabrera (cited by Riding from Cabrera's Twenty Years After).

> Freedom, equality. justice, effective suffrage. no-re-election,
> separation of powers, free municipalities, sovereignty of the states,
> international independence...words, words, words. (Riding, page
> 52.)

TABLE XIV
THE LANGUAGE OF SOCIAL REFORM

1910	"Land and Liberty" "Plan of San Luis Potosi" "Plans of Ayala" Villa's "New Day" "La Cucaracha" "House of Workers of the World"
1920	"Raza Cosmica" (Of Mestizos) "Dios No Existe" (Rivera) "Preserve Indigene" (Via Mexicanization) "Terra Y Plan" "Betrayers of the Revolution"
1930	"National Dignity" "Viva Ejidos" "Institutionalization As Solution" "Casa Del Pueblo" (Secular Education)
1940	"Problem Solving" Growth First, Justice Later" (By Critics)
1950	Avoiding "Social Dissolution" The "Economic Miracle" "Balancing the Revolution"
1960	"Race and Unity" (Versus "Agitation) "Preventative Imprisonment" "Freedom for the Middle Classes"
1970	"Renovation" of the Structure "Apertura Democratica" "Global Planning" Eliminating "Marginalidad" Pro-Socialist Text Books "Revolution in Education"
1980	"Financial Populism" "Decentralization" "Moral Renovation" "Structural Imbalances" "Preference Populations" Police 'Modernization"
1990	- Free Trade Mission - Green Nobel Prize - Pact of Economic Solidarity" - Modern = Denationalization?

Some times the words cause reactions, however. Mateos' moves were to the right, but hard words to the left - supposedly induced capital flight out of the country from the upper classes.

New words often creep into the total political "universe of discourse." Probably the early 1970s seen the political usage of terms like those referring to the "marginals." Echeverria referred to the latter, but it is not known if he saw them as really being outside of the system (thus, blaming them for their own poverty) or as linked to the system in disadvantageous ways. The use of the word "crisis" implies systemic problems, rather than problems stemming from deviants to the system, and this term has gained wider acceptance. The Mexican communist party (PSUM) would not hesitate to use words like "crisis," "structure," "struggle," and so forth, but mostly these hard words are used by left intellectuals and "jacobin" factions elsewhere. When a union faction moves from "blanco to rojo," then the language change accompanies it. Largely the language of cooperation, cooptation, and coercion dominates political and state communications. Largely we agree with Menno Vellinga in the following quotation.

> Within this strategy, the ideology has served as a safety valve. The ideological offensive directed at the popular strata has utilized revolutionary phraseology suggesting radical solutions to the problem of underdevelopment while emphasizing that the potentialities of the "regular" struggle through the existing sociopolitical structures have not been exhausted yet. (1979, page 187.)

As to the insights of our chosen academic observers of the process in Mexico, we offer the following generalizations. First, there have been great changes in the political rhetoric of the Mexican Revolution. The sexenio has much to do with the quality of the dialog, with early posturing sometimes being punctuated by late and critical parting shots. You may not be able to judge a politician's later positioning, by his earlier words. "Plazismo" lives, but so does populist-revolutionary rhetoric and premises. The demands for stability cool the language of all but a very few. Words are often a substitute for action. The words used also reflect real internal struggle, as these are used and redefined. Timing of words as well as context are important, but finally the moral attachments to words will affect actions - especially in the area of social justice.

EMPLOYMENT AND RECOVERY

Type-Location	Major Characteristics	Impact on Worker, Wages & Benefits?	Potential For Future Labor Force?
MAQUILADORES (Production Sharing)	-Assembly Line Conditions -Low wages Are Basic -Females Are Unorganized As Yet	-Old Guarantees Don't Apply -High Turnover/Absenteeism -"Soft Organization" Still Exploitive	-U.S. Policy May Reduce Scope -May Be A Model For Most of NAFTA? -Will "Foreigners" Come To Dominate?
TOURIST "Industries"	-Super Resorts From Acapulco To Huatulco -Attract Young As Well As Experienced	-No Ladder For Advancement? -"Hustle" Brings Extras -Takes Pressure Off Migration, The Border & Mexico City	-Potential Glut With Further Expansion -Deals With Airlines, Hotels, Etc. Will Sweeten the Game
AUTO "Industries"	-Use Of Already Skilled Is Very Productive -Zone Called "Little Detroit" Already -Will A "Mex Car" or "World Car" Be Produced?	-Could Last 25 Years With Export Substitution To South America -Need External Help To Unionize	-Nissan And VW Still On Cruise! -50 Dollar Wages Reinforced By Big Three Goon Tactics As In U.S.
NAFTA Created Or Stimulated	-Uncertain Because Of Global Interactions -Must Match Existing Quality of Labor -Reactions From "Partners" Still Problematic	-US Government Won't Protect Workers Anywhere? -Pemex Jobs May Be Sequestered?	-More Auto, Electronic, Glass, -Mexico Can Be Undercut By Central Americans
INFORMAL Sector	-"An Area Out Of Control" (T. Barry) -Not New, But Growing -Street Vendors Competing Strongly With Small Businesses--Not Taxed	-A Better Way To Stay Ahead Than Wages -Will Be Pressure to Tax, Regulate	-If Not Harrassed, Will Prosper -Street Vendors Now Integrated With Pri -Remains A Pressure Release, But Not As "Penny Capitalism"
NEW PROFESSIONALS	-As With Expansion Of Elementary Teachers, Social Services, Enviromental Technicians -Also Public/Private Health	-Able To Push Demands In Some (Urban?) Areas -Both Public & Private Demand Improve Situation	-Can Link Arms With Popular Causes As Health, Education Or The Environment

CHAPTER IX

CONCLUSIONS ABOUT OUR MAJOR HYPOTHESIS AND CONCERNS

Despite all the obstacles, the public sector does sometimes expand significantly and sometimes its benefits do help alleviate social ills. It is also true, however, that powerful groups often manage to maintain their privileges even under such circumstances. For one thing, they may (through their resources, contact and knowledge) reap a disproportionate share of public sector services. For another they May shun the expanding public sector in order to buy special privileges in the private sector. (Levy and Szekely, 1983, page 144.)

Cooptation, which seemed to work until the late 1960s, has not worked well into the decade of the 1970s, but Lopez Portillo is trying to make it work. However he has other non-political forces to contend with. For instance, demographic pressures: Mexico's population growth has been out of control for too long. Injustice has been the social reality of the day. There have been too many isolated massacres following those of Tlatelolco and Jueves de Corpus, too much guerrilla violence and political alienation. And surrounding all of this has been burgeoning wretchedness and poverty. (Mexican Democracy: A Critical Review, 1978, page 95.)

Mostly our evidence concerning the motive forces for Mexico's social development pattern is historical and forms a loose time series indicative of these forces. We have tried to show how each area of social enhancement has progressed and what specific initiatives should be noted. Without a full model of the Mexican political or policy process, we have speculated about the motive forces at work. Not being privy to any actual decision making process or decision makers as such, we have instead examined the shape and scope of social enhancement areas with an eye to what purposes and groups are being served. Much can be learned from the outside when one examines public activity, as when a grand highway is built between two regions or towns. Clearly the highway is meant to encourage and permit safe and efficient transport between the areas so connected and beyond. This assumption as to purposes seems clear cut and definitive. Yet, if a country were to spend most of its national budget fighting a foreign war on the opposite side of the world (certainly not Mexico!) one could perhaps tell from the effort, actions and expenditures what the national purposes seem to be - even if one had great doubts about the value of such activities. Such military activities could however mask economic or other purposes, as when John Kenneth Galbraith suggested that there was such an activity as "perverse Keynesianism" or military spending as economic pump priming. Some purposes are more obscured and latent, than manifest it seems.

Looking at Mexico's education activities after 1920; its public health efforts; its pension and clinical expansion after 1943, we can not doubt the manifest purposes that are sought and partly achieved. The coverage of specific groups with nutritional, educational, and pension programs (as ISSSTE in the 1960s) shows a selective targeting which continues to this day. The universalism of the Mexican constitution and typical political rhetoric do not, however, account for the limited application and tokenism we perceive today. To explain the less than universal outcomes we must understand the forces which can determine participation in the benefits circle. Mesa-Lago's notions about "clout" or muscle power perhaps explains why some unions have received their wage increases, IMSS largesse and housing benefits. Many beneficiaries are lucky enough to be included as participants in admittedly limited "demonstration projects" whose symbolic qualities represent a form of "plazismo" to be sure.

The period representing the "balancing of the revolution" clearly showed how the potential for causing trouble will lead to the pouring of oil upon the public waters. Manifest unrest (as noted by Judith Hellman and others) explains the "populist" expenditures and gestures of someone like Echeverria. Indeed, all of the "Explanations" we dealt with earlier have some place in helping us to understand the motive forces of Mexican social policy. The constitution of 1917 was reified later in speeches, laws and street corner pamphlets! Organized (as opposed to uncontrolled) political pressure must be given its due, as recent 1988 elections revealed. The timing of the Sexenio, and its need for an up-front, fresh appearing policy will mean that, apart from serious circumstances, new presidents and regimes must address the unmet needs, at least symbolically. In order to demonstrate that the regime is in control, and Avenida Reforma is not to be permanently blocked by demonstrators, there must also be a visible flow of projects to address unmet needs. Elites must appear to be decisive, in-charge and, of course, caring. So it must be said that most of the alternative forces do mold the shape of social policy initiatives. But critically, what explains the distribution, short as it is of a universalism? Third world "underdevelopment" mostly allows non-universalism to occur, but does not determine its particular pattern. Many 3rd world countries also approach universalism more closely than does Mexico, and even with not much greater overall levels of resources.

Probably each area of social enhancement has its own time table and operative forces, so there is no overall dynamism or master plan to account for the totality. Public education after 1925 went as far as it could have gone, considering resources and the "Cristero"-type resistance it generated. Public health received much international support for varied reasons, and its prerequisite status motivated the heroic efforts here, even though simple panaceas like iodized salt took a little longer to achieve and preventative nutrition is still mostly on the horizon.

In the 1940s the industrial modernization push meant that urban, family-detached workers would need pensions and other social guarantees - which, probably, only the government could supply. With monetary manipulation of the total economy, there had to be minimum wage adjustments or coercion would have been necessary in order to head off dissent and frustration. If children were too malnourished to stay awake in class, there had to be a school lunch program. And, free textbooks have their own compelling reasons. As the urban population took on the chronic illness pattern of industrialized, long living peoples, then clinical health care had to administer as best it could to these needs. The Mexican response has seldom gone beyond what it needed, because it has not had the luxury of this amount of "policy space." Labor redundancy, provided it did not have political clout, meant that many groups could be treated modestly, if not meanly. In the area of higher education, although not as to graduate training, Mexico seems to have gone further than it "needed" to go. Perhaps the personally inappropriate choices of too many professionals led to an over-investment here. Mexico, of course, has not done well comparatively in any area of education, but the middle class seems to have been bought off by heavy subsidies to undergraduate education.

The investment in nutrition had some early symbolic qualities as it related to children. The control of thousands of food items via CONASUPO, S.A.M. and milk producing LICONSA went beyond a "bread and circus" formulation of some social policies. However, one must not forget the efforts to create "cultural excitement" as a shunt for minds attached to bellies that are only partly satiated! Yes, we can imagine motives from crudely practical or cynical to sublimely humanitarian for each social policy initiative. Is this a sufficient scenario that we have been presenting of the policy process?

One can imagine and document a more dynamic process by which policies are achieved. Alan Riding (Distant Neighbors, 1985, page 199) has a chapter on "Indians body and soul." The policy issues centering on development and type of integration for native peoples have generated a dynamic set of positions and participants to say the least. Probably policy issues where cultural choices and dependent peoples are involved will generate more complex positions than, let us say, the need for subsidized milk for Mexico's children. Yet the natural history of any social policy area has its dynamics of conflict and synthesis. The dynamics having to do with "socialist" or secular education in the 1930s clearly involved much internal pushing and shoving, and no simple motives prevailed unscathed. Efforts to control the pharmacy business, dominated as it is by transnationals, shows the interaction of many interests, values, and constituencies as the issues slowly work themselves out. The issues of housing and rent control in Mexico City verge on open warfare by the people involved. No simple, reductionistic, functionalistic explanation of how policy arenas operate is intended in this book, although a few motives are seen as being more central than the range of other motives and forces.

We have presented no simple paradigm to represent what the Mexican system is all about. It may well be a "mobilization system" (after David Apter), an authoritarian system (after Susan Purcell), a "tutelary system" (after James Cockcroft), or some kind of modernizing machine, etc. Mexico's regime may be a mere muddling-through, pragmatic bunch of incrementalists (Albeit, a bit heavy handed at times). It might not be helpful to try to decide what the exact nature of Mexico's style is (as Koslow and Mumme have done for the "authoritarian" qualities of the Mexican political system). A more limited goal of describing how the social policy sphere operates is closer to our goal. As a "mature mobilization system" or an immature one, there still will have to be some recognition of what inspires specific policy initiatives. The Echeverria Regime expanded technical education because that is what the overall plan demanded. Even if the Revolution is mystified, the motives of social policy need not be. The problem in any country is that while labor fashioning policies can be talked about up front, it is more difficult to discuss "control" motives or the role of specific social policies to have this more or less latent function. Policy outcomes in Mexico, as elsewhere, are the results of bargaining activities and not merely the results of some groups unajudicated motives having free reign. Nor are we paranoically imputing self serving intentions. The proof of the motive force is in the pudding, not in a princely guide to Machievellean practice. In some ways our discussion could have been of "functions" of "welfare" activities, except for the unfortunate baggage which structural-functional analysis picked up (or was born with!). Mexico has "needs" (or at least the "powers that be" have) to motivate the labor force, and avoid systems changing disruption. The parallels with England of Elizabethan days or modern United States in terms of the Piven-Cloward thesis are sometimes only rough ones. "Relief' systems are not the same, and nearly absent in Mexico in terms of temporary assistance to the poor. Also not paralleling the European-U.S. experience is the more massive labor redundancy in relationship to the productive sectors. Yet there are strong reasons for allowing the Piven-Cloward thesis to be used comparatively. Benefits to the "modernized" labor segment (which can choose to withhold its labor, migrate, strike or radicalize) are "functionally" the same in any capitalist (non-capitalist?) society. The benefits allowed in Mexico through the more-or-less controlled labor organizations, are also work enforcing (as to rules, productive levels, etc.) and, hence, are a parallel phenomenon. As to the prevention of disorder, this has been well observed by many other writers on the Mexican scene (Anderson and Cockcroft, Kenneth Johnson, etc.). Overall the presidential dilemma is one of balancing opposing forces, and most government largesse is involved in this balancing act. Social benefits (as opposed to other benefits) go to the middle and lower orders, some of whom have the potential to "raise hell," if not to shut down the system. If force will not put down such groups as the "party of the poor" (Partido de los pobres) then benefits must be dispersed. The level of turmoil during the Echeverria regime shows the alternative carrot and stick actions producing a "little Vietnam" in parts of the tierra caliente. The goal then was to avoid such outbreaks before they are a complete threat to "stability."

Our discussion of the functions, purposes, or goals of social policy and development is meant to refer to the standard range of circumstances - short of the bottom falling out! Perhaps Mexico is in a permanent state of crisis as participants at a Latin American Studies Association panel in New Mexico suggested in the spring of 1985. Short of suspending its limited democracy, Mexico's choice lies in using its resources to buy loyalties and reinforce the system's fragile monopoly on "legitimacy." Short of a Cuban-style transformation, it must behave in a manner we have documented. A recent set of pool questions published in <u>NEXOS</u> magazine (Summer 1985, page 35) shows majorities favoring PRI by occupation and state (In response to the question: "CON QUE PARTIDO POLITICO SIMPATIZE?" In response to a question* on the legitimacy of the government by occupational category typically over 85% gave average to "bien" or "muy bien" responses, with businessmen and students being the most critical in the aggregate. The 1988 elections reveal a different picture however, and the country will probably follow the Federal district in the next (1994) election. What formula will then prevail for social policy? Probably not too different from what we have described!

*PREGUNTA: usted opina que la funcion del gobierno estatal es?)

The Historical Affordability of Mexico's Social Policy and Development

> Government policies took over where the marketplace left off, fostering further improvements in living standards. From 1940 to 1975, there were continuing efforts to expand the public education system, and improve the quality and volume of medical services available to the population. Although the public schools and universities still function as a mechanism for stratifying people by social class...(they) opened opportunities for many who were able to escape from their 'tracks'... "(Barkin, 1990, <u>Distorted Development</u>, p. 79).

David Barkin notes the destabilizing impact of the "stabilization" policies between 1982 and 1989. He notes (p. 105) how "The poor suffered most in the budget cutting process, which curtailed many social services and eliminated subsidies for many basic foodstuffs." It seems that the ability to fund social policies is not the same as the willingness. There are trade-offs favoring different groups and their interests, although in boom times (1979-1982) all the birds may be fed more equally.

Our counter thesis however, is that the implemented (puchased) social policy is all that the country can afford at that time. If the Piven-Cloward factors of controlling popular unrest or the labor supply enter in, then the country can switch funding priorities. How close does the country's social programs track with total revenues available? Given boom or bust times what cuts or additions are made? Time series data of the kind Wilkie offered in 1970 (<u>The Mexican Revolution: Federal Expenditure and Social Change</u>) and others such as ASPE and Sigmund in 1984, show us the ebb and flow of public-social policy expenditures. Certainly the impact of such mammoth events as the bank borrowing, the oil glut, the prescribed austerity, the international debt, the peso flight, and the various GATT "free trade" policies will impact the funds available for any purpose.

Barkin, using Nacional Financiera, SPP and INEGI data (page 92) notes the changes in the structure of public investment from 1940 to 1988. Agriculture goes down unevenly from 15 to 9%. Industry basically doubles from 21 to 42%. Transport and communication goes down from 52 to 22% because the infrastructure has been partly established. Defense is minuscule throughout the period. We are most interested in "social welfare" which goes from 10% in 1940 and 1950 to 27 to 22% in 1960,'70, 80, and '88. Data after 1988 are being sought, but may not have changed much in total.

This 23% average in the past 30 years may be spent in different ways, and we suspect that the middle class has done well recently. We are interested in motive forces, and Barkin offers (page 93) that international capital thought that "wage levels and living standards of the Mexican workers had risen too fast." Raising productivity by modernizing investments was not considered as an alternative. There are always options, and it seems that making workers hungrier solved certain labor problems (see Michael Harrington's The Next Left for a discussion of these motives north of Mexico's border). Instead of a wage cut for urban workers, Barkin advocates a rise in urban workers real wage (page 130) which "would rapidly benefit every sector of the society." We are including wages in with "welfare" as part of the "social budget." It is all part of a whole piece of cloth, whose unity will only be appreciated when it is pulled off of you - like a blanket on a cold night.

Pessimism is always called upon for such expenditures in basically capital countries. The United Nation's 1970 study on "social change and social development policy in Latin America" noted as follows:

The diagnosis also suggests that, in the face of pressures and resistance's from many directions, national authorities have only a limited or intermittent ability to guide the directions of growth of the social program. and the content of social legislation. (p. 159)

This document also notes the decreased likelihood of income distribution or full employment being implemented. We have tried to be realistic about the motive forces behind social enhancement and development. Only being privy to the decision making process or plotting an elaborate time series of expenditure and revenue data will answer this question of the affordability of any given area. Like Wilkie, we need actual spending as well. The U.N. document in question discusses the gap between social justice and actual implementation (P. 161) as exerting a force toward change. However in the next paragraph they note the "sub conscious element of primitive magic" whereby "figures symbolizing social aspirations" are transformed into reality. In this study we have from the beginning subscribed to the notion that other motives are in play.

Mexico grossly underspends by comparison to other Latin American countries of equal means as in education and on health. Our chapter VI compared Mexico with appropriate peer countries, and it performed from average downward to poor. Social security disbursements are held back in order to create a conservativizing surplus. A general foot-dragging characterizes social expenditures. Expectations are not to run ahead of "reality," and the symbolic implementation will have to carry the day. The United Nations publication (page 160) denies a universal application and, hence, holds back on "qualitative targets and time tables for improvements." We will remain in a quandary without such benchmarks, however. These authors also decry the lack of "accurate statistical information (which is needed) for social development policy."

Another study is always needed if we are dealing with the aggregate impact of social policy expenditures. Focus on the total amounts allocated or the "actual" amounts expended, may miss the action. Some citizens will always get their due. Peter Ward reflects that kind of realism that focuses upon who gets what, and why. In his article on "Political Pressure for Urban Services" (Development and Change, Volume 12, 1981, page 392) the actual pattern of negotiation shows that "affordability" is only an issue in the aggregate. As to service provision:

> Queue jumping was rife, and the largest, most troublesome, communities were most likely to be attended first. It must be appreciated, however, that a broad, well-administered programme of service provision was never the principal aim. Rather, petitioning and service-allocatory behavior can only be understood in the way in which they contributed to the political demands of the period.

Personal audiences and an "open door policy" facilitated two way communication. Both mobilization and de-mobilization of strong, independent movements were possible, given this style of presidential action, which Echeverria and others have used. Affordability would have to be very low for this pattern of entrance into the benefits circle to disappear. The result of being coopted by this kind of process leads to what Eckstein has called "the irony of organization." (Noted by Ward, 1981, page 387) Let us precede here by looking back on the pattern of dispersal by various sexenios. There still were gross, aggregate differences in these historical administrations in terms of social budget allocations. Many of the latter would not have been necessary if the trickle down effect of industrial development had been a reality.

A Review and Partial Updating of Studies of Social Expenditures

With Gini coefficients in the 48 to 53 range, economic and social well-being in Mexico for over half of the population depends on State programs and expenditures. These kinds of transfers to the lower half of the population were negligible until the middle of the 20th century. What do we know about such transfers in historical perspective? How close to the bottom of their purse did they ever go in meeting human needs? Is the rhetoric about the cupboard being bare to be taken seriously? How have available monies been distributed from the totals available? Should we relate social expenditures to the global GDPs or to the total government revenues available? Let us look at some studies of the history of the social budget.

In 1970 James Wilkie (as Howard Cline notes in the introduction to Wilkie's book) separated social from economic development. The effort was to determine the actual amounts expended in various budgets. The gem in this effort was the "poverty Index", and Chapter seven on "social expenditures" is of most value to our task. Tables cover the social expenditure per capita. Outlays for education, public health, welfare, and such amenities as potable water and sewerage are included. Let's look at Wilkie's data on the relative emphasis on social expenditure.

Wilkie notes that Cardenas spent more on economic development than on the "social revolution." (page 156) Yet there was a jump from 9% (1910) to 20-26% during Cardenas regime (1934-40). But only in one year (1938) did Cardenas come close to his goal (19.9%, actual). The social revolution was put on the back burner after 1940 (Wilkie, page 157) and bottomed out in the 1950s. Wilkie's tables go from 1869 to 1963, and he notes that rises in social expenditures came in the 1960-62 period when Lopez Mateos favored "dramatic rises." (page 161) Education did fairly well at various junctures, but Wilkie states that social aid (welfare?) and public health "have never occupied a significant share in budgetary considerations." (page 165). Social security had a generally low budget, concentrating on clinical health services, and has spent little of its accrued reserves.

Pedro Aspe and Paul Sigmund edited a volume on the period after Wilkie's study. Published in 1984 their data mostly covers the 1970s on such social areas as income maintenance, wages, employment, education, health, housing, social security, and food availability. The focus is on household rather than class as a unit. While the economic performance was "very good" from 1940 to 1980 (page 15) the issues of efficiency and justice remain unresolved. The "stabilizing" development model has not, however, changed the income distribution pattern back from 1977 to that of 1950. (page 16) The argument in some public discussions was that economic growth must precede redistribution, but growth did occur without real redistribution. The argument now offered is that redistribution creates inefficiency. The authors themselves argue that greater distributive justice must be an end in itself, and, hence, a pattern of distribution and its effects on "efficiency" is of secondary importance.

The older model that stated that economic growth comes first made claims about affordability, but never specified when it would be optimal, advantageous, or equitable for such redistribution to occur. If the thesis of our present manuscript is correct, then the above equations should be viewed skeptically. Rather, redistribution in any form has other functions for the powers that be. Affordability does not make redistribution automatic, nor it seems, based on Aspe and Sigmund's data, even likely. Wilkie observes that administrators, presidents to be exact, may ignore the budget's condition in distributing the social or economic largesse: "Indeed during the presidencies of Adolfo Ruiz Cortines and Lopez Mateos the difference between projected budgets per capita and actual expenditures was so consistently disparate as to suggest that Mexico's executives had refused to take into account the growth rate of federal expenditure."

Affordability, except at the extremes of affluence and scarcity, may have little to do with the funding of a program or of a target group's needs. The president, or indeed any other "Jefe Maximo" will not maintain their "clout", poder, or "charisma" without this ability to respond to earnest petitions. We are dealing with a formula for the dispersal of public resources, and certain prevailing interests will manifest themselves.

The attempt to counter-vail against these "faulty" theories and practices of growth and redistribution was emphasized by Lazaro Cardenas - at least symbolically. The stress on the redistribution of land, the sharing of economic returns, and the improving of human capital (See page 19 in Aspe and Sigmund) defied the alternative issue of affordability in favor of a social justice-first model. Deficit spending was in order, as the nation borrowed against itself or its future. This borrowing would not necessarily be inefficient or stifling of development. Is the question of "affordability" a total red herring? Probably, but the formula in various semi-progressive regimes after Cardenas was that redistribution would have to be comfortable or "compatible with a reasonable profit." (Page 19) Profits can indeed be made by increasing purchasing power (aggregate demand) of workers, and what has been called "fordism" in the U.S. can work to create growth, social justice and profits. Aspe and Sigmund have a table on the main objectives of presidential-sexenios from 1934 to 1976. Various economic and social goals were stressed, and we could separate the dozen objectives into these two categories. If regimes (or periods of one or two sexenios) are looked at in terms of these two, perhaps antithetical objectives, we find a balanced mix in each period (at least on these crude categorizations). The most social (3 versus 1 for economic) was during the Echeverria sexenio (1970-76), not during the Cardenas or the balancing periods.

In answer to the issue of the affordability of social policy outcomes, it seems that a mixture of national goals have been pursued together, much like the "war on poverty" in the U.S. Perhaps when the times are right, there is an attempt to feed all the birds equally. Our basic approach has been to stress the larger motives for this modicum of redistribution; it is hoped that we do not overestimate the consciousness of this effort. Aspe and Sigmund note that the Ruiz Cortines regime was without (any?) explicit goal in the area of income distribution. (page 21) These early administrations may have been more ad hoc, as well.

Aspe and Sigmund believe that the Echeverria regime sought to subordinate economic goals to social ones in terms of increased employment, redistributed income, and an improved quality of life. (page 24) Deficit financing led to an inflationary spiral and affordability issues, may indeed, have taken over other goals or motives. With the "global" planning of Lopez Portillo, redistribution went forward in the aggregate (via S.A.M. and COPLAMAR) on oil revenues and also on foreign borrowing. Enhanced social policy commitments do often raise affordability issues, but a significant effort can be made with determination for social justice or the achievement of some other agenda. The latter may include the motives to reduce unrest or to preserve a given labor market structure.

We are concerned with more than "welfare" in a restricted sense, but rather with the total social budget, and general shares of the total pie. Our analysis did focus on specific areas of social policy rather than the aggregate character of "income distribution." In the 1930s, 40s and early 50s the redistribution was with "free goods" such as undistributed land, inexpensive public health measures, and moderately expensive "casa del puebloes." Money transfers were much later! Hence there were issues of affordability, and there would be later on, as other priorities overtook the state and the nation. We are not stressing cynical manipulation nor super-conscious goal planning. Mostly it must have been a matter of putting out spot fires, yet there were such advisors as Senior Pani who advised several 20th century regimes on the deliberate craft of running a state. When 10 years of 6% growth or the influx of oil revenues later occurred, then issues of real redistribution were on the agenda.

Let us talk about the issues of affordability in the last decade of austerity. As in Estados Unitos del Norte there seems to be a fiat accompli on the acceptance of the notion that for the functioning of the total economy, there must be personal sacrifices. The basic problem, however, is that the issues of efficiency of the economic machinery seems to have been cast-upon the heads of the bottom half of the class system. Food subsidies for instance, once cut will not be restored given this "crisis" atmosphere. People have a capacity to adjust to adversity with more self-inflicted pain, and they may not understand that their pesos and wages are being watered down. The incremental devaluation of the peso has not completely leveled off as of the spring of 1992. The quality of life is often appraised correctly only from afar, even as the shoe may pinch in the short run.

One observation about sacrifice psychology's, however, is that people often expect a pay back, and may not be so readily coopted or cowed into a particular political or labor market outcome in the future. In these situations of prolonged calls for sacrifice the issues of social budget affordability may become part of the larger dialog and agenda setting as well. Gringos can understand the popular reaction to congressional rubber checks after a decade of austerity and sacrifice. On the other hand the U.S. public stood still in the 1980s for a monstrous reallocation of wealth upward in order to fuel "supply-side economics" (voodoo economics?). Great programmatic cuts are still being made and the remaining ones are seen as the cause of our problems. We have tried to discuss social policy expenditures in the "real" world where there are supposed to be zero-sum resources and actual issues of zero affordability. In the near future, however, there may be a more sophisticated response by the recipients to the "gifts" offered as social redistribution. At the extremes the issues of affordability are central to the understanding of welfare and the larger social budget. In between other scenarios can be noted. To wit:

"Relief, Labor and Civil Disorder in Mexico"

A new statecraft relative to destitution was emerging... (Piven and Cloward, quoting the Webbs, page 12, 1971)

Our major mentors in trying to understand the ebb and flow of relief note the English radical writers, the Webbs, on the impact of capitalism in western Europe. Sheer repression did not solve the problems for the emerging capitalist system, and as in Mexico, a revolution was a possible outcome of approaches like those under Diaz. Piven and Cloward nicely trace the "policy" of controlling the labor supply and alternatively civil disobedience by the manipulation of relief at a variety of historical points in Europe and the U.S. of A.

Perhaps a detailed time series for Mexico from 1920 to 1990 in terms of social expenditures and evidence of unrest is needed. Definitions of the latter probably could be operationalized with documentation of strikes, movements and repressive actions. The whole period of unbridled capitalist expansion after 1880, and especially the period of Import Substitution Development could be plotted against other indicators. Perhaps "real" wages offered could be seen as indicating the impact of various policies upon the labor force. There have been reasonable approximations of what immiserization involves, but willingness to work for others for wages is to be traced in zones short of complete destitution. How can these intervening stages be described?

Robert Kaufman has written on the economic development of Latin American countries against the rise of "bureaucratic-authoritarianism." Noting O'Donnell's ideas about the rise of these repressive forces, Kaufman cites four stages of economy, class relations and state structure, and related policy. (page 197, Reyna & Weinert, Authoritarianism in Mexico, 1977) Corresponding to the full development of I.S. Development (ISI), the state takes on "New Welfare Functions" in the second stage. The latter is after the "open" economy, and before the exhaustion of the "Early phase" of ISI. Some regimes, as in the southern cone used the military to "tame labor and close down elections." (page 203 in Reyna & Weinert) The strongest source of validation for our basic approach in this book, is that if the "welfare" system does not perform these functions, then repression will be the tune for the day! Kaufman believes that Mexico's problems, after the "early phase" of ISI "did not reach the crisis proportions characteristic of the southern countries." (page 207) Still there was considerable unrest in Mexico in the 1951-1970 period. Kaufman, using I.L.O. statistics, sees a build up of labor strikes from 1951 to

1958, and then they "level off sharply" in the late 1960s. We can use other indicators of unrest or of capital's need for labor control. Kaufman's comparison of the southern Latin American states with Mexico leads him to see Mexico as having more "strength and flexibility." Even appearing muddled and indecisive, the Mexican state (although they have used extreme brutality) may more typically use the carrot than the stick.

The strongest responses by workers and government were after the "early phases" of I.S.I. and led to repression against a variety of workers and other groups. Workers may not present the only threat to the system, but the thesis may hold. The 1968 blood bath at Tlateloco, where many hundreds of students and sympathizers were killed does not detract from the Piven-Cloward model, nor particularly add to it. The student motivations do reflect the tension in the system, and do reveal the governments intent vis "unrest." As noted elsewhere, the Mexican government does consider using both the carrot and the stick. To use a playing card analogy, "clubs are trump." As students, railroad workers, teachers and others have found out. The regime clearly sees that its inability to control students, would embolden other groups.

Our purposes have been to get a grasp on the role of "relief" and the broader "social budget" in the manipulation of labor and expressions of unrest. We know that there are other motives for the distribution of society's cornucopia. It would be very hard to believe that the powers that be, however, will ignore a chance to control the worker's motivations to produce or to throw sand into the machinery.

CHAPTER X

SOURCES OF SOCIAL STATISTICS: EXAMPLES AND AN EVALUATION

> Statistics in Mexico are unreliable, but the mishandling of the 1980 census was unprecedented: Beyond general population figures, no results had been published by 1984, forcing different departments to develop their own parallel social indicators. (Distant Neighbors, Alan Riding, 1985, page 224.)

Many writers assume that there is little solid data about Mexico in general. The economist John E. Koehler in his article "Economic policy making with little information and few instruments...." notes that an outcome of this lack of data can lead to uncertainty and "side effects" for countries like Mexico. Luis Salas and Raymond Surette writing in Volume 23 of the Statistical Abstract of America (Wilkie and Perkal, 1984, page 792) show hopes that the lack of adequate statistics will in fact stimulate their development:

> Although prospects for research on crime data are bleak for the foreseeable future and there are at present few crime data to report on or to analyze, this realization has stimulated Latin American social researchers to give increased attention to criminology within the last few years. Victimization surveys, self-report studies, and analyses of official statistics will substantially increase our knowledge of the criminological situation in the region.

Noting a "reality that is hidden from us," these authors still have hopes in the area. Crime statistics may be more bleak, than say, data on participation in higher education or other specific social services offered (as the number of free text books, etc.).

So, Mexico is not a terra incognito or a dark land - as data in the S.A.L.A. volumes sometimes indicate. Nationwide data are published and made readily available by such agencies as the Instituto Nacional de Estadistica Geografia Informatica and the related Programacion Y Presupuesto (SPP). Additional examples of governmental sources include the materials put out by the various ministries of social security (IMSS), education (Secretaria de Education Publica), agriculture, and so forth. Typical of the indigenous studies based on such available data are the two volumes <u>Mexico Ante La Crisis</u> (1985) coordinated by Pablo Gonzalez Casanova and Hector Aguilar Camin (based on work done by the Instituto de Investigaciones Sociales de la UNAM). The latter collections on wide ranging aspects of society, economy, ecology, and culture follow the previous collections <u>Mexico, Hoy</u> and the 3 volume compendium <u>El Perfil de Mexico en 1980</u>. These volumes cited many data points from the Censo de Poblacion, 1970 under the Direccion General de Estadistica. The Banco Nacional de Comercio Exterior was also a valuable source. There are excellent private sector sources (primary as well as secondary) such as the major universities like UNAM and El Colegio de Mexico with their various institutes. Many of the state universities and the newer metropolitan schools (like Universidad Autonoma Metropolitana-Xochimilco) put out surprising materials.

Some of the additional solid sources include Banco de Mexico, which publishes <u>Informes Anuales</u> amongst a wide range of other materials. S.P.P. noted above, publishes such valuable materials as <u>Manual de Estadisticas Basicas Sociodemographicas: Sector Salud Y Seguridad Social</u>. The Depatmento de Estadistica Y Actuary of I.S.S.S.T.E. has materials relevant to their programs that can be obtained. S.P.P. also gathers data, that might be hard to obtain on your own, from other agencies such as PEMEX, F.F.C.C., S.D.N., and SRIA.MARINA on their health and pension activities. The national president's office can be an excellent source as can the D.D.F., the Federal District. The following secretarias probably would have the most to offer on social policy and development.

- Secretaria de Education Publica, whose function is to implement article 123 of the Federal constitution with respect to schools and libraries

- Secretaria de Programacion Y Presupuesto, whose functions include planning and information gathering in economic and social sectors

- Secretaria de Salubridad Y asistencia, who originates health and public assistance programs, enforces the sanitary code, and regulates service institutions

- Secretaria del Trabajo Y Prevision Social, which looks after worker's health and well-being

The sources mentioned in the above paragraph are very adequately used by Mexico's major universities and research centers. Equally prestigeful to the National Autonomous University of Mexico (UNAM) is the constant flow from El Colegio de Mexico. The latter source includes such useful journals as <u>Demografia Y Economia</u> and such more general offerings as are found in <u>Historia Mexicana</u> - the latter containing excellent articles on such matters as minimum salaries over the decades, and so on. There has been a steady flow of social development studies from El Colegio even before they moved to their new buildings in Mexico City in 1976. This fine graduate school has maintained its "relevance" to Mexican society by its constant production and utilization of social data and analysis. Vivane de Marquez' <u>Dinamica de la Empresa Mexicana</u> and the volume put out by the Centro de Estudios y Demograficos of El Colegio, <u>Dinamica de la Poblacion de Mexico,</u> are two examples of the excellent work done here. The latter volume has an appendix on "Conceptos Utilizados en Los Censos de Poblacion de Mexico, 1895-1970" and it is probably the single most important article that we could recommend on this topic. (See Primera Edicion, 1970, page 255.)

Currently, there is much apparent cooperation in the production of statistical data, and the various secretariats and national banks will often work with the research institutes in the major universities. This author is also conscious of possible elements of competition, both ideological and professional between the latter. But, joint efforts at data production and analysis are quite apparent, what ever affinities are involved in individual cases. One writer who suspects strong ideological competition and power conflict is Dr. Perissonotto who observes that:

The creation of a new and huge university in Mexico City, whose functionaries come for the most part from the government, has given rise to the common belief that it is being founded to divide - geographically as well as ideologically - the highly flammable Mexican student body that has erupted violently and regularly since the Massacre of Tlateloco in 1968. (Page 226.)

Apart from these general sources and their users, each area of social development has its own sources and users. Let us examine them individually, starting with sources and studies on the distribution of Income.

Data On Income Distribution

Enrique Hernandez and Jorge Cordoba writing in 1982 (La Distribucion del Ingreso en Mexico) note the "Antecedentes sobre la distribucion del ingreso en Mexico." Research covering various time periods is cited before preceding on their own analysis. Thus, Noyola y Lopez Rozado analyzed salaries in the 1939-1955 period. Ifigenia Martinez de Navarrete noted the increased concentration of income in the 1950-1956 period. Lorenz curves and Gini coefficients were used to confirm this thesis. Studies by Jose de Jesus Prieto, Morris Singer, Jose Pescador and William R. Cline, Clark Reynolds and Richard Weisskoff seem to have the same conclusions for the 1950 to 1964 period. De Navarrete's materials and some from the Bank of Mexico are used by the latter analysts. In moving the data forward into the 1970s Hernandez and Cordoba utilize materials gathered by the Bank of Mexico, the Secretaria de Industria y Comercio (SIC), Centro nacional de Informacion y Estadisticas del Trabajo (CENIET) and Coordination General del Sistema Nacional de Information (SPP). Their (Hernandez and Cordoba) brief 26 item bibliography is partly included in our own, and the reader should note that although some of the materials are readily available, others are mimeographed, in-house, uncirculated kinds of documents.

Most data on income distribution seemingly came into being after 1950, and Wouter Van Ginneken claims that not much was available between 1940 and 1950 (page 16). After that point, the 1950 census, Banco de Mexico (1963-68), the National Labor Information and Statistics Center (1975) all provided data on income distribution. There were also family surveys by the "statistics office" in 1958 and 1969, according to Van Ginneken. The present author is aware of a Bank of Mexico study (La Distribucion del Ingreso en Mexico, done in 1968, but published in 1974 by Fondo de Cultura Economica) that has generated such family oriented materials. Using methods and assumptions developed by Ms. de Navarrete, the attempt is to get comparable data because of the problems of under-estimation in family surveys (mostly in upper income groups). Incidentally, Van Ginneken, who works for the I.L.O., sees Mexico as having one of the most unequal income distributions in the world along with Brazil, Columbia and Venezuela. The main table this author has on income distribution by deciles is strangely, mostly drawn from a U.S. centered source, the IBRD (The Economy of Mexico, Washington, 1973). Van Ginneken does note that Mexico (page 19) is one country where income distribution data is available for over 25 years running. As to the relationship between economic development and income distribution, Van Ginneken (citing an I.L.O. publication "Income distribution during the process of development," 1977) notes that the top 5% of income units hits the maximum at a GNP level of $200 per capita, but the lower 20% of income units declines until a GNP of $500 per capita is obtained. The trickling down process, so called, takes a long time to achieve! This latter paper by the I.L.O. is mimeographed and "restricted," which illustrates another problem in obtaining adequate data.

Another outside source on Mexico's income distribution is the E.C.L.A. Carlos Filgueira and Carlo Genelitti did a study of "Estraticacion y Movilidad occupacional en Latin America in 1981." (ECLA-CC, E/Cepal/G, 1122, Oct., 1981, page 53.) These analysts, using unanchored data, placed Mexico's proportion of middle and upper classes at about 1/4th of the total population. (Cited in SALA, volume 23, table 1316, page 273.) James Wilkie and Paul Wilkin's articles on class structure (see SALA, volumes 21 and 23) of Mexico see about (estimated) 43% middle and upper class participation in 1980 and 50% in 1990! These figures seem very optimistic, and their 1970 figure of 35% is 10% higher than the previously cited ECLA study for the similar time period. Perhaps, different definitions of middle and upper classes are used in the two studies. Wilkie et al., used a model developed by Iturriaga and Cline to establish their baseline for the later projections, and evidently use data from the Mexican census. (DGE: Direccion General de Estadistica.) Wilkie and Wilkins also note earlier studies by Lewis, Cline, Erasmus, and Gonzalez Cosio who also used the census data and/or interviews and questionnaires as their data sources. Also Joseph Kahl is noted as a source based on a sample survey of Mexico City and some small towns in Hidalgo state (SALA, volume 21, chapter 36, page 588). In any case, the state of the art on income distribution (as class membership) is well represented in this discussion by Wilkie and Wilkins. These authors observe how changes in the occupational structure and in self-identification play a role in evaluating income statistics as well.

For many the real issue involved in income distribution is the amount absolutely and relatively received by groups at the bottom and at the top. Another ECLA-cc study (Cuadernos de la CEPAL) by Oscar Altimir (La Dimension de la Pobreza en America Latina, #27, Santiago, 1979) measures the percent of those below the poverty line in

Mexico at 34% (vs. 40% for all of Latin America), and 12% below the extreme poverty line (vs. 19% for all of Latin America). The latter comparison may not be all that useful. On the other end of the social-structural dimension, the existing data do show a wide gap; how wide we do not know because of sampling problems and the secretiveness about income at those levels. Next, the health area.

Sources on Health in Mexico

> Evitar el analysis con base en la mera adicion de supuestos y prescindir del traslado mecanico de categorias de analysis es una primera tarea, en este caso imperfecta, ante una reqlidad que hay que problematizar.

The above quote from Ignacio Almada Bay's article "La Crisis Y la Salud" is from the 1985 collection by Gonzalez Casanova and Hector Camin entitled Mexico Ante La Crisis. This globally oriented article draws its materials from a variety of sources in order to make a critical portrait of Mexico's health situation. The first table it offers compares 10 Latin American countries where the extremes are between Guatemala and Cuba on Mortality and Morbidity data and Mexico is much closer to the negative end. Cuba has achieved statistics from two to ten times better than those of Mexico. Bay uses data from IMSS, Coplamar, the U.N. and even U.S. government as well as various academic sources. Materials are creatively drawn from such appropriate sources as the American Journal of Public Health ("Bottled beverages and typhoid fever The Mexican epidemic of 1972-73," August 1982). The Milbank demographic journal is another such source, showing activities from outside of Mexico. UNICEF, the World Bank (Office memorandum, Mexico: Public Health Sector Investment Review), and the Panamanian Sanitation Bulletin are three other external sources. (If you can find them!) Probably this type of critical article would have to draw on scattered external sources. This did not seem to be as necessary in the previous instance of income distribution, what ever the value of those statistics.

A more "upbeat" kind of portrait of Mexico's medical achievements can be drawn by using Mexican government-agency sources. The Anuario Mexicano, 1982, for instance, has a 24 page article summarizing Mexico's medical services and general health statistics. S.P.P., IMSS, ISSSTE, PEMEX, and the Secretary of the Navy are primary sources whose materials have been pulled together by S.P.P. The data is presented against general, demographic statistics and they show a steady improvement, rather than a prelude to a "crisis."

Mortality rates, for instance, show an almost predictable improvement. If one can accept the depiction of "Avitaminosis Y Otras Deficiencias Nutricionales" as the eighth highest cause of child mortality at only 30 per 100,000, then you are probably a fit prospect for buying the Brooklyn Bridge! "Enteritis Y otras enfermedades diarreicas" are listed as the second highest cause of death in the general population and for infants, but the malnutrition connection (VIA changed agricultural practices) seemingly is being played down. The Bank of Mexico is used for financial information on money spent on health care between 1965 and 1976, and this shows a sharp (29%) drop in resources from 1977 to 1978. The amount of money spent upon "marginal" people is noted in this summary (page 154). Two very different pictures of the Mexican health situation emerge from the several summaries we have just looked at. The Anuario Mexicano, 1982 has 17 full page advertisements of which 14 are government sponsored for various agencies, and the other 3 are for newspapers. The big sell is on! So what sources should we stress?

It is conceivable to write an undergraduate paper based on materials given in the U.N.'s Statistical Yearbook or on the materials compiled by the Pan American Union (as "Health Conditions in the Americas," 1969-72). And, the Depatmento de Contabilidads of IMSS or ISSSTE will tell you how much money is being spent on how many clients, but the matter of well-being is as problematic in Mexico as elsewhere, apart from a few crude indicators.

Data on Education in Mexico

Besides the Secretary of Public Education, there are numerous studies of the involvement in education by other agencies. Banco Nacional de Mexico puts out analyses of the participation in various educational programs. The Association Nacional de Universidades e Institutos de Ensenanza Superior is another source of information about public higher education. We noted two U.S. studies over the decades on education in Mexico by Marjorie Johnston and Clark Gill, and they rely for their statistics on the above sources, especially the Secretary's Informe and its "La Educacion Publica en Mexico."

As to relevant data from Banco Nacional de Mexico, Clark Gill in 1969 says "The U.S. office education passes no judgment on figures quoted from that publication in this or subsequent citations" (see page 2). The Secretaria de Educacion Publica's "Obra Educatica en el Sexenio, 1958-1964" is also heavily utilized. The person interested in the analysis of basic statistics probably is advised to look at studies produced by such groups as the Escuela Nacional de Economia (ENE) of

UNAM and SEP which has published Estadisticas Basicas del Sistema Educativo National, Mexico (1974). Certainly work done by Victor Urquidi at El Colegio de Mexico on education should be part of anyone's analysis.

For general information on education in Mexico we could turn to UNESCO and the Economic Commission for Latin America as the Statistical Abstract of Latin America has (volume 23, 1984, page 1985). Much of the latter information probably originated with the Secretaria de Educacion Publica in Mexico so that one might as well start with them. Maria de Ibarrola at UNAM's Instituto de Investigaciones Sociales put out a 700 plus item bibliographical guide in 1970 which included many of the publications of SEP. (La Ensenanza Media En Mexico, 1900-1968.) This latter source notes dozens of statistical sources including published volumes, theses, and periodicals. Items 74 (page 19) through 97 are specifically statistical sources for this time period. Some are in-house materials, and exist "mimeografiado." The perils of statistic gathering are probably known to the reader of this chapter. A recent compendium of statistical materials on education (as well as food, incomes, health, social security, and housing) is S.P.P.'s 10 Anos de Indicadores Economicos y Sociales de Mexico (April, 1985). Definitions of their concepts and methods of getting data are an important addition from the latter volume. The sources used for the 30 odd tables here are mostly S.E.P., the general census, and a few Presidential releases. Other than the "body count" and the Peso expenditure, additional data on the quality of education may be difficult to obtain. There are many sources on the programmatic context of education at all levels, for example La Humanidades en Mexico 1950-1975 published by UNAM in 1978.

Social Security Information

When Carmelo Mesa-Lago made his critical analysis of social security inequalities in Mexico he used the Demographic Yearbook of the U.N., the 1970 Mexican census and a series of specialized sources dealing with social security. The latter included ISSSTE's Anuario Estadistico, the secretary of defense's special reports on pensions, the Ferrocarrilos Nacionales de Mexico personnel reports, and a report on Pemex's pensions by Recardo Orozco Ferrera ("Seguridad Social de Petroleos Mexicanos"). From the 1970 census he focused on labor force and occupational group data. He contrasted these aggregate numbers with what IMSS offered in Memoria de Labores and ISSSTE in Datos Estadisticos and its Anuario Estadistico. Some compelling contrasts were noted in this way and this led to an assessment of the short fall between the total of economically active and number covered by social security. Other sources cited included Tendeeencias from ISSSTE; the U.N.'s Yearbook of National Account Statistics; ISSSTE's "Seis Anos de Proyession Nacional;" and social security revenues and expenditures from the I.L.O. It would seem that many sources exist for this latter topic, but Mesa-Lago suggests that personal interviews were also necessary, especially for the sectors like the Armed Forces who did not seem willing to report as systematically, perhaps, as other sectors.

In dealing with any matter so close to the economic system one must remember the reports of Banco de Mexico, as Informes Anuales or Banco Nacional de Mexico's Examen de la Situacion de Mexico. There are also the monthly reports of the Comision National de Valores which all help to note the financial background against which social security transfers are made. The Banco de Mexico's "Bibliografia Economica de Mexico" has numerous citations on "Seguridad Social," "Salarios," "Vivienda" or housing and so on. The latter are found in our bibliography hopefully under their appropriate headings.

In a more recent volume edited by Carmelo Meso-Lago (The Crisis of Social Security and Health Care: Latin American Experiences and Lessons, 1985) Peter Thullen utilizes IMSS data. In the same volume William McGreevey makes a telling comparison of the estimated number of people actually covered by social security in 11 Latin American countries. His source is a special Consultant report to the World Bank (PHND, 1983) and the lowness of the total percent covered (9%) is startling. Again, it is surprising when such key figures exist mostly in nearly private, sponsored research.

Sources of Information on Nutrition

May and McLellan, who wrote about the Ecology of Malnutrition in Mexico, used many small scale studies to get their big picture. U.S. and U.N. reports were also heavily relied upon, as for instance their data on population, land distribution, area covered in food crops, areas covered in cash crops, and livestock and fish production were all from the U.S. Departments of Commerce or the Interior. Data on consumption of foods or of nutrients is from international (Rockefeller) and in some cases Mexican sources. This would all seem to present some special problems concerning overall views, although many small scale Mexican studies provide other essential data.

Ana Maria Flores' 1973 study La Magnitude del Hambre en Mexidco cites F.A.O. work on hunger in Mexico and goes on to show her appreciation for assistance from the Organization of American States. Internally Flores seems appreciative of materials gathered by the Secretaria de Industria and Comerico as well as the general census. Some hospital-clinical sources are also noted.

The Banco de Mexico's bibliography lists many surveys of food usage and additionally cites the Secretaries of Agriculture and of "Hidraulicos" as additional sources concerning the sheer availability of food. Its efficient distribution and utilization are other matters.

We ended our chapter on nutrition with a listing of sources that were mostly clinical, institutional or foundation surveys. International agencies were involved, and much summarizing of food availability has been done by the U.N. (F.A.O.) and the U.S. (Departments of Agriculture and Commerce, etc.). Internally, Mexican analysis of actual consumption has been carried out in order to support such programs as the late S.A.M. and current CONASUPO. Special efforts have been aimed at the nutrition of children both by institutions and general nutrition programs. S.P.P.'s 10 Anos de Indicadores... in pointing out what foods are consumed used the following sources: CONAPO (Estimaciones de CONAPO), CONASUPO, the SAHR subscretary de Ganaderia, and the Departmento de Pesca (for sea foods). What seems to be lacking is data on distribution, on the consequences of the existing distribution, on what changes would make for greater food sufficiency, what the effects of food for export are, and on the impact of existing patterns of waste and supposed "maldistribution."

Employment Information

The Banco de Mexico, S.A., puts out an extensive bibliography on economic and social studies, including employment data. The executive branch in the 1970s under Echeverria put out The Mexican Newsletter, a now discontinued source (Mexico Today is now available, but is not as informative in this area) listed sources of information about jobs. An Employment Study Group had been set up by Echeverria in the early 1970s. Obviously the Ministry of Labor and Public Welfare is a likely source as are some of the more independent unions. One suspects possible differences in data or in interpretation between the latter types of sources, and getting one's data from the International Labor Organization may or may not improve their accuracy. Besides the above sources, the Secretaria de Hacienda y Credito Publico catalogs rural employment. In any case, much data exists; and between the Mexican census, the special reports of the ministries, and international compilations, sophisticated studies can be made.

Volume 23 of SALA largely uses ILO and ECLA data on

employment. The latter source has minimal information on unemployment in Mexico, with 2 of its 3 tables not showing the country (tables 1313 and 1314). Table 1315 (SALA) having to do with "Urban open unemployment 1970-1982" shows Mexico as improving from 7% unemployed in 1970 to 3.7% in 1982 (which is better than the Latin American average of 7.4 in 1982). Personal observation and such books as <u>Los mil y Un oficios de los desocupados de la ciudad</u> by Alvaro Garmendia (Editores Mexicanos Unidos, 1982) bring into question the later statistic. Alan Riding in his recent book <u>Distant Neighbors</u> cites an open unemployment rate of 12% (rural and urban we assume) and "another 40 percent of the work force (falling) outside the formal economy into the vague category of 'underemployed'" (1984, page 221). If one were to add up all of the "workers" in such "job" categories as garbage sorters, rag and bottle pickers, vendors, bicycle deliverers, car washers and watchers, newspaper hawkers, portable repair operators, prostitutes, street musicians and actors, balloon sellers, and the involuntarily retired, then one might have a very different picture than the official estimates project.

Sources on Urbanization and Housing

> In 1950, Latin America was 70% rural and 30% urban. Today, those figures are reversed. That's the real revolution which needs the attention of U.S. policy makers. (Andrew J. Glass, "Latin America's importance to U.S. has little to do with Soviets", Cox News Service).

As noted in our chapter on Mexico's urban development, the concerns by researchers have been upon the "primacy effects" of more than 20% of the total population being in Mexico City; the crushing effects of immigration; the lack of public interest planning; and the consequent chaotic development of urban areas as shown in a multitude of social problems. In dealing with these concerns the Mexican census has been utilized in Ph.D. theses by such researchers as Claudio Stern, Fernando Greene, and Arlene Rengert in the late 1970s. Most of the latter research utilizes data up to 1970, and each study also contributes original data Stem's thesis on <u>The Growth of Mexico City: Varying Sources of its Migrant Inflow, 1900-1970</u> (1977) involved the collection via "a census-like questionnaire" which was given to 25o0 households and 13,000 individuals and generated much new data (page 248). Rengert's thesis on <u>The Process of Cityward Migration for Women and Men in Mexico</u> (1978) used personal interviews (number = 1912) in completing her analysis. Fernando Greene used census data plus special distillations of national data by Luis Unikel (El Colegio de Mexico, 1975) in order to arrive at comparative measures of the socioeconomic conditions in various parts of Mexico's cities and states (Analysis of Major Mexican Urban Centers, 1960 1970). Unikel's "Centro de Estudios Economicos y Demograficos" continues to digest and create worthwhile urban data

S,P.P.'s 10 Anos de Indicadores... summarizes data from the 9th and 10th Censos Generales de Poblacion y Vivienda and from Primer Informe de Gobierno, 1983. SALA in volume 23 has a few tables on housing and amenities, some of which are derived from the Pan American Health Organization (and other tables lead you in a circle, trying to figure out their origins - see pages 181-182). Despite some disappointments from the super-sources, one occasionally scores from unexpected sources. The April, 1984 issue of Revista A from the Division de Ciencias Sociales y Humanidades de Azcapokalco has an article by Rosemond Cheetham on "Estado del Conocimiento Sobre el Fenomeno Metropolitano." The whole issue of this bi-monthly journal is focused on "La Ciudad de Mexico." Ms. Cheetham's article involves an historical survey of urban studies as well as a current assessment of current sources of information. She even offers an overall description of the theoretical perspectives available. Studies on all of the major Mexican cities are noted, not just of Mexico City. The alphabet soup of agencies who are involved in urban social needs, including housing, are noted and evaluated. The latter include INFONAVIT, SAHOP SEDUE, IMSS-Coplamar, and CONASUPO. There are, of course, other recent reviews of urban studies in Mexico, such as Claude Bataillion's 1983 article in Estudios Sociologicos entitled "Dos decadas de Investigacion Urbana en Mexico: Un analisis critico y perspectivas" (Volume 1, No. 1). No real shortage of studies exist, but one wonders if one can get a grip on the real urban situation in Mexico's growing urban centers and regions. The 1985 horrendous earthquake and subsequent government action (and inaction!) may have opened a window into the study of urban
processes. See Ward and Gilbert for a discussion of the latter and housing in general.

Data on Crime and Criminal Justice in Mexico

We observed above in this chapter the shortage of data on crime, delinquency, and the functioning of the criminal justice system. Wilkie and Perkal are hopeful, as we noted, that the absence of data will somehow be a stimulant for its achievement. Data on homicides and on bank robberies probably is fairly accurate, as any where else. Given all of the criticisms of data on crime, etc., in the United States to the north, we would expect that "property crimes" would be understated and various forces (the need to report them in order to collect insurance, etc.), would effect their reporting one way or another. "Crimes against people" probably have an historical tendency toward fuller reporting, and may appear to be increasing - contrary to reality. "White collar," "Corporative crime" and "political crime" may be going from low reporting to some middling level, and much depends upon the societal emphasis. We expect that the presidential leadership in the direction of "moral renovation" may have its effects here.

Luis de La Barrera Solorzano in his article "La Crisis y la Criminalidad" (in Casanova and Camin, 1985, page 119) presents statistics from the Federal District which he got from the Direccion General de Averiguaciones Previas de la Procuraduria General de Justica del Distrito Federal. The increased number of robberies is seen as indicating the "crisis." Indeed, if the figures are correct and generalizable, then the economic crisis in the early 1980s is resulting in a great increase in crime. In our chapter on crime we discussed it as a form of unrest and facilitated like any other social action; but the desparate economic nature of much of the increase in crime can lead to that kind of an interpretation. A couple of Mexican sources that should be included in any in-depth research include the Revista Mexicana de Derecho Penal and the proceedings of the recently formed National Congress on Criminology. Much of our concern for crime in this volume would focus upon public concern and how this might generate one or another kind of social policy. Public concern may be more affected by the mass media, than by actual exposure to increased levels of "delitos." The middle class public may be more worried about the policy than the potential robber or burglar. News accounts, popular television, and even the blood and mayhem from the pages of their detective-type magazine Alarma could be analyzed to understand public concern.

A Brief Note on Bibliographical and Archival Holdings on Mexico

Aside from personal observations, newspaper clippings, and occasional colleague debriefing, a volume like this present survey is reliant upon libraries, bookstores, government offices, and other people's collections and analyses. The author's previous publications and papers have largely been based upon questionnaires, content analyses, and the like, and only recently with a joint effort on the political culture of his own state has he turned to the kind of materials used in this study. We have relied here instead, upon histories, institutional studies, and available social statistics. Let us concern ourselves with the bibliographic experiences that led to this volume, and those additional resources that are available to scholars.

Mexico as we have noted is not terra-incognito, or a dark land. As we have noted in the context of this volume, the Mexicans are more than capable of analyzing their own society and the various institutes connected with UNAM, El Colegio de Mexico; and the several governmental ministries will doubtlessly present the last words on these several topics. But, there is a role for a non-Mexican, with comparative interests in social development and social policy. To try to synthesize, Mexico is rife with common problems of social development and social policy, and in the cooperative spirit of the various International Congresses of Mexican History, the social scientists of the two countries do share their efforts. Let us now review what these past efforts have been, and how the serious scholar and social activist can utilize them.

First, as to libraries and archives in the U.S., most of these holdings are spread across our southern states. From California State in San Francisco, to Los Angeles Public Library, to San Diego State, to Texas Western in El Paso, to the incredible holdings at the University of Texas at Austin, to the Degolyer Foundation in Dallas, there is a great library richness on Mexico. Many of the holdings are overlapping one might expect, but there are specialization's in collections of drama, Codices, and literature. These collections do not merely arise from regional interests, but like the Caribbean orientation of the Latin American collection at Tulane University, regionalism has much to do with their shaping. One would expect collections about the nature of the U.S.-Mexican border in El Paso, and so on. What also shapes these libraries are dedicated staff people, and although the present author has never met Nettie Lee Benson who developed the Latin American collection at Austin, her efforts meet one at many intersections.   Let us spend a minute on the University of Texas, Austin and its collection on Mexico.

What has recently been relabeled the "Benson Latin American Collection" was noted in 1978 as having 335,000 volumes and a yearly budget of $28,000. Based on the author's utilization of this library on several occasions, it is estimated that about 40,000 volumes are oriented toward Mexico. More important is the research oriented quality of the materials in the stacks, despite their somewhat confusing placement. This is not a collection of readily available paperbacks or of coffee table splashes of color. There are government records, public and private agency releases, and International compendiums - including those of the Pan American Union, the U.N., and the O.A.S. As of April of 1985, they listed holdings of dozens of Mexican newspapers on a regular basis, including El Dia, Excelsior, El Nacional, El Norte, and El Zocalo. The current director, Ann Graham (1985), has compiled, with the help of others, some fine reference sheets that quickly reveal the strengths and limitations of the total collection. Let us look at some other serious collections in the U.S. as these are revealed in general resources and the authors personal experience.

Bowker's Subject Collections for 1978 also stresses library holdings along our southern and western flanks. University of Arizona, Las Cruces, California State at Fresno, Los Angeles Public Library, Fort Worth Public Library, El Paso Public Library, University of California at Fullerton, San Diego's Occidental College, Standford, Roswell Public Library, Southern Methodist, and Rice are examples of the latter. Also, there are good holdings at Carbondale (in literature); Pennsylvania State (general); Yale (historical); Columbia (historical); New York Public Library (general); Indiana (historical); Temple (on industries); and the University of Wisconsin (general).

Not listed in Subject Collections are most of the Big Ten schools whose giant libraries must have considerable holdings on Mexico. If the University of Minnesota is a guide to these latter holdings, these caches are indeed substantial, but depend for their research strengths upon key personnel. Minnesota has many of the conventional works but lacks a focused research collection. Maintaining subject matter personnel seems to be the critical variable. Only a few of the Mexican government productions (as Mexico, 1973) put out by the Foreign Exchange Bank are available, and one looks in vain for systematic collections to provide for solid research as Austin's library does. Many contemporary journals on Latin America are to be found in the Big Ten libraries, and Austin has over 100. Usually missing in the typical Big Ten library are systematic materials from the Pan American Union or the O.A.S. Much work remains to be done by dedicated individuals in order to build these holdings outside of the few centers of note.

The Libraries of Mexico

The author is familiar only with the UNAM library, the old Hemeroteca Nacional, and has missed the new library of El Coligio de Mexico. UNAM's library has been hit by budget cuts in the past decades, and one suspects political motivations beyond those of austerity. Yet the UNAM card catalogue is extensive and is reasonably solid. There were considerable holdings under "Social Conditions" although "Serguridad Social" was only minimally represented.

Much more current and thorough treatments of the latter topic are books offered by street vendors by the IMSS local offices in Mexico City. The latter book vendors have always hawked the social policy legislation in little paperbacks - whose paper is rough, but clearly imprinted. The libraries of El Cologio de Mexico constitute a graduate school concentration the author is authoritatively told, with more materials on foreign relations, diplomacy, and the formal political process. Studies of social conditions are only a minor part of this collection, and social reactions to the social policies are not their forte. Indeed, the newspapers found in the new Hemerotica may provide the best source of this reaction; as full page ads by various groups proclaim their legitimate right to various benefits, etc. Generally, Mexico's library budgets at the graduate or research level are meager, and there is much reliance upon benefactors - as is true in the U.S. Just how much exchange of materials goes on is not known by the author, but libraries certainly do have different kinds of holdings. One suspects that the librarian's taxonomy of the world of sources determines all too much of what is drawn together. A complete list of Mexico's libraries is to be found in the Encyclopedia of Mexico.

Other Mexican Sources: Bookstores

If one is a late riser, then Mexico's bookstores along Cinco Mayo, Insurjentes Sur, Reforma and Juarez will be moving into high gear to greet them after 1 p.m. Some of these bookstores allow you to inspect and fondle the books and in others they must be called down from the shelf via the clerks. There are used bookstores on Cinco Mayo; radical bookstores on Juarez and Reforma and good, small stores on Insurjentes Sur near the University City. The 1985 earthquake led to some relocation toward UNAM. These collections are current, in-depth, and recently cheap in devaluated pesos! And, one should buy a book now before its limited edition is run out! In the latter instance, one would need to visit the stores often or rely on book traders from Southern California for a used copy. These Mexico City bookstores are excellent in literature, economics, public affairs and the arts, but many topics seem to be ignored. Paperbacks outnumber hard covers, but one suspects that the intelligentsia is more interested in reading the volumes than in displaying them in leather bound copies. Some of the best work in our area of concern is published by Siglo Vientiuno, Editores, Sa, as well as by the various institutes connected with UNAM. Volumes on Mexico City are now collected in the Portals de la Ciudad de Mexico on Avenue L. Cardenas.

If one wants to see a fun display of UNAM S volumes (not journals), they can be seen but not purchased, in the Museo Universitario de Ciencias y Arte which is about two city blocks southeast of the UNAM library. The remaindered volumes from UNAM are sold downtown near the main post office.

Periodicals are available on numerous magazine stands, but one of the better collections are on tables (sometimes) near the UNAM library. Most of the Walgreen's owned Sanborn stores have popular magazines, but only a few of the Sanborn bookstores have adequate room for a fair book and magazine collection. The beautiful Belles Artes building has a good bookstore and magazine offering - but the volumes are mostly in the arts and in history. The 1985 earthquake closed several bookstores - as Sotanos on Juarez. The earthquake also temporarily closed the downtown office of S.P.P., an important source of statistics, but the office now has a small, public library. The Insusgentes metro station has an outlet for SEP and SPP past publications, at reasonable costs. There is also a library near UNAM with all of the out of print publications of this agency. If one has $1,020 to spend then one can get a reprint set of Direccion General de Estadistica: Anuario 1894-1969 from Chadwyck-Healey publishing company in Alexandria, Virginia. Materials are becoming more available one can hope.

TABLE XV
STATE OF THE ART SOURCES OF SOCIAL DATA: SOME EXAMPLES

INCOME DIST.	Van Ginneken (based on Naverrete) sees income inequality as increasing as investment capital (bonds) concentrates; also weak unions accounts for the low end.	SALA volume 23: 1316 % middles and upper class. 1970 - 24.4% (L.A. range 12%, Guat. to 38% Argent.)	ILO: Mercado de Trabajo en Cifras, 1950-80. Minimum monthly wages in various sectors. SALA, vol. 23:1417.
HEALTH	PAHO/HC: Pan American Health Organization - Health Conditions in the Americas (See SALA, vol. 23, chapter 8).	S.P.P.'s 1981 review of the Plan Global de Desarrollo (Primer informe de avance) noted that 18 million Mexicans had no modern medical access.	Coordinacion de los Servicios de Salud Hacia un sistema nacional de salud. Presidencia de la Republica, 1982
SOCIAL SECURITY	IMSS, MEMORIA Various years.	Income and expenditures, IMSS 1982-85, 19.16% of insurable wages, contributions.	ILO's Yearbook of Labor Statistics % of economically active covered by Social Security, 1970 - 28.10%
NUTRITION	SPP Dept. de Co dinacion de Alimentacion y Nutricion. Retail cost in Mexico per minimum required nutritional intake. June, 1978	S.A.M., before and during its brief duration there was nutritional research to justify the various programs.	Barkin & Suarez used data from Direccion General de Agriculture to show the extent of external control over seed varieties. (El fin del Principio, 1983)
EDUCATION	UNESCO: Almost all of SALA's sources come from data which the Mexican Ministry of Education supplies to the U.N.	ANUIES, coordinating higher education since 1975, has some data on enrollment, programs, success rates, etc...	SPP, "Cuenta anual de la hacienda publica federal 1978-81 for amounts spent on education.
EMPLOYMENT	PREALC, Employment in Latin America; also ECLA's Economic Survey of Latin America	The Inter-Amer. Dev. Bank (1984) cites PREALC and the ILO for its labor force data, including unemployment data.	Anuario Estadistico del Federal, 1984 Data on Employment and Salaries in the Federal District, Volume 1, page 371
CRIME	World Health Organization	INTERPOL data is limited to 5 major cities - Mexico may not contribute (SALA: Volume 23, Ch	UN's ILANUD collected sentencing data from Mexico, 1972 - 5 general categories (SALA, Volume 23, Chapter 36)
URBAN PLANNING	SALA-LAPUA, Supplement #8, Latin American Population & Urban Analysis	CONAMUP, a militant organization has gathered and presented some urban martial to the powers that be - in order to get action within the system	Centro de Estudios Sociologicos El Colegio de Mexico, various volumes on absorption of migrants and other urban concerns.

TABLE XVI
SOCIAL STATISTICS NEEDED FOR MEXICO

AREA	SPECIAL NEEDS	WHAT'S AVAILABLE: EXAMPLES	ADDITIONAL CONCERNS
Income	Need income distribution by Quintiles & Deciles. Should be published in a paper of record.	I. de Navarrete and Combined Working Party data from 1950s-1960s. FONACUT - government source.	Need to show the "causes" of poverty; sources and distribution of wealth, and effects of redistribution.
Employment	Sub-employment or unemployment. On migration and jobs.	The President's Employment Study Group. E.N.E. studies at UNAM.	Need information on the effects of the current pattern of growth - impact of the growthmanship on jobs. Also the NAFTA.
Health	Impact of malnutrition and bad weather. Effects of extension of clinical sources.	May & McLellan have summarized nutrition data. Servicios Medicos del IMSS is comprehensive.	De-mystify the causes of mortality. Individual risks must be clarified about emerging morbidity patterns.
Education	Need materials on fate of graduates. Adult needs poorly understood.	Ministry of Education annual reports. HEW's periodic reviews from U.S. or international sources.	Level of education beyond needed by economic system should be gauged. Much of latter is aimed at citizenship values.
Social Security	Breakdown by transfers and services is needed.	IMSS and ISSSTE occasional reports are detailed. Mesa-Lago's reports allow comparisons.	Comparisons of benefits that groups have will stimulate public discussion.
Nutrition	Showing role in infant mortality would get results.	See chapter V of this volume.	Contrast of traditional and modern diets is still useful.

BIBLIOGRAPHY

A SELECT BIBLIOGRAPHY ON SOCIAL POLICY AND SOCIAL DEVELOPMENT IN MEXICO: TO 1993

Aguilar Monteverde, Alonso and Carmona. Mexico: Riqueza Y Miseria, Mexico City: Editorial Nuestro Tiempo, 1974

Alba, F. and Ricardo Alvarado. "Algunas Observaciones Sobre La Mortalidad Por Causes En Mexico: 1950-1967," Demografia Y Economia, 148-68, 1971

Almada Bay, Ignacio. Salud Y Crisis En Mexico: Textos Para Un Debate, Siglo Veintiuno, Mexico City, 1990

Alonso, Jose Antonio. The Domestic Seamstresses of Nezahualcoyotl: A Case Study of Feminine Over-Exploitation In a Marginal Urban Area. University Microfilms International

Anderson, Bo, and Cockcroft, James. "Control and Co-optation in Mexican Politics," in Latin American Radicalism, edited by Irving Horowitz and Jose De Castro, New York, Vintage Books, 1963

Arizpe, S., Lourdes. Indigenos En La Ciudad De Mexico, El Caso De Las Marias, 1975

Baerresen, D.W. "Unemployment and Mexico's Border Industrialization Program," Inter-American Economic Affairs, 29, 1975, Cambridge University Press

Banco Nacional De Mexico, "Feeding the Mexicans: Levels are Still Very Low," July, 1970

Banco Nacional De Mexico, "Final Census Figures: Indicators of Social Development," Review of the Economic Situation of Mexico, 1971

282

Banco De Mexico, S.A., La Distribution De Ingresso En Mexico, Mexico, Fondo De Cultura Economico, 1974

Barkin, David. "Mexico's Albatross: The U.S. Economy Latin American Perspectives, II, Summer, 1975, pgs. 64-80

Barta, Roger. "The Indigenous Problem and Indigenous Ideology," Revista Mexicana De Sociologia, July-Sept. 1974, Vol. 36, No. 3, pgs. 459-482

Borzutzky, Silvia. "Social Security and Health Policies in Latin America," Latin American Research Review, Vol. 28, No. 2, 1993, p.246

Brown, Jane Cowan. "Patterns of Intra-Urban Settlement in Mexico City," Ithaca: Cornell University, Latin American Studies Program Dissertation Series, 40, 1972

Camara, F. and Kemper, R.V. eds., Migration Across Frontiers: Mexico and the United States, Albany, NY, 1979

Camp, Roderic Ai. The Role of Economists in Policy Making: A Comparative Study of Mexico and the U.S., University of Arizona Press, 1977

Carr, Barry. Marxism and Communism in 20th Century Mexico, University of Nebraska, 1992

Cockcroft, James. "Coercion and Ideology in Mexican Politics," in Dependency and Underdevelopment: Latin America's Political Economy, by Cockcroft, Frank, and Johnson, Garden City, New York, Doubleday, 1972

Combined Mexican Working Party, The Economic Development of Mexico, Baltimore, Johns Hopkins Press, 1973

Cornelius, Wayne A. "Nation Building, Participation,a nd Distribution: The Politics of Social Reform Under Cardenas," in Crisis, Choice and Change, edited by Gabriel Almond, et al., Boston, Little Brown, 1973, p. 392

Cornelius, Wayne A. Politics and the Migrant Poor in Mexico City, Stanford, 1975

Cornelius, W.A. "Urbanization as an Agent in Latin American Political Instability: The Case of Mexico," The American Political Science Review, 63, 1969, pg. 833-836

Eckstein, Susan. The Poverty of Revolution: The State and Urban Poor in Mexico, Princeton University Press, 1977

Fried, Robert C. "Mexico City" in William A. Robson, ed., Great Cities of the World: Their Government, Politics and Planning, 3rd Edition, London, Allen and Unwin, 1971

Gill, Clark. The Educational Systems of Mexico, H.E.W., 1974

Gonzalez Casanova, Pablo. Democracy in Mexico, Oxford, 1970

Gonzalez Casanova, Pablo. "Dynamics of Class Structure," in Comparative Perspectives on Stratification: Mexico, Great Britain, Japan, edited by Joseph Kahl, 1968

Grayson, George. The Politics of Mexican Oil, University of Pittsburgh Press, 19__

Grindle, Merilee Serrill. Bureaucrats, Politicians, and Peasants in Mexico, University of California Press, 1977

Green, Fernando. Analysis of Major Mexican Urban Centers, 1960-1970, University Microfilms International

Instituto Mexicano Del Seguro Social, 1943-1983, anos De Historia, Director: Gabino Fraga (Notes the works of Lorenzo Meyers, Clark Reynolds, and Carlos Tello)

Jackman, Robert W. Politics and Social Equality: A Comparative Analysis, New York, John Wiley and Sons, 1975

Jimenez, Hernandez, Dalmasio, et al. La Marginalidad: El Comportamiento Adaptativo De Las Familias Marginadas En La Colonia Santa Anita, Deligacion Iztacalco, Mexico, D.F. UNAM, 1984

Johnson, Kenneth. Mexican Democracy: A Critical View, Boston, Houghton Mifflin, 1971

Kaim-Caudle, P.R. Comparative Social Policy And Social Security: Ten Country Study, New York, Durellen Co., Inc., 1973

Lomnitz, Larissa Adler. Networks and Marginality: Life in a Mexican Shantytown, Academic Press, 1977

Lopez Acuna, Daniel. "Salud, Seguridad Social Y Nutricion" Mexico Hoy, 1979

May & McLellan, The Ecology of Malnutrition in Mexico and Central America, 1972

McGreevey, William P. Social Security in Latin America: Issues and Options for the World Bank, World Discussion Paper No. 110, Washington, D.C., 1990

Mesa Lago, Carmelo. Ascent to Bankruptcy: Financing Social Security in Latin America, University of Pittsburgh, 1989

Mexico Hoy Mexico, Siglo Veintiuno, 1979

Morse, Richard M. and Jorge Hardoy, eds. Rethinking the Latin American City, Woodrow Wilson Center Press, Johns Hopkins, 1992

Navarrete, Ifigenia, et al., Biensstar Campesino Y Desarrollo

284

Economico, Mexico, Fondo De Cultura Economico, 1971

Navarrete, Ifigenia M. De, "La Distribution De Ingresso En Mexico: Tendencies Y Perspectivas, in El Perfil De Mexico En 1980, Mexico, Siglo Veintiuno, ed., 1970, pg. 17-62

De La Pena, Guillermo. A Legacy of Promises: Agriculture, Politics, and Ritual in the Morelos Highlands of Mexico, University of Texas Press, 1981

Piven, Frances Fox and Richard A. Cloward. Regulating the Poor: The Functions of Public Welfare, New York, Random House, 1971

Purcell, Susan K. The Mexican Profit Sharing Decision, University of California Press, Berkeley, 1975

Ryan, John Morris. Area Handbook for Mexico, 1st Ed., U.S. Government Printing Office, Washington, 1970

Reynolds, Clark W. The Mexican Economy: 20th Century Structure and Growth, Yale University, New Haven, 1970

Sanchez, Manuel, Arturo Olvera, Otoniel Ochoa, et al. "The Privitization Process in Mexico: Case Studies," Working Papers from IDB, 1992

Schendel, Gordon. Medicine in Mexico: From Aztec Herbs to Betatrons, University of Texas Press, 1968

Serron, Luis A. Scarcity, Exploitation and Poverty: Malthus and Marx in Mexico, University of Oklahoma Press, 1980

Spaulding, Rose Johnson. Social Security Policy Making: The Formation and Evolution of the Mexican Social Security Institute, University Microfilm International, 1978

Stern, Claudio. La Regiones De Mexico Y Sus Niveles De Dearrollo Socioeconomico, Mexico, El Colegion De Mexico, 1973

United Nations Development Programme Human Development Report 1992, New York, Oxford University Press, (see human development index, p. 127)Ward, Peter. Mexico City: The Production and Reproduction of an Urban Environment, Boston, G.K. Hall, 1990

Ward, Peter. Welfare Politics in Mexico: Papering Over The Cracks, Boston, Allen and Unwin, 1986

Wilkie, James W. "Mexico's 'New' Financial Crisis of 1982 in Historical Perspective," in Wilkie and Haber, Statistical Abstract of Latin America, Vol. 22, Los Angeles, Latin American Publication Center

Wilkie, James W. The Mexican Revolution: Federal Expenditures and Social Change Since 1910, 2nd Edition, University of

285

California Press, Berkeley, 1970
Wilkie, James W. (Editor). Society and Economy in Mexico, UCLA
   Latin American Center Publications, Los Angeles, 1990
Wilson, Richard. "The Corporatist Welfare State: Social Security and
   Development in Mexico," PhD., University of Pittsburgh, 1981

INDEX